Math Pathways & Pitfalls® Lessons and Teaching Manual

Place Value and Whole Number Operations *with Algebra Readiness*

Carne Barnett-Clarke
Alma B. Ramírez
with Debra Coggins

WestEd.org

Printed in the United States of America.

ISBN: 978-0-914409-59-5

Library of Congress Control Number: 2009938863

The book cover is printed on 50% recycled paper. The text paper is certified by the Sustainable Forest Initiative.

WestEd, a national nonpartisan, nonprofit research, development, and service agency, works with education and other communities to promote excellence, achieve equity, and improve learning for children, youth, and adults. WestEd has 17 offices nationwide, from Washington and Boston to Arizona and California. Its corporate headquarters are in San Francisco.

WestEd books and products are available through bookstores and online booksellers. WestEd also publishes its books in a variety of electronic formats.

To order books from WestEd directly, call our Publications Center at 888-293-7833, or visit us online at www.WestEd.org/bookstore.

For more information about WestEd:

Visit www.WestEd.org

Call 415-565-3000 or toll free 877-4-WestEd

Write WestEd, 730 Harrison Street, San Francisco, CA 94107-1242

Editor: Noel White

Design: Christian Holden

Production: Allan Ferguson, Fredrika Baer

Graphics: Celia Stevenson

Cover Illustration: Federico Jordán

Poster Design: Jennifer Novakoski

Video Production: Dellaruth Video

Publications Director: Mark Kerr

Business Development Manager: Aylin Bell

Proofreaders: Joan Saunders, Rosemary De La Torre, Tanicia Bell

Publications Manager and Print Buyer: Danny S. Torres

Video Consultant: Melissa Sydeman

Table of Contents

Acknowledgments v

Math Pathways & Pitfalls: Linking Research, Standards, and Practice 1

Getting Started: Professional Development 19

Getting Started: Introducing Students to *MPP* 27

Clipboard Prompts 37

References 38

Unit 2: Number, Place Value, & Operations*		TEACHING GUIDE	STUDENT PAGES
Lesson 1	Number Line Points	43	214
Lesson 2	Marking Points on a Number Line	51	220
Lesson 3	Add a Few	59	226
Lesson 4	What's the Difference?	67	232
Lesson 5	Don't Squeeze the Digits	75	238
Lesson 6	Adding On More Tens or Ones	83	244
Lesson 7	What Goes in the Blank? ALGEBRA READINESS	91	250
Lesson 8	Place Value Hints ALGEBRA READINESS	99	256
Lesson 9	Minus a Few	107	262
Lesson 10	Regroup and Subtract	115	268

Unit 3: Number, Regrouping, & Operations*		TEACHING GUIDE	STUDENT PAGES
Lesson 1	Number Line Sense	125	276
Lesson 2	Marking Points for Numbers	133	282
Lesson 3	Add On a Bit More	141	288
Lesson 4	A Little Less	149	294
Lesson 5	Finding the Difference	157	300
Lesson 6	Add On Using Place Value	165	306
Lesson 7	What Number Is Missing? ALGEBRA READINESS	173	312
Lesson 8	Values of Digits ALGEBRA READINESS	181	318
Lesson 9	Regroup a Ten	189	324
Lesson 10	When Do You Multiply?	197	330
Lesson 11	Making Sense and Multiplying	205	336

This book is part of a series that includes Units K–1, Units 4–5, and Units 6–7 in separate books.

Additional Resources

DVD Resources

Video for Students

Video for Teachers

CD Resources

Black Line Masters: Lessons

Black Line Master: Professional Development Handout

Discussion Builders Teaching Guide

Pitfalls Quiz Item Bank

Discussion Builders **Poster**

Acknowledgments

This book represents the culmination of the work of many people and organizations. We especially appreciate the contributions of the hundreds of teachers across the nation who participated in our research studies, piloted and field-tested *Math Pathways & Pitfalls (MPP)* lessons with thousands of students, and attended *MPP* professional development. Your insights, professional integrity, and flexibility will have an impact on students and teachers for years to come.

In developing this curriculum, we have often called on our colleagues at WestEd, and they have been generous in sharing their experiences and expertise in everything from data collection to publishing. WestEd's outstanding Communications department has provided exemplary design, editing, and publishing services. None of this work would have been possible without the financial support of our funders. We wish to thank the Stuart Foundation, which funded the development of the earliest prototypes of *MPP* lessons; the National Science Foundation, which funded further development of *MPP* and a nationwide research study with diverse teachers and students; and the U.S. Department of Education's Institute of Education Sciences, which funded our most recent work studying the impact of *MPP* on English learners and Latino/a students.

We owe a debt of gratitude to so many individuals that we cannot begin to name everyone. However, Kate D. Darling, *MPP* research coordinator, has contributed so much to the publication of this book and to the success of the *MPP* research projects that we want to thank her publicly. Her expertise in design and technology, her seemingly endless energy, and her meticulous organization have facilitated our ability to bring this work to fruition.

In addition, the individuals below played pivotal roles on the *MPP* research teams and advisory boards. Through their review of materials, feedback, and analyses, they helped ensure that the materials we developed are useful, practical, and effective for students and teachers.

Gunnar Carlsson, Department of Mathematics, Stanford University

Deborah A. Curtis, College of Education, California State University, San Francisco

José Franco, EQUALS program, University of California, Berkeley

Donna Goldenstein, teacher, Hayward Unified School District, California

Thomas L. Hanson, Health and Human Development Program, WestEd

Joan I. Heller, Heller Research Associates

Lena Licón Khisty, College of Education, University of Illinois, Chicago

Della R. Leavitt, doctoral student, College of Education, University of Illinois, Chicago

Robert Linquanti, Comprehensive School Assistance Program and REL West, WestEd

Nora Ramírez, Mathematics Professional Development, CRESMET, Arizona State University

Aria Razfar, College of Education, University of Illinois, Chicago

Edward A. Silver, School of Education and Department of Mathematics, University of Michigan

Guillermo Solano-Flores, School of Education, University of Colorado, Boulder

Mary Kay Stein, LRDC and School of Education, University of Pittsburgh

James W. Stigler, Department of Psychology, University of California, Los Angeles

William Yslas Vélez, Department of Mathematics, University of Arizona

Aída Walqui, Teacher Professional Development Program, WestEd

To all of you who contributed, we hope that you are as proud of *Math Pathways & Pitfalls* as we are. It would not have been possible without each of you.

Math Pathways & Pitfalls
Linking Research, Standards, and Practice

What Is *Math Pathways & Pitfalls*?

Math Pathways & Pitfalls is founded on a vision that has driven a decade of work and research in classrooms nationally. In this vision, students are engaged in mathematical discussions, talking about mathematical concepts, addressing important mathematical standards, and tackling mathematical pitfalls, head-on. Students who traditionally might not talk, whether because they are not confident in mathematics or because English is not their first language, are engaged in providing examples and counterexamples and using mathematical language to prove their ideas. In this vision, mistakes provide fodder for even deeper discussion, and students engage in intellectual risk-taking by exposing their own misconceptions for the benefit of the class. And teachers have the tools they need to facilitate and deepen discussion, ensuring their students walk away with a robust understanding of mathematical ideas that will carry them into high school and beyond.

As former classroom teachers, we understand the responsibility teachers feel for their students' success in conquering important mathematical standards. We also know that the art of conducting discussion in pursuit of those standards is not easy. To achieve our vision, we first worked with small groups of teachers to develop the initial ideas for *Math Pathways & Pitfalls (MPP)*. Then we conducted field tests and rigorous research on *MPP* in more than 300 classrooms. This work was funded by the Stuart Foundation, the National Science Foundation, and the U.S. Department of Education's Institute of Education Sciences.

The result is an easy-to-use set of tools that provide effective, equitable, discussion-based lessons and boost students' mastery of key mathematical standards.

Mathematical Topics of *MPP*	
Units K–1	**Units 2–3**
Early math concepts	Place value
Whole number concepts	Whole number operations
Algebra readiness	Algebra readiness
Units 4–5	**Units 6–7**
Fractions	Percents
Decimals	Ratios and proportions
Algebra readiness	Algebra readiness

MPP helps students make sense of mathematical problems (in context or symbolic form) and motivates them to produce solutions that don't cave in to pitfalls. This is a broader goal than just understanding how procedures work, solving problems, or preventing errors.

MPP supports increasingly sophisticated reasoning and academic language use — two competencies that are fundamental to learning mathematics from early grades through college. *MPP* also provides scaffolding for students of all language backgrounds to cultivate respectful discussions and achieve equitable learning.

MPP is designed to be used in conjunction with any adopted textbook. Not only can the lessons be used to enrich and enhance the core curriculum, but they also easily adapt to a variety of teaching and learning goals. For example, *MPP* lessons may be used as an intervention in the core curriculum or as part of an after-school program.

How Does *MPP* Use Research Findings to Boost Learning?

More than a hundred research papers about children's mathematical thinking, academic language development, and effective and equitable instructional practices have guided the substance and design of *MPP*. Examples of the research that provide the foundation for *MPP* include: Fuson, 1992; Carpenter & Moser, 1983; Behr, Lesh, Post, & Silver, 1983; Lamon, 1999; Spanos, Rhodes, Corasaniti, Crandall, & Crandall, 1988; Thompson & Rubenstein, 2000; Pimm, 1995; Festinger, 1957; Borasi, 1994; Olivares, 1996; Khisty, 2002; Cobb, Wood, & Yackel, 1993.

Turns Pitfalls into Pathways for Learning

As one of our students has pointed out, "My father says you can learn from your mistakes." The pitfalls highlighted in *MPP* lessons address some of the most common misconceptions cited in the research literature on student thinking and used as distractors on state and national assessments. During each lesson, students contrast correct and incorrect ways to solve a problem. They talk explicitly about why a particular pitfall occurs, how to avoid the pitfall, and how to think correctly about the mathematics in the problem. Experimental studies by cognitive scientists Durkin and Rittle-Johnson (2009) suggest that comparing examples of common mathematical errors to examples that are correct may prevent such errors from being made in the future. They also report that the contrast between correct and incorrect examples prompts students to recognize correct concepts. Other research supports the idea that pitfalls serve as strong motivators for inquiry and sense making (Festinger, 1957; Borasi, 1994).

Addresses Key Mathematics Standards in Number and Algebraic Reasoning

The mathematical content of *MPP* focuses on key concepts and skills that are found in the National Council of Teachers of Mathematics (NCTM) Curriculum Focal Points and in state and local standards.

The lessons in units K–3 focus on building concepts related to number sense, operations, and equality. The lessons in units 4–7 target concepts related to fractions, decimals, ratios, proportions, percents, algebraic expressions, and equations. Refer to page 17 in this book for help selecting lessons that support standards in which students need stronger development or extra reinforcement.

Provides Tools That Develop a Community of Learners

MPP draws from research about how to build communities in which students not only learn mathematics but also learn how to participate in the discourse practices of mathematics (Lampert, 1990; Ball, 1997; Cobb, Wood, & Yackel, 1993). *MPP* provides opportunities for students to participate safely while also inviting intellectual risk-taking (Beghetto, 2004). Each *MPP* lesson includes opportunities for individual, partner, and whole class participation, allowing students to take on riskier roles as they feel ready. The accompanying *Discussion Builders* poster contains sentence stems that embed the academic language used in mathematical discourse and supports risk-taking and respectful discussion. The Video for Students also models students taking risks by presenting their ideas publicly and agreeing and disagreeing respectfully.

Addresses Multiple Modalities

MPP tasks mediate learning in multiple ways, using oral, print, and other visual modes of communication. For example, mathematical concepts in an *MPP* lesson are initially developed by discussing the thinking of two fictional students. Their thinking, presented in print and supported by labeled drawings, purposefully embeds important conceptual ideas to prime the discussion. Having both text and drawings to refer to allows students to examine — and reexamine — the mathematical ideas. After the beginning of the *MPP* lesson lays a conceptual foundation, students' own solutions serve as the basis for discussion and learning. The lesson encourages students to use multiple modalities to explain their solutions, such as explaining their thinking orally and using drawings, symbols, and text labels to make their explanations clear. Learning mediated through multiple modalities is particularly important in providing access for visual learners and English learners (Echevarria, Vogt, & Short, 2004).

Provides Word Problems and Symbolic Problems

Word problems provide a meaningful context for developing number concepts and the meanings of operations (Carpenter, Fennema, Peterson, Chiang, & Loef, 1989). This idea is supported by a theory that describes the situated nature of learning (Brown, Collins, & Duguid, 1989; Lave & Wenger, 1991). Ultimately, students must also learn to work meaningfully and skillfully with mathematics in its abstract, or symbolic, form, especially if they are to be successful in higher mathematics (Sfard, 2000). *MPP* helps students make sense of — and solve — both word problems and problems in purely symbolic form. Also, *MPP* encourages mental, visual, and paper-and-pencil solution methods. Regardless of whether the problem is in context or not, students are expected to explain why their solution process makes sense.

Develops Mathematical Language

The meaning students develop for a mathematical idea is closely entwined with the way they use language to reason about the idea and learn to translate among words, symbols, and meanings of that idea (Vygotsky, 1962; Schleppegrell, 2004; Cummins, 1980; Pimm, 1995; Solomon & Rhodes, 1995). Discussion-based lessons, such as *MPP,* support language development. As Khisty (1992, 1995) points out, students develop language by talking. *MPP* teaching guides help teachers anticipate language confusion and support communication to ensure that English learners have access to the discussion. In addition to fostering oral communication, *MPP* lessons assist students in learning to comprehend complex mathematical text and write mathematical

explanations. To support vocabulary development, lessons open with a quick review of important mathematical words, including examples of how they are used. Finally, the *Discussion Builders* elicit increasingly more sophisticated use of academic language and reasoning as students progress through the grades.

Prompts a Metacognitive and Proactive Stance Toward Learning

Instructional approaches that encourage self-monitoring — or metacognition — have been shown to support learning with understanding (Donovan & Bransford, 2005). *MPP* lessons include several structures and reminders for students to become more proactively aware of their thinking and learning processes. For example, *MPP* lessons encourage students to consider where someone might make a pitfall (use incorrect reasoning) as they solve a problem. Students learn to ask themselves whether a solution makes sense or not. These opportunities for reflection help students become more conscious of how they learn and ways they can monitor their own learning and problem solving.

Incorporates Tools for Professional Learning and Lesson Study

MPP provides practical professional development options that respond to different needs, budgetary constraints, and time allocations. Teachers can learn how to use *MPP* on their own or with colleagues by viewing the *MPP* Video for Teachers (on the DVD included with this book) while completing the Professional Development Tasks found on pages 20–26. The *MPP* teaching guides, which provide mathematical insights and teaching tips for each lesson, have served as a resource for lesson study groups. Finally, each *MPP* lesson embeds structures and prompts that support the development of effective and equitable teaching habits. Further professional development opportunities are listed online at www.WestEd.org/mpp.

What Are the Research Findings on the Impact of *MPP*?

Math Pathways & Pitfalls evolved over nearly a decade of design experimentation and national field tests. Two large-scale efficacy studies and several descriptive studies have documented the positive impact of *MPP* and help explain why it is effective with diverse learners. Findings from an experimental study, funded by the National Science Foundation (ESI-9911374), demonstrated that teaching only seven *MPP* lessons in conjunction with the regular mathematics curriculum boosts student achievement during the course of one school year. The graphs on this page show students' adjusted posttest mean scores on project-designed mathematics quizzes. These quizzes assess key standards using items similar to those found on state and national assessments, such as the National Assessment of Educational Progress. Statistically significant positive effects were found (effect size statistics = 0.43 to 0.66) for *Math Pathways & Pitfalls* students in all grades. Study participants included 2,816 geographically and ethnically diverse students in grades 2, 4, and 6.

A classroom observation study of *MPP* found evidence that *MPP* practices transfer from *MPP* lessons to non-*MPP* lessons (Heller Research Associates, 2008). This may explain why incorporating only 15 hours of

MPP lessons into the regular mathematics program may amplify mathematical learning during all lessons. This study found that after experiencing *MPP* lessons, students were more likely to notice pitfalls, explain and justify their reasoning, and have a greater level of engagement in the classroom. Also, a greater variety and percentage of students participated in class discussions. This classroom observation was conducted as part of an experimental study funded by the U.S. Department of Education's Institute of Education Sciences (R305K050050). Complete findings for this study were not yet available at the time of printing, but will be available on our website: www.WestEd.org/mpp.

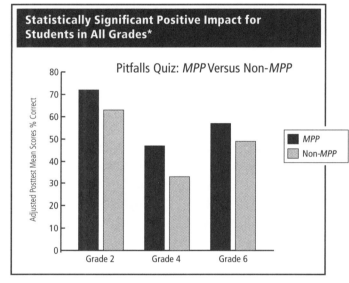

Statistically Significant Positive Impact for Students in All Grades*

Pitfalls Quiz: *MPP* Versus Non-*MPP*

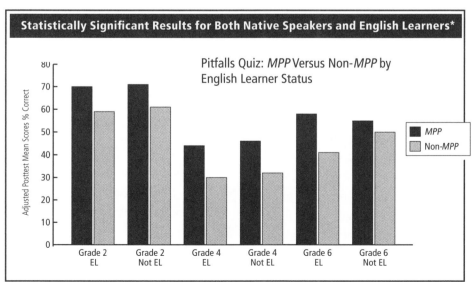

Statistically Significant Results for Both Native Speakers and English Learners*

Pitfalls Quiz: *MPP* Versus Non-*MPP* by English Learner Status

* Heller et al., 2000.

What Tools and Resources Are Included with *MPP*?

Each *MPP* book contains two units, totaling 20 to 22 lessons, and together the four books cover key mathematics topics for kindergarten through grade 8. To maximize effectiveness, each book comes with a

DVD, CD, and *Discussion Builders* poster. This set of materials is all that is needed for successful implementation for most teachers. Additional professional development is available to provide teachers with a practicum for implementing *MPP* and opportunities to further develop their expertise with the mathematical content and pedagogy of *MPP*.

Book with Lessons and Teaching Manual

Each book contains two units of lessons, including engaging teaching guides and black line masters for student pages.

DVD

Video for Students: An *MPP* lesson models respectful and productive mathematics discussion.

Video for Teachers: A Lesson in Action demonstrates effective facilitation, bolstered by helpful tips from *MPP* teachers.

CD with Black Line Masters and Resources

The student pages and professional development tasks in this book, as well as quiz items, can be printed out directly from the CD.

Poster

A poster of *Discussion Builders* sentence stems helps students engage proactively, politely, and productively in discussion.

Professional Development

Tasks for teachers to do individually or with colleagues are included in each book and are accompanied by black line masters found on the CD. Additional offerings are available online at www.WestEd.org/mpp.

What Is in This Book?

Organization of the Book

Unit 2 in this book has 10 lessons, and Unit 3 has 11 lessons. The lessons focus on number sense, operations, and algebra readiness. Sections of this book are described below.

Math Pathways & Pitfalls: Linking Research, Standards, and Practice

Every teacher who implements *MPP* should start by reading this section — some parts more than once! It provides a rationale for important design decisions, presents research findings on the impact of *MPP*, describes an *MPP* lesson, explains what is in the teaching guide, and suggests alternative ways for integrating *MPP* into a math program.

Getting Started

This section has three parts. The first part provides Professional Development Tasks for teachers to do on their own or in collaboration with other teachers. The second part provides tasks for introducing students to *MPP* and their first *MPP* lesson. The third part provides a helpful tool, the Clipboard Prompts, for teachers to use when conducting *MPP* discussions.

Teaching Guides for Units 2 and 3

These sections include teaching guides for core lessons and follow-up mini lessons.

Masters for Student Pages

These sections have the student pages for the lessons and mini lessons of units 2 and 3. Black line masters are also provided on the accompanying CD.

Mathematical Topics

The tables below and on the next page outline the mathematical topics in each unit of this book. Students have more than one opportunity to solidify, reinforce, and extend the mathematical ideas within a lesson and connect to other lessons. *MPP* is not designed to replace the regular curriculum. Instead, it is designed to enhance and reinforce learning of key mathematical concepts and skills in the regular curriculum. *MPP* also acts as a catalyst for helping teachers implement their regular lessons in ways that deepen mathematics learning and broaden participation in mathematical discussion.

Number, Place Value, and Operations Topics	Unit 2 Lessons
Identify, locate, and estimate two-digit numbers on a number line	1, 2
Relate numerical values to common benchmark numbers	1, 2, 3
Find sums mentally	3, 6
Find differences mentally	4
Understand place value concepts for two- and three-digit numbers	5, 6, 8
Understand and solve word problems	4, 5, 6
Understand the regrouping process	5, 6, 9, 10
Understand and use an algorithm to add two- and three-digit numbers	5, 8
Understand and use an algorithm to subtract one- and two-digit numbers	9, 10
Understand that addition and subtraction are related operations	9, 10
Use number sense to check if answers are reasonable	3, 5, 6, 7, 9, 10
Understand the equals sign **ALGEBRA READINESS**	7, 8
Solve missing addend equations **ALGEBRA READINESS**	7, 8
Reinforce basic addition and subtraction facts	3, 5, 6, 7, 9, 10

Number, Regrouping, and Operations Topics	Unit 3 Lessons
Identify, locate, and estimate three-digit numbers on a number line	1, 2, 3, 4
Relate numerical values to common benchmark numbers	1, 2, 3, 4, 5
Find sums mentally	3, 6, 7
Find differences mentally	4, 5, 8
Understand place value concepts for two- and three-digit numbers	6, 8
Understand and solve word problems	4, 5, 6, 10, 11
Understand the regrouping process	5, 9
Understand and use an algorithm to add one-, two-, and three-digit numbers	6, 8, 9
Understand and use an algorithm to subtract from three-digit numbers	5, 9
Understand that addition and subtraction are related operations	9
Use number sense to check if answers are reasonable	3, 4, 6, 7, 11
Understand the equals sign ALGEBRA READINESS	7, 8
Solve missing addend equations ALGEBRA READINESS	7, 8
Recognize multiplication situations	10
Understand and use an algorithm to multiply three-digit by one-digit numbers	11

What Is in Each *MPP* Lesson?

MPP lessons use a consistent, easy-to-follow format with a core lesson and two follow-up mini lessons, each accompanied by a teaching guide. Teaching guides provide sample prompts and solution keys for each part of the lesson. Lessons rely on drawings for visuals and suggest but do not require manipulatives, allowing lessons to be used in schools where such materials are not available.

The four elements of each *MPP* lesson are: Opener, Discussion, Review and Practice, and Assess and Reinforce. Together they provide multiple opportunities for students to develop, assess, and solidify their mathematical understandings.

Core Lesson	**Multiple Choice Mini Lesson**	**Writing Task Mini Lesson**
Opener, Discussion, Review and Practice	Assess and Reinforce	Assess and Reinforce
✳	✳	✳
4 student pages	1/2 student page	1/2 student page
✳	✳	✳
2 consecutive days	1–2 days later	1–2 days later
✳	✳	✳
45 minutes each day	20 minutes	25 minutes

MPP Lesson Roadmap

Use the *MPP* Lesson Roadmap below to mentally walk through a lesson and get a feel for how it flows. It gives an overview of the lesson, the sequence of the lesson parts, the groupings used, and the time frame. A condensed version of the *MPP* Lesson Roadmap is included in the teaching guide for every lesson. The consistent format of every lesson makes it easy to implement *MPP* lessons.

As you look through the Roadmap, you might be surprised to see that students are given only 5 minutes to work on the Starter Problem and that they don't share their solutions right away. Although this is an unconventional approach, it is done intentionally. The central purpose of the Starter Problem is to motivate inquiry into the mathematics and the pitfall during the discussion. The problem is often not difficult, but it elicits pitfalls, especially when students do not make sense of the mathematical symbols or words. Even students who solve the problem correctly may be simply manipulating symbols without making sense. So *MPP* lessons begin by providing students with examples of conceptually rich mathematical thinking as a vehicle for developing their conceptual understanding through discussion. This discussion provides an opportunity for students to self-correct and check their own understanding before being asked to share and justify their own solutions later on in the lesson.

CORE LESSON: DAY 1	GROUPING	TIME	INSTRUCTION
Opener			
Discussion Builders Purpose Math Words	Whole Class	5 min	Students review the *Discussion Builders*. A student reads the purpose. Students review each math word and example.
Starter Problem	Individual	5 min	Students solve the problem on their own and think about possible pitfalls.
Discussion			
Student Thinking	Individual Pairs Whole class	25 min	Using *Discussion Builders,* students discuss a fictional student's work marked OK, then a fictional student's work marked Oops!
Things to Remember Reflection	Whole class	10 min	Students generate and write Things to Remember, then look back on the learning process.
CORE LESSON: DAY 2			
Review and Practice			
Review Day 1 Lesson	Whole class	5 min	Students briefly review the lesson and Things to Remember discussed the previous day.
Our Turn	Pairs Whole class	25 min	Students work with a neighbor to solve each problem. Then they explain their solutions to their classmates.
My Turn	Individual	15 min	Students solve the problems on their own.
MINI LESSONS: 2–3 DAYS LATER			
Assess and Reinforce			
Multiple Choice Mini Lesson	Individual Pairs Whole class	20 min	Students evaluate choices and justify solutions.
Writing Task Mini Lesson	Individual Whole class	25 min	Students learn to write an explanation that is complete, comprehensive, and correct.

Detailed Overview of Lesson Elements

The information on this page and the following pages will help you understand the purpose of each lesson element and how each lesson is organized. In this overview, sample student pages for the core lesson and two mini lessons are followed by the teaching guide for that lesson. The book itself, however, includes all teaching guides in the first half and all student pages in the second half.

Student Pages — Core Lesson Day 1

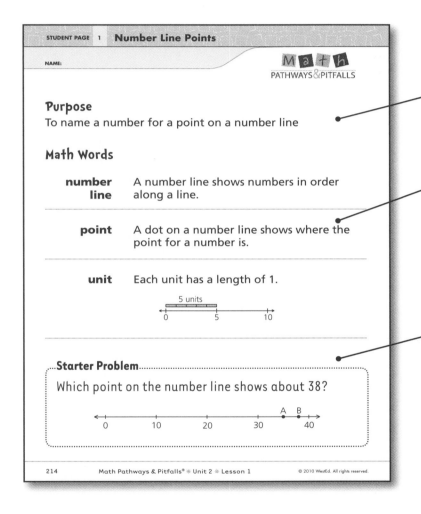

Purpose. The lesson purpose is made explicit to students to prompt intentional learning.

Math Words. Mathematical terms are used in sentences to contextualize vocabulary.

Starter Problem. This problem often elicits pitfalls, especially when students do not make sense of the mathematical symbols or words. It also motivates inquiry into the mathematics and the pitfall, or oops, during the discussion that follows.

Student Pages — Core Lesson Day 1, continued

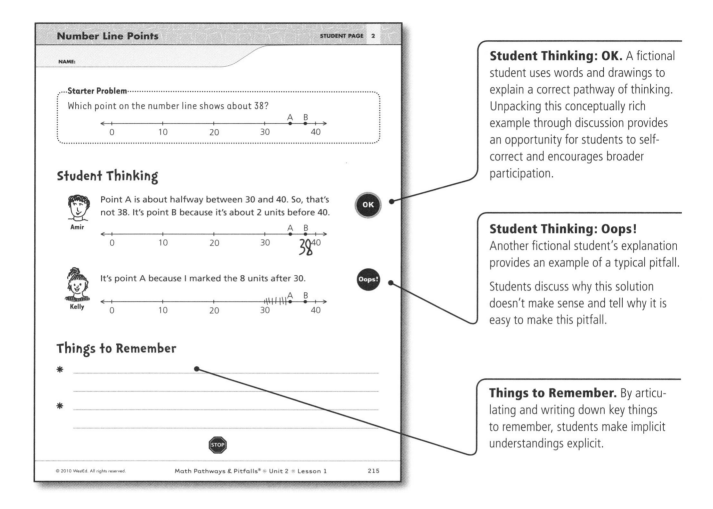

Number Line Points   STUDENT PAGE   2

NAME:

Starter Problem

Which point on the number line shows about 38?

Student Thinking

Amir

Point A is about halfway between 30 and 40. So, that's not 38. It's point B because it's about 2 units before 40.

Kelly

It's point A because I marked the 8 units after 30.

Things to Remember

*

*

STOP

© 2010 WestEd. All rights reserved.   Math Pathways & Pitfalls® ✳ Unit 2 ✳ Lesson 1   215

Student Thinking: OK. A fictional student uses words and drawings to explain a correct pathway of thinking. Unpacking this conceptually rich example through discussion provides an opportunity for students to self-correct and encourages broader participation.

Student Thinking: Oops! Another fictional student's explanation provides an example of a typical pitfall.

Students discuss why this solution doesn't make sense and tell why it is easy to make this pitfall.

Things to Remember. By articulating and writing down key things to remember, students make implicit understandings explicit.

Student Pages — Core Lesson Day 2

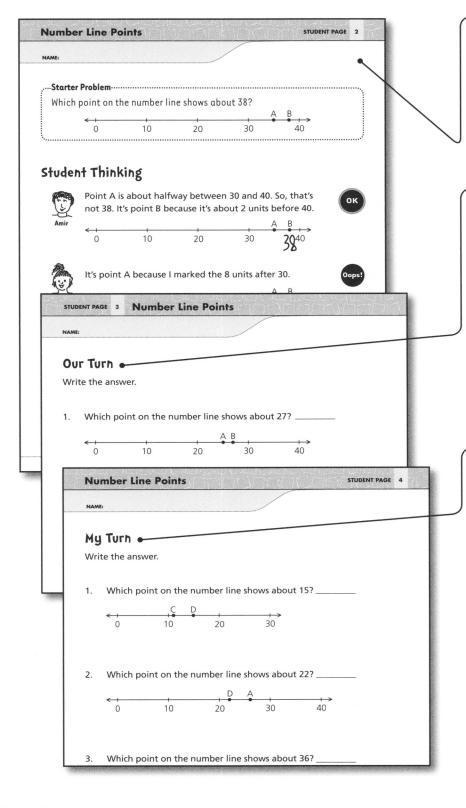

Number Line Points STUDENT PAGE 2

NAME:

Starter Problem

Which point on the number line shows about 38?

0 10 20 30 40 A B

Student Thinking

Amir: Point A is about halfway between 30 and 40. So, that's not 38. It's point B because it's about 2 units before 40. **OK**

0 10 20 30 A B 38 40

It's point A because I marked the 8 units after 30. **Oops!**

A B

STUDENT PAGE 3 **Number Line Points**

NAME:

Our Turn

Write the answer.

1. Which point on the number line shows about 27? _____

0 10 20 A B 30 40

Number Line Points STUDENT PAGE 4

NAME:

My Turn

Write the answer.

1. Which point on the number line shows about 15? _____

0 10 C D 20 30

2. Which point on the number line shows about 22? _____

0 10 20 D A 30 40

3. Which point on the number line shows about 36? _____

(Review.) Before starting the discussion on Day 2, students review the discussion from Day 1 and their list of things to remember. This review brings key mathematical ideas to the forefront and reminds students about the oops, or pitfall.

Our Turn. Students work with a partner on practice problems that extend their thinking beyond the Starter Problem.

They present and discuss alternative solutions to each problem to encourage flexibility in their mathematical understanding.

My Turn. Students practice solving the problems independently and monitoring their thinking for pitfalls.

Student Pages — Mini Lessons, 2–3 Days Later

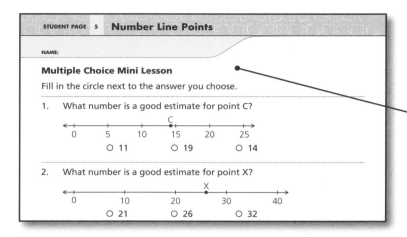

STUDENT PAGE 5 **Number Line Points**

NAME:

Multiple Choice Mini Lesson

Fill in the circle next to the answer you choose.

1. What number is a good estimate for point C?

⚬ 11   ⚬ 19   ⚬ 14

2. What number is a good estimate for point X?

⚬ 21   ⚬ 26   ⚬ 32

Number Line Points   STUDENT PAGE 6

NAME:

Writing Task Mini Lesson

Explain how you know that a good estimate for point C is 25. You may draw a picture on the back to help explain.

Multiple Choice Mini Lesson. This short lesson is used for reinforcement or informal assessment.

Students learn to look for pitfalls and eliminate unreasonable choices — valuable test-taking skills.

Writing Task Mini Lesson. This guided activity helps students learn to write mathematical explanations.

Teaching Guide — Before Starting the Core Lesson

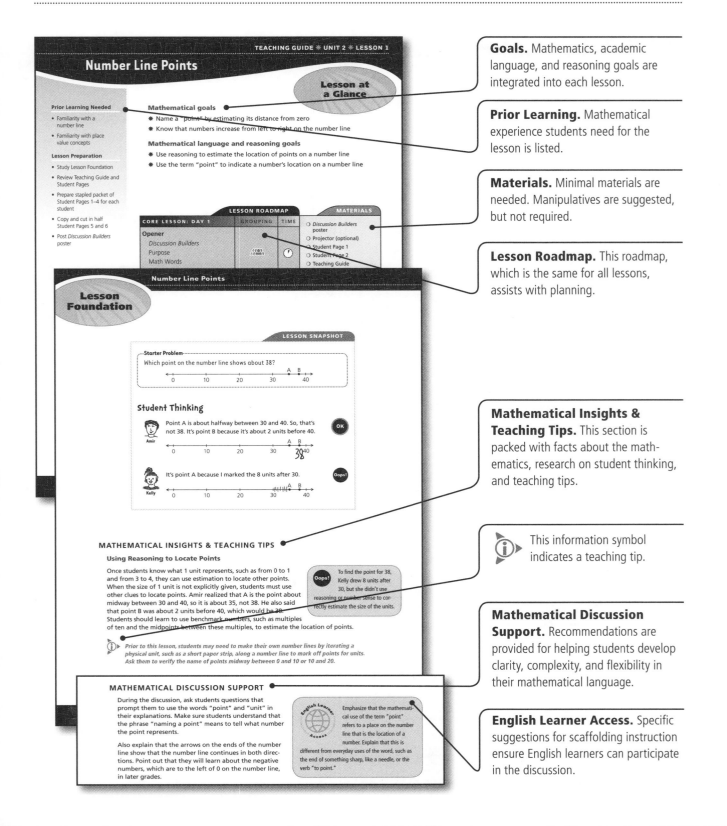

Goals. Mathematics, academic language, and reasoning goals are integrated into each lesson.

Prior Learning. Mathematical experience students need for the lesson is listed.

Materials. Minimal materials are needed. Manipulatives are suggested, but not required.

Lesson Roadmap. This roadmap, which is the same for all lessons, assists with planning.

Mathematical Insights & Teaching Tips. This section is packed with facts about the mathematics, research on student thinking, and teaching tips.

This information symbol indicates a teaching tip.

Mathematical Discussion Support. Recommendations are provided for helping students develop clarity, complexity, and flexibility in their mathematical language.

English Learner Access. Specific suggestions for scaffolding instruction ensure English learners can participate in the discussion.

Teaching Guide — Core Lesson Day 1

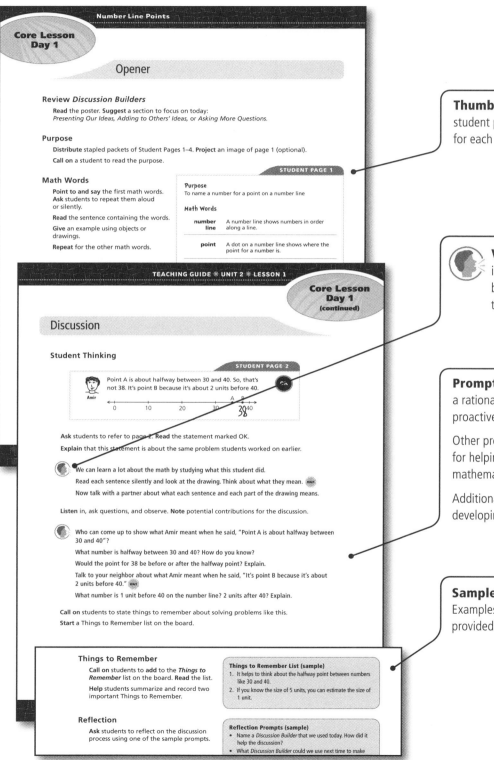

Thumbnails. A small copy of the student page gives a visual reference for each lesson section.

Visual Cues. This symbol indicates a prompt that is to be directly read or paraphrased to students.

Prompts. Some prompts convey a rationale to students to motivate proactive and intentional learning.

Other prompts suggest a pathway for helping students understand core mathematical ideas.

Additional probing is necessary for developing understanding.

Sample Student Responses. Examples of Things to Remember are provided for each lesson.

Teaching Guide — Core Lesson Day 2

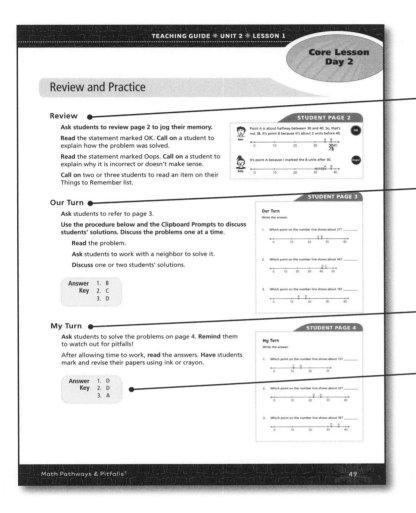

Review. Frequent review and reflection throughout the lesson help students remember and connect mathematical ideas.

Collaborative Practice. Students solve additional problems to solidify and extend their understanding. They discuss their solutions with classmates.

Individual Practice. Students work on problems by themselves to further develop their understanding.

Answer Keys. Solutions are provided for all problems.

Teaching Guide — Mini Lessons, 2–3 Days Later

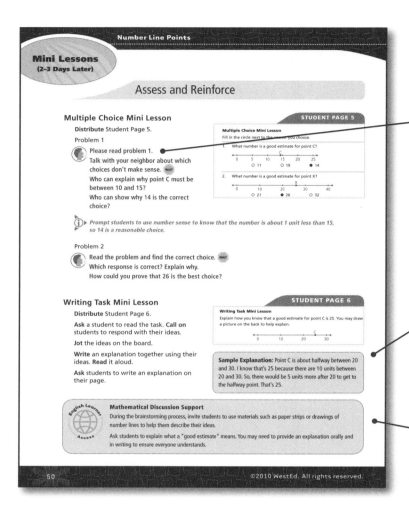

Prompts and Answer Keys. The teaching guides for the mini lessons, like for the core lessons, give lesson-specific prompts and answer keys to help teachers guide the discussions.

Sample Explanation. The teaching guide for the Writing Task Mini Lesson provides a sample written explanation.

English Learner Access. The Mathematical Discussion Support section includes helpful suggestions to anticipate language confusion and make the lesson accessible for English learners.

Implementing *MPP* Lessons

As mentioned earlier, *MPP* lessons may be used as an intervention to the core curriculum and to enhance and enrich mathematics learning during a regular school day, during after-school programs, and in summer school classes. The Getting Started section of this book provides a complete guide for implementing *MPP*. If possible, launch *MPP* lessons in the fall so that students begin to adopt the habits of mind and strategies embedded in *MPP* and transfer them to non-*MPP* lessons throughout the school year. Our research shows that *MPP* can be successful implementing as few as seven *MPP* lessons, but students will likely benefit even more with additional lessons.

Using *MPP* with Individual Students or Small Groups

MPP is an excellent intervention for pull-out or after-school programs involving individual students, pairs, or small groups. In contrast to some intervention programs, discussion is central to the learning process with *Math Pathways & Pitfalls*. Even when there is only one student, the teacher will engage the student in a thoughtful discussion of the concepts and pitfalls using the prompts in the teaching guides. The time required to complete the parts of the lesson are flexible and can be shortened when fewer students are involved. Visit www.WestEd.org/mpp for specific suggestions on using *MPP* lessons in these settings.

Selecting and Sequencing Lessons

Although the lessons in this book build on each other sequentially within each topic, they can be selected to address particular student needs or to correlate with curriculum needs. If *MPP* is being implemented schoolwide or districtwide, decisions about the selection and sequencing of lessons should be made jointly to ensure coherence for students. A good place to begin the selection and correlation process is with the tables of mathematical topics provided on pages 6–7. Also consult the teaching guides for each lesson for Mathematical Goals, Language and Reasoning Goals, and Prior Learning Needed. Or you may find it helpful to use the table below to select *MPP* lessons that correlate to the National Council of Teachers of Mathematics Curriculum Focal Points published in 2006.

Curriculum Focal Points*	Related *MPP* Lessons (Unit: Lesson)
Grade 1: Developing understandings of addition and subtraction and strategies for basic addition facts and related subtraction facts	Unit 2: L3, L4
Grade 1: Developing an understanding of whole number relationships, including grouping in tens and ones	Unit 2: L1, L2, L3, L4 Unit 3: L1, L2
Grade 2: Developing an understanding of the base-ten numeration system and place-value concepts	Unit 2: L1, L2, L5, L6, L8, L9, L10 Unit 3: L1, L2, L3, L4, L5, L6, L8, L9
Grade 2: Developing quick recall of addition facts and related subtraction facts and fluency with multidigit addition and subtraction	Unit 2: L2, L4, L5, L6, L7, L9, Unit 3: L4, L5, L6, L7, L9
Grade 3: Developing an understanding of multiplication and division and strategies for basic multiplication facts and related division facts	Unit 3: L10, L11
Grade 3: Developing quick recall of multiplication facts and related division facts and fluency with whole number multiplication	Unit 3: L10, L11

* Adapted from National Council of Teachers of Mathematics, 2006.

Getting Started
Professional Development

It takes only a little time to become acquainted with *MPP,* but teachers using the program agree that it is time well spent. The Professional Development Tasks in this section are meant to help teachers learn about the features of *MPP* lessons and gain practical advice for using them effectively. To ground the tasks in practice, watch the *MPP* Video for Teachers, which includes a Lesson in Action and Frequently Asked Questions. During the video, viewers are prompted to participate in Professional Development Tasks. There are four tasks in this section that will be used in conjunction with the video. We also make suggestions for learning about the vision, rationale, and research underlying *MPP*, and for using the teaching guides as vehicles for professional learning.

An important aim for this section is to help teachers think not only about how to teach an *MPP* lesson, but also about how to use *MPP* lessons to accomplish the broader goal of helping students assume a more proactive, metacognitive, and reflective stance toward learning in general. After teaching a lesson or two, teachers will likely benefit from revisiting this section and the *MPP* Video for Teachers.

Ideally, teachers will work through these tasks with colleagues, perhaps with the guidance of a coach or facilitator. The tasks can be flexibly adapted for different professional development formats, such as teacher study groups and facilitated discussions. However, if resources for professional learning are limited or there is little opportunity for colleagues to interact, teachers can use this section for individual study and reflection.

Research on *MPP* has shown students' math achievement improves when teachers attend as little as one day and up to four days of *MPP* professional development. Teachers report that they have also found it helpful to plan each *MPP* lesson together and debrief afterward.

Professional Development Tasks

Purpose

To increase understanding of the purpose, time frame, and process of *MPP* lessons

Materials

- ○ DVD: Video for Teachers
- ○ Professional Development Handout from the CD for each participant
- ○ *Discussion Builders* poster
- ○ DVD player and monitor

Preparation

- ○ Print the Professional Development Handout from the CD. Prepare a stapled packet of the handout for each participant.
- ○ Set up the DVD player and monitor.
- ○ Post the *Discussion Builders* poster.

Time Frame

30 minutes per task; all four tasks may be completed during one session or spread over two to four sessions

PROFESSIONAL DEVELOPMENT TASK 1

Review the student pages for the featured lesson provided in the Professional Development Handout.

View *Lesson in Action Professional Development: Task 1* on the DVD, after which you will be automatically returned to the menu.

Complete the following reflective activities individually or with colleagues. Each participant should have a copy of the Professional Development Handout. This task will take about 30 minutes.

Lesson at a Glance and Lesson Foundation

Read the Lesson at a Glance and the Lesson Foundation sections of the teaching guide for the lesson in the handout.

- ✱ About how much time is allotted for the core lesson on Day 1? on Day 2? What are the goals for the lesson? What materials are suggested?
- ✱ Highlight ideas in the Mathematical Insights & Teaching Tips section that you found interesting or helpful. Why did you choose these ideas?
- ✱ Highlight ideas from the Mathematical Discussion Support section and English Learner Access section that might be particularly important for your students. Why did you choose these ideas?

Core Lesson: Opener

Look at the *MPP* Lesson Roadmap excerpt to the right. The first part of a lesson is called the Opener. Read through the student pages and the teaching guide for this part of the lesson, thinking about the goals for this lesson.

Discussion Builders

Each lesson begins by reviewing the *Discussion Builders* posted in the front of the room. Read through the sentence stems on the poster.

✳ What did you notice about the way the *Discussion Builders* were introduced on the video?

✳ Which *Discussion Builders* do you think students will be most likely to adopt easily?

✳ How might you encourage students to expand their use of different *Discussion Builders* over time?

✳ About how much time is allotted for this activity in each lesson?

Purpose

Each lesson continues by reading the purpose.

✳ Why might it be helpful to project an image of Student Page 1 on a screen?

✳ How does reading the purpose of the lesson set the stage for purposeful and intentional learning?

Math Words

The Math Words on Student Page 1 are used in sentences to contextualize vocabulary. Notice that only about 5 minutes are allowed for this part of the lesson to help keep the lesson within the 45-minute time frame.

✳ How are these sentences similar to or different from definitions?

✳ Why might it benefit students to repeat the words aloud or silently?

✳ Why is it helpful for students to see the words in writing?

✳ On the video, how was the use of oral and written mathematical language encouraged and reinforced during the discussion?

Starter Problem

The Starter Problem is often not difficult. However, the underlying mathematical ideas are complex. If students do not make sense of the problem conceptually, their solution is very likely to have a pitfall. The Starter Problem motivates inquiry into the mathematical meaning of the problem, in part by eliciting pitfalls.

✳ What are possible pitfalls for the Starter Problem in the lesson shown on the video? Why might they occur?

MPP Lesson Roadmap

CORE LESSON: DAY 1

Opener
Discussion Builders
Purpose
Math Words
Starter Problem

Discussion
Student Thinking
Things to Remember
Reflection

CORE LESSON: DAY 2

Review and Practice
Review Day 1 Lesson
Our Turn
My Turn

MINI LESSONS: 2–3 DAYS LATER

Assess and Reinforce
Multiple Choice Mini Lesson
Writing Task Mini Lesson

✳ What mathematical concepts are foundational to understanding the meaning of the Starter Problem in this lesson? How would understanding these ideas help students make sense of their solution and avoid pitfalls?

✳ In the video, students solved the Starter Problem individually. What is the rationale given for the approach? About how much time is suggested for working on the Starter Problem?

✳ Students are asked to share their thinking, rather than their solutions, during the discussion that follows the Starter Problem. Students share their own solutions to problems after they have had an opportunity to self-correct their pitfalls and establish a conceptual foundation. Why might this strategy help lower the level of risk, broaden participation, and equalize the playing field for students?

PROFESSIONAL DEVELOPMENT TASK 2

View *Lesson in Action Professional Development: Task 2* on the DVD, after which you will be automatically returned to the menu.

Complete the following reflective activities individually or with colleagues. Each participant should have a copy of the Professional Development Handout. This task will take about 30 minutes.

Core Lesson: Discussion

Look at the *MPP* Lesson Roadmap excerpt to the right. The Discussion part of an *MPP* lesson is when students collaboratively develop their mathematical understandings. Read through the student pages and the teaching guide for this part of the lesson in the handout.

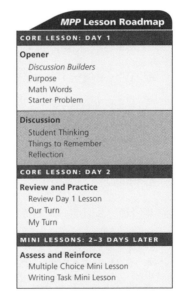

MPP Lesson Roadmap

CORE LESSON: DAY 1

Opener
Discussion Builders
Purpose
Math Words
Starter Problem

Discussion
Student Thinking
Things to Remember
Reflection

CORE LESSON: DAY 2

Review and Practice
Review Day 1 Lesson
Our Turn
My Turn

MINI LESSONS: 2–3 DAYS LATER

Assess and Reinforce
Multiple Choice Mini Lesson
Writing Task Mini Lesson

Student Thinking: OK

During this part of the lesson, students carefully analyze and discuss the thinking and drawing of a fictional student whose work is marked OK. This student's work conveys a pathway of thinking that is mathematically rich and packed with opportunities for learning. Students first work independently, then in pairs, and finally participate in a whole class discussion.

✳ What was the teacher's role during this part of the lesson in the video?

✳ How do students benefit from individually analyzing a fictional student's thinking before talking with a partner?

✳ Why is it helpful to present the thinking of the fictional student in text rather than just orally? What are the particular benefits for English learners?

✳ While students are talking in pairs, what kinds of things might the teacher take note of while listening in on students' conversations? How might these notes be helpful during the whole class discussion?

✳ What are the benefits and drawbacks of carefully unpacking the thinking and drawing of a fictional student before focusing on students' own solutions? Are there benefits for teachers?

✳ Why will it be important for students to generate and share their own solution methods later in the lesson?

Student Thinking: Oops!

Next, students analyze the work of a fictional student whose work is marked Oops! Again, they work independently, then in pairs, and finally participate in a whole class discussion. They are asked to figure out why a solution doesn't make sense or explain why it is a pitfall.

❋ What did students in the video have to say about the pitfall? How might explaining why something is a pitfall motivate students to be more mindful of their own thinking?

❋ Why is it important for students to explain why a solution doesn't make sense? How does this reinforce the meaning of a mathematical idea?

❋ Reread the specific prompts provided in the teaching guide for the Student Thinking OK and Oops! parts of the lesson. Make a list of follow-up prompts a teacher might ask to probe student thinking further. Consider enacting this part of the lesson with a colleague to practice using follow-up questions to deepen conceptual understanding.

Things to Remember and Reflection

To close the Discussion part of the lesson, students generate a list of Things to Remember and participate in a Reflection of the discussion process.

❋ Reread the teaching guide for these parts of the lesson. How much time is suggested for the two activities? What support is provided to the teacher? How do students benefit from this part of the lesson?

PROFESSIONAL DEVELOPMENT TASK 3

View *Lesson in Action Professional Development: Task 3* on the DVD, after which you will be automatically returned to the menu.

Complete the following reflective activities individually or with colleagues. Each participant should have a copy of the Professional Development Handout. This task will take about 30 minutes.

Core Lesson: Review and Practice

Look at the *MPP* Lesson Roadmap excerpt to the right. The second day of the lesson provides students opportunities to review the previous day's discussion and to practice by solving additional problems in the Our Turn and My Turn parts of the lesson. Read through the student pages and the teaching guide for this part of the lesson in the handout.

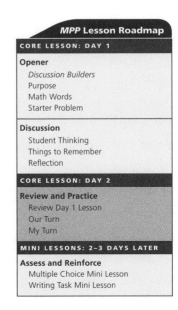

MPP **Lesson Roadmap**

CORE LESSON: DAY 1

Opener
Discussion Builders
Purpose
Math Words
Starter Problem

Discussion
Student Thinking
Things to Remember
Reflection

CORE LESSON: DAY 2

Review and Practice
Review Day 1 Lesson
Our Turn
My Turn

MINI LESSONS: 2–3 DAYS LATER

Assess and Reinforce
Multiple Choice Mini Lesson
Writing Task Mini Lesson

❋ What is the purpose of these parts of the lesson? About how much time is spent on each part?

❋ How did the teacher in the video handle the review of Day 1?

✳ Solve the problems in the Our Turn and My Turn sections. Which problems extend students' thinking beyond the Starter Problem? In what ways are they different or more difficult?

✳ What is the benefit for students to begin working in pairs for the Our Turn part? Why is it important for students to solve and then share their solutions for each problem in the Our Turn part of the lesson? How is the My Turn part of the lesson handled differently?

✳ Find the Clipboard Prompts in your book or in the handout. How will these be helpful during the discussion of the Our Turn problems?

Mini Lessons: Assess and Reinforce

The mini lessons are completed two or three days after the core lesson. They each take approximately half of a class period and may be presented on the same day or on different days. Read through the student pages and the teaching guide for the mini lessons in the handout.

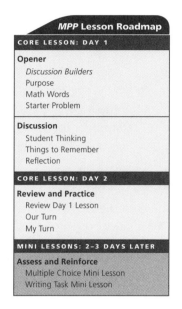

MPP Lesson Roadmap

CORE LESSON: DAY 1

Opener
Discussion Builders
Purpose
Math Words
Starter Problem

Discussion
Student Thinking
Things to Remember
Reflection

CORE LESSON: DAY 2

Review and Practice
Review Day 1 Lesson
Our Turn
My Turn

MINI LESSONS: 2–3 DAYS LATER

Assess and Reinforce
Multiple Choice Mini Lesson
Writing Task Mini Lesson

✳ How does the Multiple Choice Mini Lesson format help students be more metacognitive and aware of pitfalls in their own thinking?

✳ How does discussing the choices prepare students for achievement testing?

✳ Notice the sequence of the Writing Task Mini Lesson: read the problem, brainstorm, write together on the board, and write an explanation on the student's own page. How will this sequence be helpful to English learners and students who have difficulty reading, writing, or using mathematical language?

PROFESSIONAL DEVELOPMENT TASK 4

View the *Frequently Asked Questions* part of the video.

Read the questions and answers below.

Reflect individually or work with a partner to generate or find answers to additional questions that you may have. This task will take about 30 minutes.

Frequently Asked Questions

How much time do I need to teach one lesson?

Each core lesson is designed to take approximately two 45-minute class periods. These class periods correspond to Day 1 and Day 2 of the lesson. Each mini lesson takes about 20–25 minutes.

How soon after the core lesson do I teach the mini lessons?

It is a good idea to teach the Multiple Choice Mini Lesson a day or two after the core lesson. The Writing Task Mini Lesson can be taught a day or two after the first mini lesson is complete. This timing allows students time to revisit the concepts in the core lesson in a different context.

What if the Starter Problem or lesson is too hard for my students?

These lessons have been used effectively to introduce new concepts and to reinforce concepts. If the concept is new, anticipate that the Starter Problem may be especially challenging for a lot of students. If students are having difficulty, resist the urge to explain how to do the problem or give an on-the-spot lesson. Instead, ask students to think about what the problem means and to draw or write down anything that might help them understand it so that they can participate in the discussion that follows.

When the lesson is particularly difficult and the students are having trouble contributing to the discussion, focus more attention on the meaning of the problem rather than the solution to the problem. For example, carefully walk through the OK statement and drawing, asking questions about the details of what the fictional student said and did. You may need to provide additional examples similar to the Starter Problem and collaboratively work through them, making sure to focus on the meaning of the problem before tackling the solution.

What if my students don't talk?

In the beginning, students may be reluctant to speak, especially if they have made a pitfall. Reinforce the use of the *Discussion Builders,* and revisit the idea that this is a class endeavor with the goal of getting rid of pitfalls together. This makes it easier for students to share their thinking to help the class reach its goal. Some teachers have shown the Video for Students a second or third time to their students to reinforce how to talk with a neighbor and how to ask questions of each other, in pairs and in the whole class discussions. The video shows students how even reluctant speakers can make a contribution to the class.

Is there time to let everyone share ideas at the board?

Notice that there are prompts in the teaching guide that require you to ask students to talk to a neighbor. It is in these pairs that all students will get an opportunity to think out loud with someone. When you do call a student to the board, everyone else's job is to ask questions about or comment on that student's idea. This helps keep the discussion focused and prevents it from jumping around from idea to idea.

What if my students don't feel confident using mathematical terms or speaking in English?

There are multiple opportunities for students to engage in the lessons, and each lesson includes a variety of risk structures. Over time, with the use of partner talk, whole class talk, and *Discussion Builders,* students begin to increase both their ability in academic English and their willingness to use it publicly.

Why does the Student Thinking section of the lessons include drawings so frequently?

One purpose of the lessons is to help students visualize mathematical ideas. Diagrams are important to mathematical thinking and learning because they can help students unpack the meaning of each part of a problem and make sense of the solution. Our lessons provide students with visual models and diagrams and often encourage students to generate their own. These visual models provide fertile ground for discussing and analyzing abstract mathematical ideas.

Additional Professional Development Suggestions

MPP Research and Rationale

We suggest making it a priority to read *Math Pathways & Pitfalls: Linking Research, Standards, and Practice* on pages 1–17. This section shares the vision and rationale for *MPP* and presents research findings on the impact of *MPP*. It also includes suggestions for adapting *MPP* to different situations and needs. A lot of information is presented, so it may be helpful to break it into parts. Also, look through the research papers cited in this section to find readings that could be used for study groups or individual reflection. We encourage you to check our website for additional resources: www.WestEd.org/mpp.

Lesson Study Groups

An excellent way to learn from colleagues while teaching *MPP* lessons is by meeting with fellow teachers once or twice monthly to plan new lessons and debrief *MPP* lessons previously taught. Consider meeting with teachers at the same grade level so that you can teach the same lessons. The Lesson Foundation and Discussion sections of the teaching guide for each lesson are excellent resources for study groups. To become more familiar with the mathematics and to practice questioning techniques, enact the lesson with colleagues in pairs or small groups. Study group leaders or coaches will find many ways to adapt the teaching guides for professional learning.

Getting Started
Introducing Students to *MPP*

ACTIVITY 1: INTRODUCE THE *DISCUSSION BUILDERS* POSTER

The *Discussion Builders* poster provides an easy way to help students learn how to participate productively in discussions. The *Discussion Builders* teaching guide on the CD provides a rationale and lesson plans for introducing students to the *Discussion Builders*. With a little encouragement and practice, students quickly adapt this language to their regular mathematics classes, as well as other subject areas.

Materials
- ○ *Discussion Builders* poster
- ○ CD: *Discussion Builders* teaching guide

Preparation
- ○ Print one copy of the *Discussion Builders* teaching guide from the CD, or use the prompts below.

Time Frame
Introduce the *Discussion Builders* over a period of three days. Each day, conduct a 5- to 10-minute discussion in any subject area. Ask students to focus on one section of the *Discussion Builders*.

Day 1 — Presenting Our Ideas

Use the following suggestions to help students practice using the Presenting Our Ideas section of the *Discussion Builders* poster.

Read the poster together.

 We are going to use the *Discussion Builders* to help us learn how to have good discussions.

Point to and read the Presenting Our Ideas section.

 Why might it be important to use these during a discussion?

What might _____ sound like during a discussion?

What might someone say or ask?

Conduct a whole class discussion in any subject area and ask students to use some of the language in this first section of the poster.

Debrief after the discussion.

 What idea did someone present?

How was it helpful to the discussion?

Ask students to use these ways to share their ideas when they have other discussions.

Day 2 — Adding to Others' Ideas

Use the following suggestions to help students practice using the Adding to Others' Ideas section of the *Discussion Builders* poster.

Point to and read the Adding to Others' Ideas section.

 Why might it be important to use these during a discussion?

What might _____ sound like during a discussion? What might someone say or ask?

How are these different from Presenting Our Ideas?

Conduct a whole class discussion in any subject area and ask students to use some of the language in this second section of the poster.

Debrief after the discussion.

 Did anyone hear someone add to an idea?

How was it helpful to the discussion?

Were any other *Discussion Builders* used?

Were there any we didn't use?

Ask students to use these ways to add on to others' ideas when they have other discussions.

Day 3 — Asking More Questions

Use the following suggestions to help students practice using the Asking More Questions section of the *Discussion Builders* poster.

Point to and read the Asking More Questions section.

 Why might it be important to use these during a discussion?

How are these different from Presenting Our Ideas and Adding to Others' Ideas?

What might _____ sound like during a discussion? What might someone say or ask?

Conduct a whole class discussion in any subject area and ask students to use some of the language in this third section of the poster.

Debrief after the discussion.

Did anyone hear a question that was asked?

How was it helpful to the discussion?

Were any other *Discussion Builders* used?

Were there any we didn't use?

Ask students to use these ways of asking additional questions when they have other discussions.

ACTIVITY 2: INTRODUCE THE *MPP* VIDEO FOR STUDENTS

The Video for Students provides a visual demonstration of students discussing difficult mathematical concepts respectfully and thoughtfully. The video helps students understand the purpose and process of an *MPP* lesson. It models ways that students can be more proactive in their own learning by presenting their ideas and asking questions about others' ideas. Show this video periodically to refresh the students' memory about the purpose and the process of math discussions.

Materials
- ○ DVD: Video for Students
- ○ DVD player and monitor

Preparation
- ○ Set up the DVD player and monitor.
- ○ View the video yourself before showing it to students. Take notes and add to the set of questions on the following page as appropriate.

Time Frame
30 minutes or two 15-minute viewings that correspond to Day 1 and Day 2

Introduce the video using the following suggested instructional sequence.

Explain to students that they will be watching a short video of a *Math Pathways & Pitfalls* lesson and that later they will do *Math Pathways & Pitfalls* lessons too.

Ask students to pay special attention to the way the students work together and how they solve problems. Ask them to listen carefully to how students on the video use the *Discussion Builders*.

Explain that after the video is over, you will ask questions about what they noticed.

Show Day 1 of the lesson on the video.

Conduct a discussion using the following questions as a resource. **Ask** students to share their ideas with a neighbor before discussing as a class.

What are some of the things students in the video did to help each other understand the math?

Who can repeat some of the *Discussion Builders* students in the video used? How did the *Discussion Builders* help students discuss their ideas?

What are some of the methods the students used as they worked on the Starter Problem? Did all of them draw or did some use blocks or symbols?

Students show respect for each other's ideas in different ways. They might listen carefully to someone who is talking. They might ask questions politely. What were some things students in the video did or said to show respect for each other's ideas?

Why might it be a good idea to show a drawing at the board? How many of you think you might be nervous the first time you show your ideas at the board? What would make you feel better if you are nervous?

What math idea did you learn by watching the video?

Show Day 2 of the lesson on the video.

Conduct a discussion using the following questions as a resource. **Ask** students to share their ideas with a neighbor before discussing as a class.

What did the class do first on Day 2? Why do you think it was important to review?

Why is it a good idea to work together with a neighbor on the Our Turn problems before going to the board with your ideas?

Did anyone hear partners disagreeing about their ideas or the problems? Who can give an example of how students can be respectful to one another when disagreeing?

What can we learn from a *Math Pathways & Pitfalls* lesson that we can apply to our other math classes?

ACTIVITY 3: INTRODUCE THE PITFALLS CHALLENGE

The Pitfalls Challenge can be used as a diagnostic tool to guide the selection of *MPP* lessons. It can also be used to motivate students to learn how to monitor their thinking for pitfalls and make sense of the mathematics through *MPP* lessons.

This activity has three parts. In Part 1, students take a Pitfalls Quiz. In Part 2, the teacher corrects the quiz and provides feedback to students about how many pitfalls their class had on the quiz and presents the Pitfalls Challenge. In Part 3, students take another Pitfalls Quiz after completing several *MPP* lessons to see if they have made progress toward the Pitfalls Challenge of "No more pitfalls!"

Part 1 — Administer Pitfalls Quiz

Materials

○ Pitfalls Quiz for each student

Preparation

○ Read the Quiz How-To file in the Pitfalls Quiz folder on the CD.

○ After choosing the *MPP* lessons that you tentatively plan to use during the school year, make a Pitfalls Quiz by selecting quiz items from the CD that correspond to the lessons.

○ Print a quiz for each student.

Time Frame

30 minutes

Introduce the Pitfalls Quiz using the following suggested instructional sequence.

Invite students to explain what a pitfall is and to give an example. **Ask** why it might be important to know if they have any pitfalls.

Explain to your students that they will be taking a Pitfalls Quiz to see how many pitfalls they have as a class. **Point out** that you will collect the quizzes and report the number of pitfalls for the class, not for individuals.

Distribute the Pitfalls Quiz to students. **Ask** students to do their best to complete the problems correctly and to watch out for pitfalls! **Allow** time for students to work.

Collect the completed quizzes and score them privately. **Count** the total number of pitfalls (incorrect responses) for the whole class. This number may be reported to students as a challenge (see Part 2) to motivate them to learn how to avoid pitfalls.

Do not hand the quizzes back unless you plan to use different items for the post-challenge quiz. We suggest using this quiz as a diagnostic tool to guide selection of *MPP* lessons for the school year. Formative assessments embedded in the *MPP* lessons will provide students and the teacher ongoing feedback during the year.

Part 2 — Introduce the Pitfalls Challenge

Materials
- ○ Pitfalls Challenge chart

Preparation
- ○ Make a Pitfalls Challenge chart:

  Our class made _____ pitfalls!
  Our challenge is "No more pitfalls on the next Pitfalls Quiz!"
- ○ Post the Pitfalls Challenge chart.

Time Frame
10 minutes

Introduce the Pitfalls Challenge using the following suggested instructional sequence.

Refer to the Pitfalls Challenge chart. **Point out** how many pitfalls the whole class made on the Pitfalls Quiz taken earlier.

Explain to students that the *Math Pathways & Pitfalls* lessons will help them learn to spot their own pitfalls and make sense of the mathematics.

Part 3 — Follow Up on the Pitfalls Challenge

Materials
- ○ Pitfalls Challenge chart
- ○ Pitfalls Quiz for each student

Preparation
- ○ Post the Pitfalls Challenge chart made previously:

  Our class made _____ pitfalls!
  Our challenge is "No more pitfalls on the next Pitfalls Quiz!"
- ○ Create and print a post-assessment Pitfalls Quiz for each student using the assessment items from the CD.

Time Frame
30 minutes, after completing several *MPP* lessons

Use the following suggested instructional sequence to follow up on the Pitfalls Challenge that was given to students before their first *MPP* lesson.

Give students a post-assessment Pitfalls Quiz to check their progress toward meeting the Pitfalls Challenge.

Go over the quiz in class to see which kinds of items are still problematic for students and may need a review.

Collect the quizzes and count the number of incorrect responses for the whole class.

Write on the board the number of pitfalls from the quizzes so that students can compare how well they are meeting the Pitfalls Challenge. **Talk about** what everyone can do to make fewer pitfalls.

ACTIVITY 4: INTRODUCE THE FIRST *MATH PATHWAYS & PITFALLS* LESSON

The purpose of this activity is to introduce students to their first *MPP* lesson in a way that motivates their personal responsibility for contributing to — and learning from — *MPP* discussions. It will also help students understand how *MPP* discussions are related to the challenge: "No more pitfalls on the next Pitfalls Quiz!" By making the expectations and purpose of *MPP* lessons transparent to students, they become partners in the learning process. Part 1 of this activity introduces the core lesson; Parts 2 and 3 introduce the mini lessons.

Part 1 — Introduce the Core Lesson

Materials
- ○ *Discussion Builders* poster
- ○ Pitfalls Challenge chart
- ○ Stapled lesson packet of Student Pages 1–4 for each student
- ○ *MPP* book

Preparation
- ○ Choose the first lesson by using the tables on pages 6, 7, and 17 that correlate *MPP* to key mathematical topics in widely adopted textbooks and standards. Review the Prior Learning section of the lesson's teaching guide to make sure students have the necessary preparation.
- ○ Review the teaching guide and student pages for the lesson you choose.
- ○ Just prior to beginning the core lesson introduction, post the Pitfalls Challenge chart:

  Our class made _____ pitfalls!
  Our challenge is "No more pitfalls on the next Pitfalls Quiz!"

Time Frame
10 minutes, immediately prior to teaching your first *MPP* lesson

Introduce the first *MPP* core lesson using the following suggested instructional sequence.

Explain to students that today they have their first *Math Pathways & Pitfalls* discussion like the one they saw in the video. **Invite** students to give their ideas about what a *mathematical* pitfall, or oops, is. **Jot** their ideas on the board.

Explain that a pitfall is a mistake that is easy to make unless we're careful. **Point out** that in math we can avoid pitfalls by checking to see if our answers make sense.

Point to and read the Pitfalls Challenge chart previously posted in the front of the room: "Our class made _____ pitfalls! Our challenge is 'No more pitfalls on the next Pitfalls Quiz!'"

Explain that the purpose of these lessons will be to help them learn to make sense of the math so they catch their own pitfalls.

Refer to the *Discussion Builders* poster. **Ask** why using a variety of *Discussion Builders* helps the discussion. **Ask** students to pick a *Discussion Builder* and take turns telling a neighbor what someone might say that is an example of that *Discussion Builder*.

Distribute the lesson packets to students and use the teaching guide to begin the lesson. Another activity will introduce the first mini lessons.

Part 2 — Introduce the Multiple Choice Mini Lesson

Materials
- ○ Pitfalls Challenge chart
- ○ Student Page 5, half page for each student
- ○ *MPP* book

Preparation
- ○ Copy and cut in half the Multiple Choice Mini Lesson that corresponds to the first core lesson chosen.
- ○ Review the teaching guide and student page.
- ○ Just prior to beginning the mini lesson, post the Pitfalls Challenge chart:

  Our class made _____ pitfalls!
  Our challenge is "No more pitfalls on the next Pitfalls Quiz!"

Time Frame
10 minutes, immediately prior to teaching your first *MPP* Multiple Choice Mini lesson

Introduce the Multiple Choice Mini Lesson using the following suggested instructional sequence.

Explain to students that today they have their first *Math Pathways & Pitfalls* Multiple Choice Mini Lesson. **Explain** that in this lesson they will be asked to make some choices.

Write the following problem on the board. **Call on** a student to read the problem.

> About how much does an adult cat weigh?
>
> O   70 to 90 pounds
>
> O   7 to 9 tons
>
> O   7 to 9 pounds

Ask students to explain why the first choice doesn't make sense.

 This choice doesn't make sense because 70 to 90 pounds is about how much a school-age child might weigh! A cat can't weigh that much!

Ask students to decide whether or not the second choice makes sense.

 This choice doesn't make sense because 7 to 9 tons is really heavy. That's how much elephants weigh, not cats!

Call on a student to explain whether the third choice makes sense.

 This is a possibility. The answer makes sense.

Explain that the correct choice is 7 to 9 pounds. **Ask** a student to fill in the bubble next to the correct choice.

Explain that the way we figured out the correct choice was going through the choices one at a time and eliminating those that didn't make sense. **Ask** why this is a good strategy to use when choices are given.

Explain that sometimes one of the choices will have a pitfall, so they need to be careful. For example, it would be a pitfall to choose 7 to 9 tons because you didn't notice that it was tons, not pounds. **Call on** someone to explain why it is important to check back to see if the answer makes sense.

Distribute the Multiple Choice Mini Lesson and use the teaching guide to begin the lesson.

Part 3 — Introduce the Writing Task Mini Lesson

Materials
- ○ Pitfalls Challenge chart
- ○ Student Page 6, half page for each student
- ○ *MPP* book

Preparation
- ○ Copy and cut in half the Writing Task Mini Lesson that corresponds to the first core lesson chosen.
- ○ Review the teaching guide and student page.
- ○ Just prior to beginning the mini lesson, post the Pitfalls Challenge chart:

  Our class made _____ pitfalls!
  Our challenge is "No more pitfalls on the next Pitfalls Quiz!"

Time Frame
10 minutes, immediately prior to teaching your first Writing Task Mini Lesson

Use the suggestions in this section to introduce students to their first Writing Task Mini Lesson.

Explain to students that today they will do their first *Math Pathways & Pitfalls* Writing Task Mini Lesson.

Explain that any time they write an explanation, they need to make sure it is clear, correct, and makes sense.

Write the following two explanations for how to pour a glass of milk. **Ask** a student to read the explanations.

> You open it and pour it.

> You open the top of the milk carton. Then you hold the carton over the glass and pour the milk into the glass.

Call on students to explain which is the better explanation and why. **Jot** their ideas on the board. **Encourage** suggestions for improving the explanations.

Ask students to keep these ideas in mind when they write a mathematical explanation in today's *Math Pathways & Pitfalls* mini lesson. **Invite** ideas for ways to check whether their mathematical explanations are clear, correct, and make sense.

Distribute the Writing Task Mini Lesson and use the teaching guide to begin the lesson.

Clipboard Prompts

Effective instructional dialogue digs deep into one student's thinking or one idea at a time. To unfold understanding, begin with a broader question and then follow up with probes for more detail. Use the first set of prompts below to focus students' attention on what the problem means. Use the second set of questions to delve into students' solutions. Finally, use the third set of prompts to invite reflection and ask for other approaches.

1 Understanding the Problem

- ☐ Who can explain what this problem means — not how to solve it — what does it mean?

- ☐ How do you read this (point to a word, phrase, number, symbol, or equation)? What does it mean?

- ☐ Could someone show us how to use a drawing or materials to show what it means? Please explain _____. Please label _____. How does this help us understand?

- ☐ Do you think the answer will be greater or less than _____? Maybe you're not sure yet, but what do you think …?

2 Understanding the Solution Process

- ☐ Who would like to show us how they solved the problem?

- ☐ Please say more. Could you help us understand why you _____? What does _____ mean? Why does it make sense to _____? How is this different from _____?

- ☐ Some of you seem to have questions about this idea. Who has a question? What is confusing?

- ☐ Can someone else help us clarify this idea? Who has another way to help us understand it?

3 Reflecting On and Extending the Problem

- ☐ Explain how you know this answer makes sense. How could you check? How can we show or prove it is correct?

- ☐ Does someone have another approach? Could we use a drawing? Could we use a paper-and-pencil procedure?

References

Ball, D. L. (1997). From the general to particular: Knowing our own students as learners of mathematics. *Mathematics Teacher, 90,* 732–737.

Beghetto, R. A. (2004). Toward a more complete picture of student learning: Assessing students' motivational beliefs. *Practical Assessment, Research, & Evaluation, 9*(15).

Behr, M., Lesh, R., Post, T., & Silver, E. (1983). Rational number concepts. In R. Lesh & M. Landau (Eds.), *The acquisition of mathematical concepts and processes* (pp. 91–126). New York: Academic Press.

Borasi, R. (1994). Capitalizing on errors as "springboards for inquiry." *Journal for Research in Mathematics Education, 25*(2), 166–208.

Brown, J. S., Collins, A., & Duguid, P. (1989). Situated cognition and the culture of learning. *Educational Researcher, 18*(1), 32–42.

Carpenter, T. P., Fennema, E., Peterson, P. L., Chiang, C., & Loef, M. (1989). Using knowledge of children's mathematics thinking in classroom teaching: An experimental study. *American Educational Research Journal, 26*(4), 499–531.

Carpenter, T. P., & Moser, J. M. (1983). The acquisition of addition and subtraction concepts. In R. Lesh & M. Landau (Eds.), *The acquisition of mathematical concepts and processes* (pp. 7–44). New York: Academic Press.

Cobb, P., Wood, T. L, & Yackel, E. L. (1993). Discourse, mathematical thinking, and classroom practice. In N. Minick, E. Forman, & C. A. Stone (Eds.), *Contexts for learning: Sociocultural dynamics in children's development* (pp. 91–119). New York: Oxford University Press.

Cummins, J. (1980). The construct of proficiency in bilingual education. In J. E. Alatis (Ed.), *Georgetown University Round Table on Languages and Linguistics: Current issues in bilingual education,* 81–103.

Donovan, M. S., & Bransford, J. D. (2005). Pulling threads. In M. S. Donovan and J. D. Bransford (Eds.), *How students learn: Mathematics in the classroom* (pp. 569–590). Washington, DC: National Research Council.

Durkin, K., & Rittle-Johnson, B. (2009, June 7). *Comparing incorrect and correct examples when learning about decimals and the effects on explanation quality.* Poster session presented at the Institute of Education Sciences Research Conference.

Echevarria, J., Vogt, M. E., & Short, D. (2004). *Making content comprehensible for English learners: The SIOP model.* Boston: Allyn & Bacon.

Festinger, L. (1957). *A theory of cognitive dissonance.* Evanston, IL: Row, Peterson & Company.

Fuson, K. C. (1992). Research on learning and teaching addition and subtraction of whole numbers. In G. Leinhardt, R. T. Putnam, & R. A. Hattrup (Eds.), *The analysis of arithmetic for mathematics teaching* (pp. 53–187). Hillsdale, NJ: Erlbaum.

Heller, J., Gordon, A., Curtis, D., Rabe-Hesketh, S., Clarke, C., & Ramírez, A. (2000). *The effects of the* Math Pathways & Pitfalls *lessons on elementary school students' mathematics achievement.* Paper presented at the Research Presession of the National Council of Teachers of Mathematics, April 2006, St. Louis, MO.

Heller Research Associates (2008). Math Pathways & Pitfalls *transfer study summary.* Unpublished manuscript.

Khisty, L. (1992, August). *A naturalistic look at language factors in mathematics teaching in bilingual classrooms.* Proceedings of the Third National Research Symposium on Limited English Proficient Student Issues: Focus on middle and high school issues. Washington, DC: U.S. Department of Education Office of Bilingual Education and Minority Languages Affairs.

Khisty, L. (1995). Making inequality: Issues of language and meanings in mathematics teaching with Hispanic students. In W. G. Seced, E. Rennema, & L. B. Adajian (Eds.), *New direction for equity in mathematics education* (pp. 279–297). New York: Cambridge University Press.

Khisty, L. (2002). Mathematics learning and the Latino student: Suggestions from research for classroom practice. *Teaching Children Mathematics, 9*(1), 32–35.

Lamon, S. J. (1999). *Teaching fractions and ratios for understanding.* London and New Jersey: Lawrence Erlbaum Associates.

Lampert, M. (1990). When the problem is not the question and the solution is *not* the answer: Mathematical knowing and teaching. *American Educational Research Journal, 27,* 29–64.

Lave, J., & Wenger, E. (1991). *Situated learning: Legitimate peripheral participation.* Cambridge, England: Cambridge University Press.

National Council of Teachers of Mathematics. (2006). *Curriculum focal points for prekindergarten through grade 8 mathematics: A quest for coherence.* Reston, VA: NCTM.

Olivares, R. A. (1996). Communication in mathematics for students with limited English proficiency. In P. C. Elliot & M. J. Kenney (Eds.), *Communication in mathematics: K–12 and beyond — 1996 yearbook* (pp. 219–230). Reston, VA: National Council of Teachers of Mathematics.

Pimm, D. (1995). *Symbols and meanings in school mathematics.* London and New York: Routledge.

Schleppegrell, M. J. (2004). *The language of schooling: A functional linguistics perspective.* Mahwah, NJ: Erlbaum.

Sfard, A. (2000). Limits of mathematics discourse. *Mathematical thinking and learning, 2*(3), 157–189.

Solomon, J., & Rhodes, N. (1995). *Conceptualizing academic language (Research Rep. No. 15).* Santa Cruz: University of California, National Center for Research on Cultural Diversity and Second Language Learning.

Spanos, G., Rhodes, N., Corasaniti, T., Crandall, D., & Crandall, J. (1988). Linguistic features of mathematical problem solving: Insights and applications. In *Linguistic and cultural influence on learning mathematics.* London: Lawrence Erlbaum Associates.

Thompson, D. R., & Rubinstein, R. N. (2000). Learning mathematics vocabulary: Potential pitfalls and instructional strategies. *Mathematics Teacher, 93,* 568–573.

Vygotsky, L. S. (1962). *Thought and language.* (E. Hanfmann & G. Vakar, Trans. and Eds.). New York: John Wiley.

Vygotsky, L. S. (1978). *Mind in society: The development of higher psychological processes.* Cambridge, MA: Harvard University Press.

Teaching Guides

Number Line Points

Lesson at a Glance

Prior Learning Needed

- Familiarity with a number line
- Familiarity with place value concepts

Lesson Preparation

- Study Lesson Foundation
- Review Teaching Guide and Student Pages
- Prepare stapled packet of Student Pages 1–4 for each student
- Copy and cut in half Student Pages 5 and 6
- Post *Discussion Builders* poster

Mathematical goals

✳ Name a "point" by estimating its distance from zero

✳ Know that numbers increase from left to right on the number line

Mathematical language and reasoning goals

✳ Use reasoning to estimate the location of points on a number line

✳ Use the term "point" to indicate a number's location on a number line

LESSON ROADMAP			MATERIALS
CORE LESSON: DAY 1	GROUPING	TIME	○ *Discussion Builders* poster
Opener			○ Projector (optional)
Discussion Builders			○ Student Page 1
Purpose	👥	🕐	○ Student Page 2
Math Words			○ Teaching Guide
Starter Problem	👤	🕐	○ Paper strips of equal length for making number lines (suggested)
Discussion			
Student Thinking	👤 👥 👥	🕑	
Things to Remember	👥	🕐	
Reflection			
CORE LESSON: DAY 2			○ Clipboard Prompts, page 37
Review and Practice			○ Student Page 2 (completed day 1)
Review Day 1 Lesson	👥	🕐	○ Student Pages 3 and 4
Our Turn	👥 👥	🕐	○ Teaching Guide
• My Turn	👤	🕐	○ Paper strips of equal length for making number lines (suggested)
MINI LESSONS: 2–3 DAYS LATER			○ Student Pages 5 and 6
Assess and Reinforce			○ Teaching Guide
Multiple Choice Mini Lesson	👤 👥 👥	🕐	○ Paper strips of equal length for making number lines (suggested)
Writing Task Mini Lesson	👤 👥	🕐	

Lesson Foundation

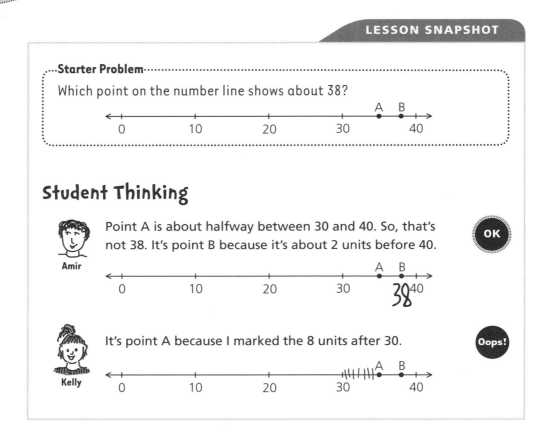

Starter Problem

Which point on the number line shows about 38?

Student Thinking

Amir

Point A is about halfway between 30 and 40. So, that's not 38. It's point B because it's about 2 units before 40.

OK

Kelly

It's point A because I marked the 8 units after 30.

Oops!

MATHEMATICAL INSIGHTS & TEACHING TIPS

Using Reasoning to Locate Points

Once students know what 1 unit represents, such as from 0 to 1 and from 3 to 4, they can use estimation to locate other points. When the size of 1 unit is not explicitly given, students must use other clues to locate points. Amir realized that A is the point about midway between 30 and 40, so it is about 35, not 38. He also said that point B was about 2 units before 40, which would be 38. Students should learn to use benchmark numbers, such as multiples of ten and the midpoints between these multiples, to estimate the location of points.

Oops! To find the point for 38, Kelly drew 8 units after 30, but she didn't use reasoning or number sense to correctly estimate the size of the units.

 Prior to this lesson, students may need to make their own number lines by iterating a physical unit, such as a short paper strip, along a number line to mark off points for units. Ask them to verify the name of points midway between 0 and 10 or 10 and 20.

MATHEMATICAL INSIGHTS & TEACHING TIPS (CONTINUED)

Estimating Equal-Sized Units to Locate Points

The name of a point on a number line is determined by how far it is from 0. For whole numbers, this distance is measured in equal-sized whole units. For fractions and decimals, it is measured with parts of whole units. Kelly drew 8 fairly equal-sized units along the number line to find the point for 38, but she incorrectly estimated the size of each unit. Since she put in 8 units between 30 and 35 (the midpoint between 30 and 40), her units were too small. Exactly 5 units can fit into this space.

 Have students estimate the length of 1 unit using a known distance on the number line, such as the distance between 30 and 35. Then they can mark off units on the number line to see if 5 units fit between 30 and 35. If they know the length of 5 units, then 2 units is a little less than half of this length and 3 units is a little more. Some students will try to draw 5 marks between 30 and 35 rather than 5 units. A unit is a length, not a point.

Infinite Number of Points

A number line has an infinite number of points and represents different kinds of numbers. For example, the value of a point placed half of the distance from 0 to 1 is 1/2, or 0.5. The point halfway between 0 and 1/2 is 1/4, or 0.25. The distance between any two numbers can always be split in half to make a new number. The value of numbers on a number line increases from left to right, regardless of whether their values are positive or negative. (Note that numbers to the left of 0 are negative.)

MATHEMATICAL DISCUSSION SUPPORT

During the discussion, ask students questions that prompt them to use the words "point" and "unit" in their explanations. Make sure students understand that the phrase "naming a point" means to tell what number the point represents.

Also explain that the arrows on the ends of the number line show that the number line continues in both directions. Point out that they will learn about the negative numbers, which are to the left of 0 on the number line, in later grades.

Emphasize that the mathematical use of the term "point" refers to a place on the number line that is the location of a number. Explain that this is different from everyday uses of the word, such as the end of something sharp, like a needle, or the verb "to point."

Opener

Review *Discussion Builders*

Read the poster. **Suggest** a section to focus on today:
Presenting Our Ideas, Adding to Others' Ideas, or *Asking More Questions.*

Purpose

Distribute stapled packets of Student Pages 1–4. **Project** an image of page 1 (optional).

Call on a student to read the purpose.

Math Words

Point to and say the first math words. **Ask** students to repeat them aloud or silently.

Read the sentence containing the words.

Give an example using objects or drawings.

Repeat for the other math words.

Starter Problem

Read the Starter Problem. **Call on** a student to restate it in his/her own words.

 Please use what you already know to help you solve this problem on your own. This will prepare you to talk about the math and how to avoid pitfalls in our discussion later on.

I'll walk around and make notes about things we need to discuss. Look out for oops, or pitfalls! (WAIT)

Look at your work. It's easy to have an oops, or pitfall, in this type of problem. You might also have made a pitfall if you thought point A showed 38.

Don't worry. Next we'll discuss how two imaginary students solved this problem. One has a pitfall! You may keep your solution private, but bring up your ideas in the discussion.

STUDENT PAGE 1

Purpose
To name a number for a point on a number line

Math Words

number line	A number line shows numbers in order along a line.
point	A dot on a number line shows where the point for a number is.
unit	Each unit has a length of 1.

5 units

0   5   10

Starter Problem

Which point on the number line shows about 38?

                                A B

0   10   20   30   40

Discussion

Student Thinking

Point A is about halfway between 30 and 40. So, that's not 38. It's point B because it's about 2 units before 40.

OK

Amir

Ask students to refer to page 2. **Read** the statement marked OK.

Explain that this statement is about the same problem students worked on earlier.

 We can learn a lot about the math by studying what this student did.

Read each sentence silently and look at the drawing. Think about what they mean. **WAIT**

Now talk with a partner about what each sentence and each part of the drawing means.

Listen in, ask questions, and observe. **Note** potential contributions for the discussion.

 Who can come up to show what Amir meant when he said, "Point A is about halfway between 30 and 40"?

What number is halfway between 30 and 40? How do you know?

Would the point for 38 be before or after the halfway point? Explain.

Talk to your neighbor about what Amir meant when he said, "It's point B because it's about 2 units before 40." **WAIT**

What number is 1 unit before 40 on the number line? 2 units after 40? Explain.

Call on students to state things to remember about solving problems like this.

Start a Things to Remember list on the board.

MORE DAY 1

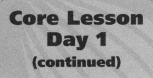

Discussion

Student Thinking, continued

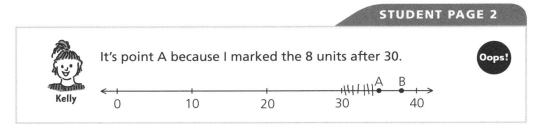

It's point A because I marked the 8 units after 30.

Oops!

Kelly

Read the statement marked Oops. **Remind** students that this is a common pitfall.

Kelly made a pitfall when she marked off 8 units between 30 and point A. Talk with your neighbor about why her answer doesn't make sense. **WAIT**

About how many units should fit between 30 and point A? Should the length of each unit be longer or shorter than Kelly's? Explain.

Who can explain why about 5 units should fit between 30 and point A?

Who can mark off units to show us why 38 makes sense for point B?

Draw a number line like in the Starter Problem and show points for 15 and 25. **Ask** students to talk with a neighbor about which point shows 25. **Remind** them to look out for pitfalls. **Call on** students to show why their answers make sense.

Things to Remember

Call on students to **add** to the Things to Remember list on the board. **Read** the list.

Help students summarize and record two important Things to Remember.

Things to Remember List (sample)
1. It helps to think about the halfway point between numbers like 30 and 40.
2. If you know the size of 5 units, you can estimate the size of 1 unit.

Reflection

Ask students to reflect on the discussion process using one of the sample prompts.

Reflection Prompts (sample)
- Name a *Discussion Builder* that we used today. How did it help the discussion?
- What *Discussion Builder* could we use next time to make the discussion even better?
- What did someone do or say today that helped you understand the math?

**Core Lesson
Day 2**

Review and Practice

Review

Ask students to review page 2 to jog their memory.

Read the statement marked OK. Call on a student to explain how the problem was solved.

Read the statement marked Oops. Call on a student to explain why it is incorrect or doesn't make sense.

Call on two or three students to read an item on their Things to Remember list.

Point A is about halfway between 30 and 40. So, that's not 38. It's point B because it's about 2 units before 40. **OK**

It's point A because I marked the 8 units after 30. **Oops!**

Our Turn

Ask students to refer to page 3.

Use the procedure below and the Clipboard Prompts to discuss students' solutions. Discuss the problems one at a time.

   Read the problem.

   Ask students to work with a neighbor to solve it.

   Discuss one or two students' solutions.

Answer Key	1. B
	2. C
	3. D

STUDENT PAGE 3

Our Turn

Write the answer.

1. Which point on the number line shows about 27? _____
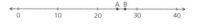

2. Which point on the number line shows about 44? _____

3. Which point on the number line shows about 18? _____

My Turn

Ask students to solve the problems on page 4. Remind them to watch out for pitfalls!

After allowing time to work, read the answers. Have students mark and revise their papers using ink or crayon.

Answer Key	1. D
	2. D
	3. A

STUDENT PAGE 4

My Turn

Write the answer.

1. Which point on the number line shows about 15? _____

2. Which point on the number line shows about 22? _____

3. Which point on the number line shows about 36? _____
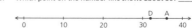

Mini Lessons
(2–3 Days Later)

Assess and Reinforce

Multiple Choice Mini Lesson

Distribute Student Page 5.

Problem 1

 Please read problem 1.

Talk with your neighbor about which choices don't make sense. **WAIT**

Who can explain why point C must be between 10 and 15?

Who can show why 14 is the correct choice?

 Prompt students to use number sense to know that the number is about 1 unit less than 15, so 14 is a reasonable choice.

Problem 2

 Read the problem and find the correct choice. **WAIT**

Which response is correct? Explain why.

How could you prove that 26 is the best choice?

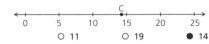

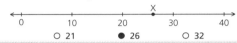

STUDENT PAGE 5

Multiple Choice Mini Lesson

Fill in the circle next to the answer you choose.

1. What number is a good estimate for point C?

   0   5   10   15   20   25

   ○ 11   ○ 19   ● 14

2. What number is a good estimate for point X?

   0   10   20   30   40

   ○ 21   ● 26   ○ 32

Writing Task Mini Lesson

Distribute Student Page 6.

Ask a student to read the task. **Call on** students to respond with their ideas.

Jot the ideas on the board.

Write an explanation together using their ideas. **Read** it aloud.

Ask students to write an explanation on their page.

STUDENT PAGE 6

Writing Task Mini Lesson

Explain how you know that a good estimate for point C is 25. You may draw a picture on the back to help explain.

0   10   20   30

Sample Explanation: Point C is about halfway between 20 and 30. I know that's 25 because there are 10 units between 20 and 30. So, there would be 5 units more after 20 to get to the halfway point. That's 25.

Mathematical Discussion Support

During the brainstorming process, invite students to use materials such as paper strips or drawings of number lines to help them describe their ideas.

Ask students to explain what a "good estimate" means. You may need to provide an explanation orally and in writing to ensure everyone understands.

Marking Points on a Number Line

Prior Learning Needed

- Familiarity with a number line
- Familiarity with place value concepts

Lesson Preparation

- Study Lesson Foundation
- Review Teaching Guide and Student Pages
- Prepare stapled packet of Student Pages 1–4 for each student
- Copy and cut in half Student Pages 5 and 6
- Post *Discussion Builders* poster

Mathematical goals

✳ Locate whole numbers on a number line by thinking of units of distance

✳ Understand the relative magnitude of numbers on a number line

Mathematical language and reasoning goals

✳ Use benchmark numbers on a number line to find other numbers

✳ Estimate the length of one unit using a given distance

LESSON ROADMAP			MATERIALS
CORE LESSON: DAY 1	GROUPING	TIME	○ *Discussion Builders* poster
Opener			○ Projector (optional)
Discussion Builders			○ Student Page 1
Purpose	👥	🕐	○ Student Page 2
Math Words			○ Teaching Guide
Starter Problem	👤	🕐	○ Paper strips of equal length for making number lines (suggested)
Discussion			
Student Thinking	👤 👥 👥	🕐	
Things to Remember	👥	🕐	
Reflection			
CORE LESSON: DAY 2			○ Clipboard Prompts, page 37
Review and Practice			○ Student Page 2 (completed day 1)
Review Day 1 Lesson	👥	🕐	○ Student Pages 3 and 4
Our Turn	👥 👥	🕐	○ Teaching Guide
My Turn	👤	🕐	○ Paper strips of equal length for making number lines (suggested)
MINI LESSONS: 2–3 DAYS LATER			○ Student Pages 5 and 6
Assess and Reinforce			○ Teaching Guide
Multiple Choice Mini Lesson	👤 👥 👥	🕐	○ Paper strips of equal length for making number lines, large copies of premade number lines (suggested)
Writing Task Mini Lesson	👤 👥	🕐	

Lesson Foundation

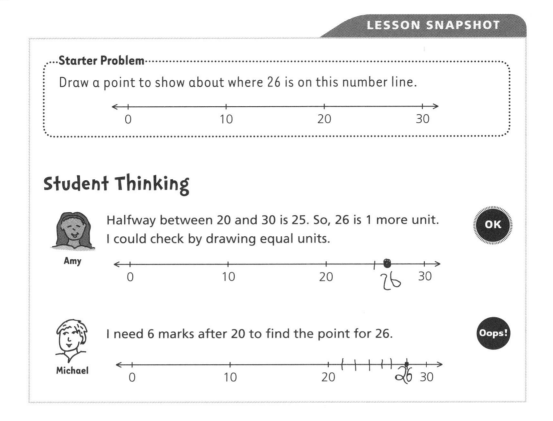

LESSON SNAPSHOT

Starter Problem

Draw a point to show about where 26 is on this number line.

0   10   20   30

Student Thinking

Amy

Halfway between 20 and 30 is 25. So, 26 is 1 more unit. I could check by drawing equal units.

OK

0   10   20   26   30

Michael

I need 6 marks after 20 to find the point for 26.

Oops!

0   10   20   26 30

MATHEMATICAL INSIGHTS & TEACHING TIPS

Using Reasoning to Locate Points

Amy used 25, the halfway point between 20 and 30, to find the approximate location of 26 on the number line. She estimated about how long 1 unit would be and drew the point for 26 about 1 unit to the right of 25. Students need to develop several skills to locate numbers on a number line that has only some of the benchmarks (such as 10, 20, and 30) marked. For example, they need to know that there are 10 units between 20 and 30, 5 units between 20 and 25, and 5 units between 25 and 30. They also need to learn how to estimate the length of 1 unit.

Oops! Michael made 6 marks after the 20 to show 26, but his units were too long to fit 10 units between 20 and 30.

Estimating the Size of 1 Unit

To determine the location of 26 on the number line, Michael understood that 10 equal-sized units are supposed to fit between 20 and 30. He drew 6 units that were approximately equal in size, but he didn't think about how long the unit should be so that 10 units would fit between 20 and 30. Since his unit was too long, the point he drew for 26 didn't make sense.

MATHEMATICAL INSIGHTS & TEACHING TIPS (CONTINUED)

 Students may benefit from practice estimating the size of a unit on a number line prior to this lesson. A simple activity is to have each student draw a line on his or her paper. The goal is to divide the line into a number of parts (3, 4, 5, or 10) of equal size. Have them first estimate about how long 1 part will be and then use visual estimation to mark off more parts of equal size.

Marks on a Number Line

Like rulers, number lines have marks that show a number of units of length. However, on a number line, each mark represents both a point as a location in comparison to other numbers and a distance from 0. Arrows show that number lines continue in both directions, both positive (to the right of 0) and negative (to the left of 0).

The marks on a number line, corresponding to numbers, give a spatial feeling to abstract numbers: 5 is to the left of 7, 8 is between 6 and 11, 10 is halfway between 9 and 11. This spatial feeling may help students understand the relationships between numbers. It also sets the stage for geometry.

MATHEMATICAL DISCUSSION SUPPORT

Ask students questions that prompt them to explain their reasoning for placing a point between two particular numbers. Be sure that the phrase "halfway between" is clear. Halfway between 20 and 30 means there are the same number of units from 20 to 25 as there are from 25 to 30.

 Help students understand that when we say "1 unit after 25," we mean 1 unit to the right of 25 on the number line. Similarly, when we say "1 unit before 25," we mean 1 unit to the left of 25 on the number line. Show them how numbers increase as we move to the right on the number line.

**Core Lesson
Day 1**

Opener

Review *Discussion Builders*

Read the poster. Suggest a section to focus on today:
Presenting Our Ideas, Adding to Others' Ideas, or *Asking More Questions.*

Purpose

Distribute stapled packets of Student Pages 1–4. Project an image of page 1 (optional).

Call on a student to read the purpose.

Math Words

Point to and say the first math words. Ask students to repeat them aloud or silently.

Read the sentence containing the words.

Give an example using objects or drawings.

Repeat for the other math words.

Starter Problem

Read the Starter Problem. Call on a student to restate it in his/her own words.

 Please use what you already know to help you solve this problem on your own. This will prepare you to talk about the math and how to avoid pitfalls in our discussion later on.

I'll walk around and make notes about things we need to discuss. Look out for oops, or pitfalls! (WAIT)

Look at your work. It's easy to have an oops, or pitfall, in this type of problem. You might also have made a pitfall if your point is very close to 30.

Don't worry. Next we'll discuss how two imaginary students solved this problem. One has a pitfall! You may keep your solution private, but bring up your ideas in the discussion.

STUDENT PAGE 1

Purpose
To use estimation to mark a point for a number on a number line

Math Words

halfway between — 15 is halfway between 10 and 20 on the number line.

(number line marked 0, 10, 15, 20)

point — A dot on a number line shows where the point for a number is.

units — 10 equal units fit between 0 and 10 on a number line.

Starter Problem
Draw a point to show about where 26 is on this number line.

(number line marked 0, 10, 20, 30)

Discussion

Student Thinking

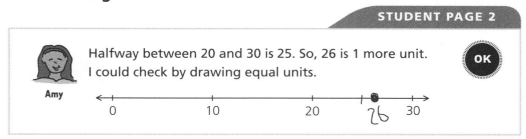

STUDENT PAGE 2

Amy

Halfway between 20 and 30 is 25. So, 26 is 1 more unit.
I could check by drawing equal units.

OK

Ask students to refer to page 2. **Read** the statement marked OK.

Explain that this statement is about the same problem students worked on earlier.

We can learn a lot about the math by studying what this student did.

Read each sentence silently and look at the drawing. Think about what they mean. WAIT

Now talk with a partner about what each sentence and each part of the drawing means.

Listen in, ask questions, and observe. **Note** potential contributions for the discussion.

Who can come up and explain why 25 is halfway between 20 and 30? How many units are on the number line between 20 and 25? between 0 and 26?

Amy knew that 26 is 1 more unit than 25. Talk to your neighbor about how she knew where to put 26 on her number line. WAIT

Who would like to come up to show how Amy estimated where to put 26 on her number line? (**Call** student(s) up to demonstrate their method.)

Amy said she could check by drawing equal units. How do you know about how long 1 unit will be? Who can show us a way to check by drawing equal units?

Who can show about where we would draw the point for 18 on our number line?

Call on students to state things to remember about solving problems like this.

Start a Things to Remember list on the board.

MORE DAY 1

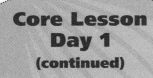

**Core Lesson
Day 1**
(continued)

Discussion

Student Thinking, continued

STUDENT PAGE 2

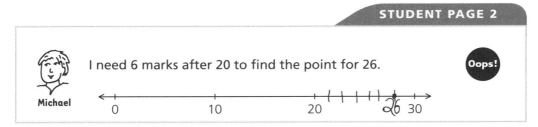

Michael: I need 6 marks after 20 to find the point for 26. **Oops!**

Read the statement marked Oops. **Remind** students that this is a common pitfall.

 Michael made a pitfall when he made his units too long. Talk with your neighbor about why his answer doesn't make sense. WAIT

How many units must fit between 20 and 30? How do you know Michael's units are too long? What is a better way to figure out where to draw a point for 26?

Draw a number line like in the Starter Problem. **Ask** students to talk with a neighbor about where to draw a point on the number line to show 14. **Remind** them to look out for pitfalls. **Call on** students to show why their answers make sense.

Provide another example to solve as a class, if time permits. **Ask** students to look out for pitfalls.

Things to Remember

Call on students to **add** to the Things to Remember list on the board. **Read** the list.

Help students summarize and record two important Things to Remember.

> **Things to Remember List (sample)**
> 1. It helps to know what number is halfway between two other numbers.
> 2. Estimate the length of 1 unit to help you draw the point on a number line.

Reflection

Ask students to reflect on the discussion process using one of the sample prompts.

> **Reflection Prompts (sample)**
> * Name a *Discussion Builder* that we used today. How did it help the discussion?
> * What *Discussion Builder* could we use next time to make the discussion even better?
> * What did someone do or say today that helped you understand the math?

Core Lesson Day 2

Review and Practice

Review

Ask students to review page 2 to jog their memory.

Read the statement marked OK. **Call on** a student to explain how the problem was solved.

Read the statement marked Oops. **Call on** a student to explain why it is incorrect or doesn't make sense.

Call on two or three students to read an item on their Things to Remember list.

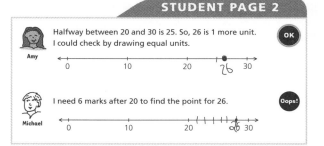

Amy: Halfway between 20 and 30 is 25. So, 26 is 1 more unit. I could check by drawing equal units. **OK**

Michael: I need 6 marks after 20 to find the point for 26. **Oops!**

Our Turn

Ask students to refer to page 3.

Use the procedure below and the Clipboard Prompts to discuss students' solutions. **Discuss** the problems one at a time.

> **Read** the problem.
>
> **Ask** students to work with a neighbor to solve it.
>
> **Discuss** one or two students' solutions.

Answer Key

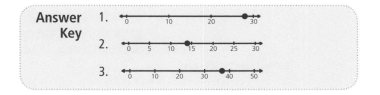

STUDENT PAGE 3

Our Turn

Draw a point to show about where the number is on each number line. Label the point.

1. 28

2. 14

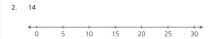

3. 37

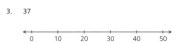

My Turn

Ask students to solve the problems on page 4. **Remind** them to watch out for pitfalls!

After allowing time to work, **read** the answers. **Have** students mark and revise their papers using ink or crayon.

Answer Key

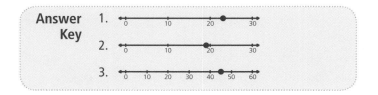

STUDENT PAGE 4

My Turn

Draw a point to show about where the number is on each number line. Label the point.

1. 23

2. 19

3. 45

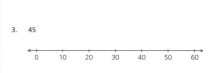

Mini Lessons
(2–3 Days Later)

Assess and Reinforce

Multiple Choice Mini Lesson

Distribute Student Page 5.

Problem 1

Please read problem 1.

Talk with your neighbor about which choices don't make sense. **WAIT**

Who can explain which number line has 14 marked correctly?

Remind students to use benchmarks, such as 15, the halfway point between 10 and 20. Help them see that 14 is 1 unit less than 15.

Problem 2

Read the problem and find the correct choice. **WAIT**

Which response is correct? Explain why.

How can you check that a point is in about the right place if not all the numbers are written on the number line? Explain.

Multiple Choice Mini Lesson

Fill in the circle next to the answer you choose.

1. Which number line correctly shows the point for 14?

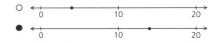

2. Which number line correctly shows the point for 27?

Writing Task Mini Lesson

Distribute Student Page 6.

Ask a student to read the task. **Call on** students to respond with their ideas.

Jot the ideas on the board.

Write an explanation together using their ideas. **Read** it aloud.

Ask students to write an explanation on their page.

Writing Task Mini Lesson

Explain how you know where to mark and label the number 39 on this number line.

Sample Explanation: I remembered 39 is 1 less than 40. I can mark 10 equal units between 30 and 40 on the number line. Then I move 1 unit back from 40 and mark the point for 39.

Mathematical Discussion Support

English Learner Access

When generating ideas, invite students to use materials or drawings, such as a large copy of the number line and a 10-unit paper strip, to mark off groups of 10 units. This may help them describe their ideas.

Ask students to explain what 1 unit and 10 units mean.

Talk with students about the meanings of terms such as "point" and "label" and how they are used in this lesson.

Add a Few

Lesson at a Glance

Prior Learning Needed

- Use a number line
- Add using an algorithm

Lesson Preparation

- Study Lesson Foundation
- Review Teaching Guide and Student Pages
- Prepare stapled packet of Student Pages 1–4 for each student
- Copy and cut in half Student Pages 5 and 6
- Post *Discussion Builders* poster

Mathematical goals

✳ Increase a number by a specific amount

✳ Count forward from one decade to the next

Mathematical language and reasoning goals

✳ Use a mental number line to add

✳ Count up in easy steps using benchmarks

LESSON ROADMAP			MATERIALS
CORE LESSON: DAY 1	GROUPING	TIME	
Opener			○ *Discussion Builders* poster
Discussion Builders			○ Projector (optional)
Purpose	👥	🕐	○ Student Page 1
Math Words			○ Student Page 2
Starter Problem	👤	🕐	○ Teaching Guide
Discussion			○ Place value materials (suggested)
Student Thinking	👤 👥 👥	🕐	
Things to Remember	👥	🕐	
Reflection			
CORE LESSON: DAY 2			○ Clipboard Prompts, page 37
Review and Practice			○ Student Page 2 (completed day 1)
Review Day 1 Lesson	👥	🕐	○ Student Pages 3 and 4
Our Turn	👥 👥	🕐	○ Teaching Guide
My Turn	👤	🕐	○ Place value materials (suggested)
MINI LESSONS: 2–3 DAYS LATER			○ Student Pages 5 and 6
Assess and Reinforce			○ Teaching Guide
Multiple Choice Mini Lesson	👤 👥 👥	🕐	○ Base ten blocks, beans or counters, copies of number lines (suggested)
Writing Task Mini Lesson	👤 👥	🕐	

Lesson Foundation

Starter Problem

Think about the meaning. Solve.

$$68 + 7 = \underline{\qquad}$$

Student Thinking

Katie

I added 7 in my head using easy steps. 68 and 2 more made 70. Then 5 more made 75. I could add on paper too.

OK

$$68 + 7 = \underline{75}$$

Sam

I just lined them up and added. It's 138.

Oops!

$$\begin{array}{r} 68 \\ + 7 \\ \hline 138 \end{array}$$

MATHEMATICAL INSIGHTS & TEACHING TIPS

Adding Using a Mental Number Line

Katie thought of a number line in her head to visualize adding 68 + 7. She added on 2 units to 68 to get to 70. Then, she added on 5 more units to get to 75. So, 68 + 7 (or 68 + 2 + 5) equals 75. Notice that she added on in easy steps, taking advantage of the benchmark number 70, which is a multiple of 10.

She also could have added 68 + 1 + 6. In fact, she could have used hops for any combination of 7, such as 5 + 2, 4 + 3, or 3 + 3 + 1, because 7 more than 68 is always 75. Since the addition operation is commutative, the order of the hops doesn't matter. So, she could have made a hop for 5, then a hop for 2, and still have gotten the sum of 75. A mental number line is a powerful model that helps students visualize addition whether they are computing with whole numbers, fractions, or decimals.

Oops! Sam used the addition algorithm to add 68 and 7, but when he wrote down the numbers, he lined them up beginning with the digits on the left instead of the right.

Lesson Foundation (continued)

MATHEMATICAL INSIGHTS & TEACHING TIPS (CONTINUED)

 Katie's number line shows a long hop for 68 and two little short hops for +2 and +5. Encourage students to make the hops somewhat proportional to the size of the numbers, but do not require them to be exact in their drawing. In this lesson, the drawing is used as a tool to help students visualize and support their reasoning.

Place Value and Addition Algorithm Pitfalls

Sam used the traditional addition algorithm to add 68 and 7. However, he lined up the digits beginning on the left side rather than the right so that digits with different place values were added together. In other words, he mistakenly added 70, not 7, by placing the 7 under the 6 (tens) instead of under the 8 (ones).

Gaining Facility with Both Mental and Paper-and-Pencil Methods

Katie solved the problem mentally, and she said she could have added on paper too. Sam used a paper-and-pencil algorithm but did it incorrectly. Sam also failed to use number sense to realize that 138 is not a reasonable sum when adding 68 and 7. Students should gain facility with both methods and monitor how reasonable their answers are, regardless of the method they choose. Mental math is an efficient way to calculate many problems and is often used to check if an answer makes sense. Paper-and-pencil algorithms are helpful in more complicated multidigit computation.

 Students need to be convinced that counting up on a mental number line results in the same sum as when they add using the paper-and-pencil algorithm. Ask them to prove it (perhaps using base ten blocks or expanded notation) and to explain why.

MATHEMATICAL DISCUSSION SUPPORT

Ask students questions that prompt them to use place value ideas and reasoning to explain or show why it doesn't make sense to get 138 as the sum of 68 and 7.

Remind students that Katie used a mental number line to add 7 in easy steps by keeping in mind benchmarks like multiples of 5 and 10. Draw number lines using numbers similar to the ones in the Starter Problem so that the size of each hop is related to benchmark numbers.

Help students understand the relationship between the hops on the number line and what Katie refers to as "easy steps." Have students trace the long hop that Katie drew, which gets her to 68. Ask what the next hop is. Where does it land? Explain that the hops represent easy steps because they got Katie to benchmark numbers like 70, which are easy to work with.

**Core Lesson
Day 1**

Opener

Review *Discussion Builders*

Read the poster. **Suggest** a section to focus on today:
Presenting Our Ideas, Adding to Others' Ideas, or *Asking More Questions.*

Purpose

Distribute stapled packets of Student Pages 1–4. **Project** an image of page 1 (optional).

Call on a student to read the purpose.

Math Words

Point to and say the first math words. **Ask** students to repeat them aloud or silently.

Read the sentence containing the words.

Give an example using objects or drawings.

Repeat for the other math word.

Purpose
To add a few more to a number

Math Words

add on	I can start with 28 shells and add on 2 more to make 30.
sum	When you add 8 and 5, you get 13 as the sum.

Starter Problem

Think about the meaning. Solve.

$$68 + 7 = \underline{\qquad}$$

Starter Problem

Read the Starter Problem. **Call on** a student to restate it in his/her own words.

 Please use what you already know to help you solve this problem on your own. This will prepare you to talk about the math and how to avoid pitfalls in our discussion later on.

I'll walk around and make notes about things we need to discuss. Look out for oops, or pitfalls!

Look at your work. It's easy to have an oops, or pitfall, in this type of problem. You might also have made a pitfall if your answer is more than 100.

Don't worry. Next we'll discuss how two imaginary students solved this problem. One has a pitfall! You may keep your solution private, but bring up your ideas in the discussion.

Discussion

Student Thinking

STUDENT PAGE 2

Katie

I added 7 in my head using easy steps. 68 and 2 more made 70. Then 5 more made 75. I could add on paper too.

OK

$68 + 7 = \underline{75}$

Ask students to refer to page 2. **Read** the statement marked OK.

Explain that this statement is about the same problem students worked on earlier.

We can learn a lot about the math by studying what this student did.

Read each sentence silently and look at the drawing. Think about what they mean. WAIT

Now talk with a partner about what each sentence and each part of the drawing means.

Listen in, ask questions, and observe. **Note** potential contributions for the discussion.

Who can come up to explain how Katie showed 68 on her number line?

She drew two hops after 68. Who can explain what the two hops stand for?

Who can come up and explain how she showed that 68 plus 7 is 75?

Talk to your neighbor about what Katie meant by "I added using easy steps." WAIT

Why do you think she first added on 2 more in her head and then added 5 more? Why is it easy to add 5 to 70?

What would happen if Katie started at 68 and made a hop for 1 and a hop for 6 more? Why is that like adding 7 all at once? Would she still get 75?

How could we use Katie's way to add 54 + 8? What is another way?

Call on students to state things to remember about solving problems like this.

Start a Things to Remember list on the board.

MORE DAY 1

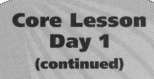

Discussion

Student Thinking, continued

 I just lined them up and added. It's 138.

Sam

 Oops!

$$\begin{array}{r} 6\ 8 \\ +\ 7 \\ \hline 1\ 3\ 8 \end{array}$$

Read the statement marked Oops. **Remind** students that this is a common pitfall.

 Sam made a pitfall when he wrote the 7 under the 6 instead of under the 8. Talk with your neighbor about why his answer doesn't make sense. WAIT

Did Sam line up the 7 with the tens place or the ones place? Explain how he mistakenly added 70 instead of 7.

Write the following problems on the board. **Ask** students to talk with a neighbor about which two of these problems show how to add 3 + 59 by lining up the digits with the same place values. **Remind** students to look out for pitfalls. **Call on** students to explain.

$$\begin{array}{r} 3 \\ +\ 59 \end{array} \qquad \begin{array}{r} 3 \\ +\ 59 \end{array} \qquad \begin{array}{r} 59 \\ +\ 3 \end{array} \qquad \begin{array}{r} 59 \\ +\ 3 \end{array}$$

Things to Remember

Call on students to **add** to the Things to Remember list on the board. **Read** the list.

Help students summarize and record two important Things to Remember.

> **Things to Remember List (sample)**
> 1. To add on a few in your head, think of a number line and add using easy steps and benchmarks.
> 2. To add using paper, line up the numbers so you add ones to ones and tens to tens.

Reflection

Ask students to reflect on the discussion process using one of the sample prompts.

> **Reflection Prompts (sample)**
> - Name a *Discussion Builder* that we used today. How did it help the discussion?
> - What *Discussion Builder* could we use next time to make the discussion even better?
> - What did someone do or say today that helped you understand the math?

Review and Practice

Review

Ask students to review page 2 to jog their memory.

Read the statement marked OK. **Call on** a student to explain how the problem was solved.

Read the statement marked Oops. **Call on** a student to explain why it is incorrect or doesn't make sense.

Call on two or three students to read an item on their Things to Remember list.

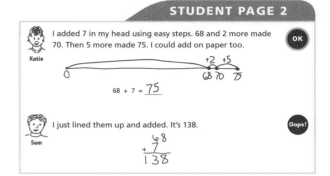

STUDENT PAGE 2

Katie: I added 7 in my head using easy steps. 68 and 2 more made 70. Then 5 more made 75. I could add on paper too. **OK**

$68 + 7 = 75$

Sam: I just lined them up and added. It's 138. **Oops!**

$$\begin{array}{r} 68 \\ + 7 \\ \hline 138 \end{array}$$

Our Turn

Ask students to refer to page 3.

Use the procedure below and the Clipboard Prompts to discuss students' solutions. **Discuss** the problems one at a time.

> **Read** the problem.
>
> **Ask** students to work with a neighbor to solve it.
>
> **Discuss** one or two students' solutions.

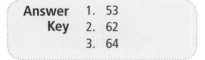

Answer Key	
1.	53
2.	62
3.	64

STUDENT PAGE 3

Our Turn

Write the sum for each problem.

1. $45 + 8 =$ _____

2. $59 + 3 =$ _____

3. $4 + 60 =$ _____

My Turn

Ask students to solve the problems on page 4. **Remind** them to watch out for pitfalls!

After allowing time to work, **read** the answers. **Have** students mark and revise their papers using ink or crayon.

Answer Key	
1.	54
2.	75
3.	47

STUDENT PAGE 4

My Turn

Write the sum for each problem.

1. $48 + 6 =$ _____

2. $70 + 5 =$ _____

3. $8 + 39 =$ _____

Mini Lessons
(2–3 Days Later)

Assess and Reinforce

Multiple Choice Mini Lesson

Distribute Student Page 5.

Problem 1

 Please read problem 1.

Talk with your neighbor about which choices don't make sense. **WAIT**

What is the correct choice?

Who can show why 71 is the correct choice?

Remind students that they can use benchmark numbers to add on mentally in easy steps. Help them see that 63 and 7 more is equal to 70, plus 1 more is 71.

Problem 2

 Read the problem and find the correct choice. **WAIT**

Which response is correct? Explain why.

How can you use a number line to check that 59 + 6 is 65? Explain.

STUDENT PAGE 5

Multiple Choice Mini Lesson

Fill in the circle next to the answer you choose.

1. 63 + 8 = _____

    ○ 143   ○ 61   ● 71

2. 59 + 6 = _____

    ○ 55   ● 65   ○ 119

Writing Task Mini Lesson

Distribute Student Page 6.

Ask a student to read the task. **Call on** students to respond with their ideas.

Jot the ideas on the board.

Write an explanation together using their ideas. **Read** it aloud.

Ask students to write an explanation on their page.

STUDENT PAGE 6

Writing Task Mini Lesson

Explain how to add 36 + 7 in easy steps. You may draw on this number line to help you explain.

0   10   20   30   40   50

Sample Explanation: I start with 36 and need to add on 7. First, I draw a hop of 4 to show that I used an easy step to get from 36 to 40. Then, I need to add on 3 more, which is easy. So, I've really added 7. That's 43.

 Mathematical Discussion Support

When generating ideas, invite students to use drawings or materials such as number lines or base ten blocks to help them describe their thinking.

Ask students to explain what using easy steps and benchmark numbers mean. Ask them to write or give oral examples of benchmark numbers.

What's the Difference?

Lesson at a Glance

Prior Learning Needed

- Use a number line
- Solve subtraction word problems using invented strategies
- Count up from a given number

Lesson Preparation

- Study Lesson Foundation
- Review Teaching Guide and Student Pages
- Prepare stapled packet of Student Pages 1–4 for each student
- Copy and cut in half Student Pages 5 and 6
- Post *Discussion Builders* poster

Mathematical goals

✳ Find a difference by counting the number of units between two values on a number line

✳ Find a difference by subtracting

Mathematical language and reasoning goals

✳ Recognize what it means when a word problem asks you to find the difference

✳ Use reasoning to find a difference by counting up or back

LESSON ROADMAP			MATERIALS
CORE LESSON: DAY 1	GROUPING	TIME	○ *Discussion Builders* poster
Opener			○ Projector (optional)
Discussion Builders Purpose Math Words	👥👥	🕐	○ Student Page 1 ○ Student Page 2
Starter Problem	👤	🕐	○ Teaching Guide
Discussion			○ Scratch paper for drawing number lines (suggested)
Student Thinking	👤 👥 👥👥	🕜	
Things to Remember Reflection	👥👥	🕐	
CORE LESSON: DAY 2			○ Clipboard Prompts, page 37
Review and Practice			○ Student Page 2 (completed day 1)
Review Day 1 Lesson	👥👥	🕐	○ Student Pages 3 and 4
Our Turn	👥👥 👥👥	🕜	○ Teaching Guide
My Turn	👤	🕐	○ Scratch paper for drawing number lines (suggested)
MINI LESSONS: 2–3 DAYS LATER			○ Student Pages 5 and 6
Assess and Reinforce			○ Teaching Guide
Multiple Choice Mini Lesson	👤 👥👥 👥👥	🕜	○ Scratch paper for drawing number lines (suggested)
Writing Task Mini Lesson	👤 👥👥	🕐	

Lesson Foundation

Starter Problem

Adam has 11 toy trains. Marcos has 8 toy trains. What is the difference between the number of trains Adam has and the number of trains Marcos has? _____

Student Thinking

Dan

To find the difference, I started with Marcos' trains and counted up 3 units between 8 and 11. It's easier to count up in easy steps than to take away in this problem. The difference is 3.

OK

$$11 - 8 = 3$$

Olivia

I counted up from 8 to 11. There are 4 numbers: 8, 9, 10, 11. The difference is 4.

Oops!

$$8, 9, 10, 11 \qquad 11 - 8 = 4$$

MATHEMATICAL INSIGHTS & TEACHING TIPS

Using a Number Line to Represent Word Problem Situations

Dan made sense of the word problem, recognizing that he could subtract or find the difference by counting up from 8 to 11. Notice that he started with the number of trains Marcos had, 8, and counted up to the number of trains Adam had. He also used a number line to represent his ideas.

Oops! To find the difference between 11 and 8, Olivia counted "8, 9, 10, 11" instead of counting the units from 8 to 11. She incorrectly concluded that the difference was 4.

A number line is a geometric model that helps students visualize a difference, and this visualization allows students to invent techniques for solving simple problems mentally. One way to think about difference is to think about the distance between two numbers on a number line. Dan found the difference between the numbers by showing a hop from 8 to 10 and then from 10 to 11.

Lesson Foundation
(continued)

MATHEMATICAL INSIGHTS & TEACHING TIPS (CONTINUED)

Counting Up to Find the Difference

To find the difference, Olivia mistakenly counted the number of numerals from 8 through 11 rather than counting the number of units from 8 to 11. She should count up from 8 to 11 by saying "9, 10, 11." Each count stands for 1 unit between 8 and 11. Since there are 3 counts, the difference is 3 units. She could also count back to find the difference, but this is a less common choice.

 When using the counting up method, students may incorrectly count "8 (the starting number), 9, 10, 11" and think that the difference is 4, not 3. Another common error for this problem is to count only the numerals that are between or in the middle: "9, 10." Again emphasize counting the number of units, not the numerals.

Finding a Difference Is Also Subtraction

Students may think of subtraction exclusively as take-away. However, finding the difference is also a subtraction situation, although nothing is taken away. It is especially easy to find the difference when numbers are close in size. The answers to problems such as 21 – 18 and 400 – 398 are obvious when students think about differences rather than taking away — and there are likely to be fewer errors. The answer is the same whether you use an algorithm, count up mentally, or compare on a number line.

 Ask students to explain why it is easy to count up to find the solution to problems such as 50 – 48, 33 – 29, and 200 – 198.

MATHEMATICAL DISCUSSION SUPPORT

Ask students questions that prompt them to explain why the difference between 11 and 8 is 3. Encourage flexibility in the models and language students use. For example, they should be equally comfortable with modeling subtraction as a difference and with modeling subtraction as taking away.

In this lesson, students are required to make sense of the word problem. The word problem asks them to find the difference between two numbers. The difference can be thought of as the distance between two numbers on a number line, a comparison of two numbers, or a subtraction. Make sure students understand that the word "difference" and the phrase "difference between" have special meaning in mathematics related to subtraction.

**Core Lesson
Day 1**

Opener

Review *Discussion Builders*

Read the poster. Suggest a section to focus on today: *Presenting Our Ideas, Adding to Others' Ideas,* or *Asking More Questions.*

Purpose

Distribute stapled packets of Student Pages 1–4. Project an image of page 1 (optional).

Call on a student to read the purpose.

Math Words

Point to and say the first math words. Ask students to repeat them aloud or silently.

Read the sentence containing the words.

Give an example using objects or drawings.

Repeat for the other math words.

Starter Problem

Read the Starter Problem. Call on a student to restate it in his/her own words.

Purpose
To find the difference between two numbers

Math Words

difference between	Since I am 2 years older than my sister, the difference between our ages is 2 years.
find the difference	To find the difference between 5 and 3, find how much more 5 is than 3.

2 units

0 1 2 3 4 5 6

difference	The difference is the answer you get when you subtract.

Starter Problem

Adam has 11 toy trains. Marcos has 8 toy trains. What is the difference between the number of trains Adam has and the number of trains Marcos has? _____

 Please use what you already know to help you solve this problem on your own. This will prepare you to talk about the math and how to avoid pitfalls in our discussion later on.

I'll walk around and make notes about things we need to discuss. Look out for oops, or pitfalls! **WAIT**

Look at your work. It's easy to have an oops, or pitfall, in this type of problem. You might also have made a pitfall if you said the difference is equal to 4.

Don't worry. Next we'll discuss how two imaginary students solved this problem. One has a pitfall! You may keep your solution private, but bring up your ideas in the discussion.

Discussion

Student Thinking

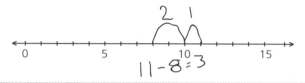

> To find the difference, I started with Marcos' trains and counted up 3 units between 8 and 11. It's easier to count up in easy steps than to take away in this problem. The difference is 3.
>
> **OK**
>
> Dan

Ask students to refer to page 2. **Read** the statement marked OK.

Explain that this statement is about the same problem students worked on earlier.

 We can learn a lot about the math by studying what this student did.

Read each sentence silently and look at the drawing. Think about what they mean. **WAIT**

Now talk with a partner about what each sentence and each part of the drawing means.

Listen in, ask questions, and observe. **Note** potential contributions for the discussion.

 Dan read the word problem and decided to start with Marcos' trains. He counted up the units between 8 and 11 on the number line to find the difference. Who can trace the units with their finger?

Dan used 2 hops to count the number of units between 8 and 11. Why did he draw a hop of 2 units first? How did he know he needed another hop of 1 unit? How do both hops together show a difference of 3 units?

Explain how Dan used easy steps to show the difference between 11 and 8.

Talk to your neighbor about why Dan said it was easier to count up than to take away in this problem. **WAIT**

Why is it easy to count up when two numbers are close together on the number line? Is the answer the same when we start with 11 and take away 8?

How can you use the number line to show the difference between 22 and 19?

Call on students to state things to remember about solving problems like this.

Start a Things to Remember list on the board.

MORE DAY 1

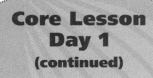

Discussion

Student Thinking, continued

 I counted up from 8 to 11. There are 4 numbers: 8, 9, 10, 11. The difference is 4.

 Oops!

Olivia

$8, 9, 10, 11$ $11 - 8 = 4$

Read the statement marked Oops. **Remind** students that this is a common pitfall.

 Olivia made a pitfall when she counted up from 8 to 11 by counting "8, 9, 10, 11." Talk with your neighbor about why this is incorrect. **WAIT**

Who can explain the correct way to count up to find the difference?

Why should we start counting with 9 instead of 8?

Write the following problems on the board. **Ask** students to talk with a neighbor about which two of the problems have a difference of 4. **Remind** them to look out for pitfalls. **Call on** students to explain.

$$9 - 5 = \underline{\quad} \qquad 9 - 6 = \underline{\quad} \qquad 6 - 3 = \underline{\quad} \qquad 6 - 2 = \underline{\quad}$$

Things to Remember

Call on students to **add** to the Things to Remember list on the board. **Read** the list.

Help students summarize and record two important Things to Remember.

> **Things to Remember List (sample)**
> 1. You can find the difference between two numbers by using a number line, by counting up in your head, or by taking away.
> 2. When two numbers are close together on the number line, it is easy to find the difference by counting up.

Reflection

Ask students to reflect on the discussion process using one of the sample prompts.

> **Reflection Prompts (sample)**
> • Name a *Discussion Builder* that we used today. How did it help the discussion?
> • What *Discussion Builder* could we use next time to make the discussion even better?
> • What did someone do or say today that helped you understand the math?

Core Lesson Day 2

Review and Practice

Review

Ask students to review page 2 to jog their memory.

Read the statement marked OK. **Call on** a student to explain how the problem was solved.

Read the statement marked Oops. **Call on** a student to explain why it is incorrect or doesn't make sense.

Call on two or three students to read an item on their Things to Remember list.

STUDENT PAGE 2

To find the difference, I started with Marcos' trains and counted up 3 units between 8 and 11. It's easier to count up in easy steps than to take away in this problem. The difference is 3. **OK**

Dan

$11 - 8 = 3$

I counted up from 8 to 11. There are 4 numbers: 8, 9, 10, 11. The difference is 4. **Oops!**

Olivia

$8, 9, 10, 11$ $11 - 8 = 4$

Our Turn

Ask students to refer to page 3.

Use the procedure below and the Clipboard Prompts to discuss students' solutions. **Discuss** the problems one at a time.

> **Read** the problem.
>
> **Ask** students to work with a neighbor to solve it.
>
> **Discuss** one or two students' solutions.

Answer Key	
1.	8
2.	3
3.	15

STUDENT PAGE 3

Our Turn

Find the difference. Use the number line to help you.

1. Eva's bean plant is 17 inches tall. Sophia's bean plant is 9 inches tall. Find the difference between the heights of Eva's and Sophia's plants. _____

2. 21
   − 18

3. Find the difference between 20 and 5. _____

My Turn

Ask students to solve the problems on page 4. **Remind** them to watch out for pitfalls!

After allowing time to work, **read** the answers. **Have** students mark and revise their papers using ink or crayon.

Answer Key	
1.	4
2.	4
3.	6

STUDENT PAGE 4

My Turn

Find the difference. Use the number line to help you.

1. Avery is 13 years old. His little brother, Tom, is 9 years old. Find the difference in their ages. _____

2. 21
   − 17

3. Find the difference between 25 and 19. _____

Assess and Reinforce

Multiple Choice Mini Lesson

Distribute Student Page 5.

Problem 1

 Please read problem 1.

Talk with your neighbor about which choices don't make sense. (WAIT)

Who can show why the difference between 10 and 7 is 3?

 Some students may mistakenly say there are 4 units between 7 and 10 because they count the numerals from 7 to 10 (i.e., 7, 8, 9, 10), instead of counting the difference in units by counting up from 7 (i.e., 8, 9, 10).

Problem 2

 Read the problem and find the correct choice. (WAIT)

Which response is correct? Explain why.

Who can explain how to check if the difference between 31 and 25 is 6?

Writing Task Mini Lesson

Distribute Student Page 6.

Ask a student to read the task. Call on students to respond with their ideas.

Jot the ideas on the board.

Write an explanation together using their ideas. Read it aloud.

Ask students to write an explanation on their page.

Multiple Choice Mini Lesson

Fill in the circle next to the answer you choose.

1. Aida has 10 stuffed animals. Marta has 7 stuffed animals. Find the difference between the number of stuffed animals Aida has and the number of stuffed animals Marta has.

    ○ 17   ○ 7   ● 3

2. Find the difference.
    $$\begin{array}{r} 31 \\ -25 \end{array}$$
    ● 6   ○ 4   ○ 14

Writing Task Mini Lesson

Explain how to find the difference between 15 and 7. You may make a drawing to help you explain.

Sample Explanation: It's like finding how many units fit between the two numbers on a number line. I start at 7. From 7 to 10 is 3 units. From 10 to 15 is 5 more units. The difference is 8 units. It's the same answer for 15 − 7.

Mathematical Discussion Support

When generating ideas, invite students to draw a large number line on the board so they can show their ideas.

Ask students to explain what the phrase "difference between" means in this mathematical problem. The mathematical meaning is similar to, but not the same as, the everyday meaning of this phrase. In this problem, "difference" means a comparison of the numerical values, i.e., how much greater or less one number is than the other.

Don't Squeeze the Digits

Lesson at a Glance

Prior Learning Needed

- Count and group objects in tens and ones
- Solve addition word problems using invented strategies
- Add using an algorithm

Lesson Preparation

- Study Lesson Foundation
- Review Teaching Guide and Student Pages
- Prepare stapled packet of Student Pages 1–4 for each student
- Copy and cut in half Student Pages 5 and 6
- Post *Discussion Builders* poster

Mathematical goals

✷ Find the sum of two two-digit numbers

✷ Understand and use regrouping when adding two-digit numbers

Mathematical language and reasoning goals

✷ Recognize addition situations in word problems

✷ Recognize whether a solution is reasonable or not

LESSON ROADMAP			MATERIALS
CORE LESSON: DAY 1	GROUPING	TIME	○ *Discussion Builders* poster
Opener			○ Projector (optional)
Discussion Builders			○ Student Page 1
Purpose	👥	🕐	○ Student Page 2
Math Words			○ Teaching Guide
Starter Problem	👤	🕐	○ Place value materials such as base ten blocks (suggested)
Discussion			
Student Thinking	👤 👥 👥	🕐	
Things to Remember			
Reflection	👥	🕐	
CORE LESSON: DAY 2			○ Clipboard Prompts, page 37
Review and Practice			○ Student Page 2 (completed day 1)
Review Day 1 Lesson	👥	🕐	○ Student Pages 3 and 4
Our Turn	👥 👥	🕐	○ Teaching Guide
My Turn	👤	🕐	○ Place value materials such as base ten blocks (suggested)
MINI LESSONS: 2–3 DAYS LATER			○ Student Pages 5 and 6
Assess and Reinforce			○ Teaching Guide
Multiple Choice Mini Lesson	👤 👥 👥	🕐	○ Place value materials such as base ten blocks (suggested)
Writing Task Mini Lesson	👤 👥	🕐	

Lesson Foundation

LESSON SNAPSHOT

Starter Problem

Ellen has 36 seashells. Hillary has 28 seashells.
How many seashells do they have in all? _____

Student Thinking

Jerry

I added because I want to know how many shells in all.
I regrouped when I added 6 and 8. I got 64.

$$\begin{array}{r} \overset{1}{3}6 \\ +\ 28 \\ \hline 64 \end{array}$$

OK

Li Nan

I added. 6 and 8 is 14. 3 and 2 is 5. It's 514.

$$\begin{array}{r} 36 \\ +\ 28 \\ \hline 514 \end{array}$$

Oops!

MATHEMATICAL INSIGHTS & TEACHING TIPS

Place Value and Regrouping

Both students used the standard addition algorithm to add 36 and 28. Jerry added the digits in the ones column and got 14 ones. Then he regrouped to make 1 ten and 4 ones. After adding the tens digits, he got the correct answer, 64. When Li Nan added the ones digits, she got 14 ones but didn't regroup. After adding the tens digits, she got an unreasonable answer of 514.

Students often approach multidigit addition problems as if they were several single-digit addition problems that just happen to be next to each other. This works when no regrouping is needed, but students may stumble when regrouping is needed.

Oops! When Li Nan added the digits in the ones column to get 14 ones, she incorrectly squeezed 2 digits into the ones column of the answer instead of regrouping.

Lesson Foundation
(continued)

MATHEMATICAL INSIGHTS & TEACHING TIPS (CONTINUED)

We may actually reinforce this pitfall when a similar situation arises in the tens column. When adding the tens in the problem, 65 + 82, for example, we may say, "Write 14 down, since there is no place to carry." Students get the correct answer, but the actual meaning is masked. They may not realize that the 14 is actually 14 tens or 1 hundred and 4 tens.

 Students may have difficulty understanding why in the problem 65 + 82 you can write down 14 when you add the tens. Provide contrasting examples, such as 16 + 48, in which it does not work to write down 14 in the ones place.

Using Number Sense

Li Nan would benefit by learning to think about 36 as 30 and 6 and about 28 as 20 and 8. Then, she could use number sense to predict that the sum will be between 60 and 70. This will also help her decide if a problem will have a two-digit or a three-digit sum. She might also learn to scan a problem before calculating to notice whether regrouping will be needed.

 Encourage students to develop the habit of checking to see whether or not their solution is reasonable. Encourage them to use their number sense to explain how they know an answer is reasonable or not.

MATHEMATICAL DISCUSSION SUPPORT

Ask students questions that prompt them to say numbers in different ways, such as 36 is thirty-six, 30 and 6, or 3 tens and 6 ones.

Invite students to show or explain how they know their solutions are reasonable. They may choose to use mental math, number lines, or base ten materials.

Point out that each place in a number is designed to hold only one digit, so in the addition algorithm, when we get a sum of 14 ones, we can't squeeze two digits into the ones place. Instead, we regroup 14 ones into 1 ten and 4 ones and put the 1 in the tens column.

Make place value language clear by pointing out that an amount such as 2 tens means 2 groups of ten, or 20 ones. Have students practice using the language by describing the meaning of other amounts, such as 4 tens or 40 ones.

Core Lesson Day 1

Opener

Review *Discussion Builders*

Read the poster. **Suggest** a section to focus on today: *Presenting Our Ideas, Adding to Others' Ideas,* or *Asking More Questions.*

Purpose

Distribute stapled packets of Student Pages 1–4. **Project** an image of page 1 (optional).

Call on a student to read the purpose.

Math Words

Point to and say the first math word. **Ask** students to repeat it aloud or silently.

Read the sentence containing the word.

Give an example using objects or drawings.

Repeat for the other math words.

Starter Problem

Read the Starter Problem. **Call on** a student to restate it in his/her own words.

STUDENT PAGE 1

Purpose
To understand how to regroup when finding the sum of two numbers

Math Words

digit	There are ten digits: 0, 1, 2, 3, 4, 5, 6, 7, 8, and 9. The digits in 42 are 4 and 2.
regroup	I can regroup 14 ones into 1 ten and 4 ones, and 14 tens into 1 hundred and 4 tens.
place	The number 54 has 4 in the ones place and 5 in the tens place.

Starter Problem

Ellen has 36 seashells. Hillary has 28 seashells.

How many seashells do they have in all? _____

 Please use what you already know to help you solve this problem on your own. This will prepare you to talk about the math and how to avoid pitfalls in our discussion later on.

I'll walk around and make notes about things we need to discuss. Look out for oops, or pitfalls!

Look at your work. It's easy to have an oops, or pitfall, in this type of problem. You might also have made a pitfall if your answer is more than 64.

Don't worry. Next we'll discuss how two imaginary students solved this problem. One has a pitfall! You may keep your solution private, but bring up your ideas in the discussion.

Discussion

Student Thinking

STUDENT PAGE 2

Jerry

I added because I want to know how many shells in all. I regrouped when I added 6 and 8. I got 64.

OK

$$\begin{array}{r} \overset{1}{3}6 \\ +\ 28 \\ \hline 64 \end{array}$$

Ask students to refer to page 2. **Read** the statement marked OK.

Explain that this statement is about the same problem students worked on earlier.

We can learn a lot about the math by studying what this student did.

Read each sentence silently and look at Jerry's work. Think about what they mean. WAIT

Now talk with a partner about what each sentence and each part of Jerry's work means.

Listen in, ask questions, and observe. **Note** potential contributions for the discussion.

Who can come up to explain why Jerry added? Where did he start adding? Why did he start there?

Jerry said, "I regrouped when I added 6 and 8." What did he mean? What does the little 1 over the 3 in 36 mean?

What does the 4 in the answer mean? What does the 6 mean? What is the sum?

Talk to your neighbor about how Jerry could tell before he started whether he would have to regroup or not. WAIT

Who can come up to explain or show why Jerry's answer makes sense?

Should we regroup when we add 45 + 16? Explain. What is the sum?

Call on students to state things to remember about solving problems like this.

Start a Things to Remember list on the board.

MORE DAY 1

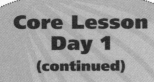

**Core Lesson
Day 1
(continued)**

Discussion

Student Thinking, continued

Li Nan

I added. 6 and 8 is 14. 3 and 2 is 5. It's 514.

$$\begin{array}{r} 36 \\ + 28 \\ \hline 514 \end{array}$$

Oops!

Read the statement marked Oops. **Remind** students that this is a common pitfall.

Li Nan made a pitfall when she squeezed 14 into the ones place and wrote 514. Talk with your neighbor about why her answer doesn't make sense. WAIT

Who would like to show why this is a pitfall?

How could Li Nan check to see if her answer is correct?

Write the following problems on the board. **Ask** students to talk with a neighbor about which of these has a sum of 814. **Remind** students to look out for pitfalls. **Call on** students to show why their answers make sense.

$$\begin{array}{r} 18 \\ + 76 \\ \hline \end{array} \qquad \begin{array}{r} 108 \\ + 706 \\ \hline \end{array}$$

Things to Remember

Call on students to **add** to the Things to Remember list on the board. **Read** the list.

Help students summarize and record two important Things to Remember.

Things to Remember List (sample)
1. Check your answer in addition problems, especially if you need to regroup.
2. Only one digit fits in each place, so regroup when you get more than 9 ones or more than 9 tens.

Reflection

Ask students to reflect on the discussion process using one of the sample prompts.

Reflection Prompts (sample)
- Name a *Discussion Builder* that we used today. How did it help the discussion?
- What *Discussion Builder* could we use next time to make the discussion even better?
- What did someone do or say today that helped you understand the math?

Review and Practice

Review

Ask students to review page 2 to jog their memory.

Read the statement marked OK. **Call on** a student to explain how the problem was solved.

Read the statement marked Oops. **Call on** a student to explain why it is incorrect or doesn't make sense.

Call on two or three students to read an item on their Things to Remember list.

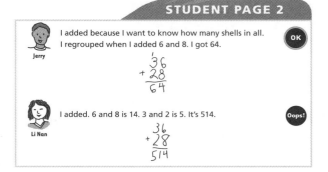

STUDENT PAGE 2

Jerry: I added because I want to know how many shells in all. I regrouped when I added 6 and 8. I got 64. **OK**

$$\begin{array}{r} \overset{1}{3}6 \\ + 28 \\ \hline 64 \end{array}$$

Li Nan: I added. 6 and 8 is 14. 3 and 2 is 5. It's 514. **Oops!**

$$\begin{array}{r} 36 \\ + 28 \\ \hline 514 \end{array}$$

Our Turn

Ask students to refer to page 3.

Use the procedure below and the Clipboard Prompts to discuss students' solutions. **Discuss** the problems one at a time.

> **Read** the problem.
>
> **Ask** students to work with a neighbor to solve it.
>
> **Discuss** one or two students' solutions.

> **Answer Key**
> 1. 93
> 2. 95
> 3. 90

STUDENT PAGE 3

Our Turn

Solve.

Is your answer reasonable? Circle Yes or No.

1. $\begin{array}{r} 64 \\ + 29 \end{array}$ Yes No

2. $\begin{array}{r} 87 \\ + 8 \end{array}$ Yes No

3. $\begin{array}{r} 55 \\ + 35 \end{array}$ Yes No

My Turn

Ask students to solve the problems on page 4. **Remind** them to watch out for pitfalls!

After allowing time to work, **read** the answers. **Have** students mark and revise their papers using ink or crayon.

> **Answer Key**
> 1. 71
> 2. 43
> 3. 108

STUDENT PAGE 4

My Turn

Solve.

Is your answer reasonable? Circle Yes or No.

1. $\begin{array}{r} 58 \\ + 13 \end{array}$ Yes No

2. $\begin{array}{r} 34 \\ + 9 \end{array}$ Yes No

3. $\begin{array}{r} 67 \\ + 41 \end{array}$ Yes No

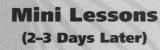

Mini Lessons
(2–3 Days Later)

Assess and Reinforce

Multiple Choice Mini Lesson

Distribute Student Page 5.

Problem 1

 Please read problem 1.

Talk with your neighbor about which choices don't make sense. **WAIT**

Who can explain why it makes sense to regroup?

 Prompt students who are using the standard algorithm to ask themselves before they start if they have to regroup.

Problem 2

 Read the problem and find the correct choice. **WAIT**

Which response is correct? Explain why.

How can you check that your answer is reasonable? Explain.

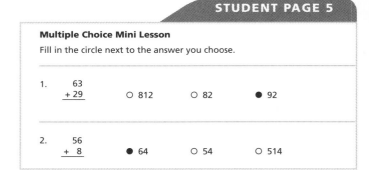

STUDENT PAGE 5

Multiple Choice Mini Lesson

Fill in the circle next to the answer you choose.

1. 63
    + 29   ○ 812   ○ 82   ● 92

2. 56
    + 8   ● 64   ○ 54   ○ 514

Writing Task Mini Lesson

Distribute Student Page 6.

Ask a student to read the task. **Call on** students to respond with their ideas.

Jot the ideas on the board.

Write an explanation together using their ideas. **Read** it aloud.

Ask students to write an explanation on their page.

STUDENT PAGE 6

Writing Task Mini Lesson

Explain how you know to regroup when you add 45 and 18.

Sample Explanation: I know to regroup because when I add the ones digits, I get more than 9. So, I regroup 13 to have a ten and 3 ones. When I put the ten with the other tens, it makes 60. That makes 63 all together.

Mathematical Discussion Support

As they generate ideas, ask students to explain what "adding the ones" and "adding the tens" means. Help them understand that they are not adding rows of single digits. Remind them to use different language to describe the numbers. For example, 45 can be described as 4 groups of ten and 1 group of five, 40 and 5, or 4 tens and 5 ones.

Adding On More Tens or Ones

Lesson at a Glance

Prior Learning Needed

- Have some understanding of place value and relative magnitude of whole numbers
- Use mental math and basic addition facts
- Add using an algorithm

Lesson Preparation

- Study Lesson Foundation
- Review Teaching Guide and Student Pages
- Prepare stapled packet of Student Pages 1–4 for each student
- Copy and cut in half Student Pages 5 and 6
- Post *Discussion Builders* poster

Mathematical goals

✳ Understand place value

✳ Use place value knowledge to add to a three-digit number

Mathematical language and reasoning goals

✳ Add more tens or ones mentally

✳ Relate place value terminology to the expanded form of writing a number

LESSON ROADMAP			MATERIALS
CORE LESSON: DAY 1	GROUPING	TIME	○ *Discussion Builders* poster
Opener			○ Projector (optional)
Discussion Builders Purpose Math Words	👥	🕐	○ Student Page 1 ○ Student Page 2
Starter Problem	👤	🕐	○ Teaching Guide
Discussion			○ Place value materials such as base ten blocks (suggested)
Student Thinking	👤 👥 👥	🕐	
Things to Remember Reflection	👥	▶	
CORE LESSON: DAY 2			○ Clipboard Prompts, page 37
Review and Practice			○ Student Page 2 (completed day 1)
Review Day 1 Lesson	👥	🕐	○ Student Pages 3 and 4
Our Turn	👥 👥	🕐	○ Teaching Guide
My Turn	👤	🕐	○ Place value materials such as base ten blocks (suggested)
MINI LESSONS: 2–3 DAYS LATER			○ Student Pages 5 and 6 ○ Teaching Guide
Assess and Reinforce			○ Place value materials such as base ten blocks (suggested)
Multiple Choice Mini Lesson	👤 👥 👥	🕐	
Writing Task Mini Lesson	👤 👥	🕐	

Lesson Foundation

Starter Problem

What number is 30 more than 328? _____

Student Thinking

Carla

328 has 2 in the tens place. So 3 more tens is 358.

300 20 50 8 358
+30

OK

Russ

30 more than 328 is 628. You just add.

328
+ 30
628

Oops!

MATHEMATICAL INSIGHTS & TEACHING TIPS

Place Value and Mental Computation

Carla added 30 more simply by increasing the tens digit by 3. This understanding is a key place value concept because it enables students to perform mental calculations and judge the reasonableness of their answers. This is an extension of the idea of adding more ones, such as adding 3 more by increasing the ones digit by 3.

 Students will soon catch on to the pattern of adding on to the tens digit to add multiples of ten or adding on to the ones digit to add more ones and may forget why. Therefore, it is important to ask them to explain their reasoning and to justify their answers.

Oops! Russ understood that he needed to add 30, but when he wrote the numbers down, he mistakenly lined them up beginning with the digits on the left instead of the right.

Lesson Foundation (continued)

MATHEMATICAL INSIGHTS & TEACHING TIPS (CONTINUED)

Choosing When to Use the Paper-and-Pencil Algorithm

Russ saw the words "30 more" in the problem and tried to quickly add 30 using the paper-and-pencil algorithm. Although this is a viable method to use, it is not the most efficient method for this problem. Students who rely exclusively on paper-and-pencil algorithms are often not confident in their abilities to compute mentally using place value concepts or to use reasoning to solve a problem. Developing their flexibility, confidence, and competence to compute both mentally and with paper and pencil is important.

 Russ' incorrect method provides an opportunity to discuss several important ideas: Why is it important to line up the digits so that like place values are added together? Why is it important to review an answer to see if it is reasonable or not? Why is it important to make a conscious choice about the methods we use?

Relating to Expanded Notation

Notice that Carla's drawing relates place value representations to expanded notation. Her drawing shows that the 3 in 328 means 300; the 2 means 20; and the 8 means 8. She also seems to understand that 300 + 50 + 8 (expanded form) is 358 (standard form). Part of understanding place value is knowing that the 2 in the tens place means both 2 tens and 20 and that 30 more is 3 tens more.

MATHEMATICAL DISCUSSION SUPPORT

Ask students to explain why a number such as a 2 in the tens place is 2 tens or 20, but not 2 ones.

Practice writing numbers in standard form (e.g., 358) and expanded form (e.g., 300 + 50 + 8). Point out the relationship of the written forms of the number and how they are read orally.

English Learner Access

Have students act out what Carla did using base ten blocks. First, they should show 3 hundreds, 2 tens, and 8 ones, and then put in 3 more tens.

Students need to understand that the blocks in Carla's drawing are the same number whether you count by hundreds, tens, and ones; by tens and ones; or by ones.

**Core Lesson
Day 1**

Opener

Review *Discussion Builders*

Read the poster. **Suggest** a section to focus on today:
Presenting Our Ideas, Adding to Others' Ideas, or *Asking More Questions.*

Purpose

Distribute stapled packets of Student Pages 1–4. **Project** an image of page 1 (optional).

Call on a student to read the purpose.

Math Words

Point to and say the first math word. **Ask** students to repeat it aloud or silently.

Read the sentence containing the word.

Give an example using objects or drawings.

Repeat for the other math words.

Starter Problem

Read the Starter Problem. **Call on** a student to restate it in his/her own words.

STUDENT PAGE 1

Purpose
To add on more tens or ones to a number

Math Words

place	In the number 257, 7 is in the ones place, 5 is in the tens place, and 2 is in the hundreds place.
ones	In the number 257, 7 means 7 ones.
tens	In the number 257, 5 means 5 tens.
hundreds	In the number 257, 2 means 2 hundreds.

Starter Problem

What number is 30 more than 328? _____

 Please use what you already know to help you solve this problem on your own. This will prepare you to talk about the math and how to avoid pitfalls in our discussion later on.

I'll walk around and make notes about things we need to discuss. Look out for oops, or pitfalls!

Look at your work. It's easy to have an oops, or pitfall, in this type of problem. You might also have made a pitfall if your answer is more than 600.

Don't worry. Next we'll discuss how two imaginary students solved this problem. One has a pitfall! You may keep your solution private, but bring up your ideas in the discussion.

Discussion

Student Thinking

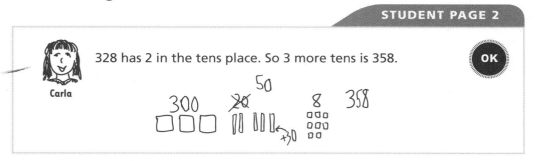

328 has 2 in the tens place. So 3 more tens is 358.

OK

Carla

Ask students to refer to page 2. **Read** the statement marked OK.

Explain that this statement is about the same problem students worked on earlier.

 We can learn a lot about the math by studying what this student did.

Read each sentence silently and look at the drawing. Think about what they mean. **WAIT**

Now talk with a partner about what each sentence and each part of the drawing means.

Listen in, ask questions, and observe. **Note** potential contributions for the discussion.

 Look at the number Carla started with. Why do we say "three hundred twenty-eight" and not "three-two-eight" when we read this number?

What did Carla mean by "328 has a 2 in the tens place"? Why did she write 20 in her drawing? What number is in the hundreds place? the ones place?

Talk to your neighbor about what Carla did to find 30 more than 328. **WAIT**

How did Carla show that she added 30 more in her drawing? Why did she cross out 20 and write 50? How do you know that 30 more is the same as 3 more tens?

What if Carla were adding 3 more instead of 30 more to 328?

What is an easy way to add 4 + 345? Why is the answer 349 and not 385 or 745?

Call on students to state things to remember about solving problems like this.

Start a Things to Remember list on the board.

MORE DAY 1

Core Lesson Day 1 (continued)

Discussion

Student Thinking, continued

Russ

30 more than 328 is 628. You just add.

$$
\begin{array}{r}
328 \\
+\ 30 \\
\hline
628
\end{array}
$$

Read the statement marked Oops. **Remind** students that this is a common pitfall.

 Russ made a pitfall when he lined up the numbers incorrectly to add. Talk with your neighbor about why this answer doesn't make sense. WAIT

Is Russ' answer too high or too low? Explain.

Why is it important to add digits with the same place values?

Who can show a correct way to add 30 to 328 using paper and pencil?

Write the following problems on the board. **Ask** students which problem shows how to line up numbers with the same place values to find 6 more than 271. **Remind** them to look out for pitfalls. **Call on** students to explain.

$$
\begin{array}{r}
6 \\
+\ 271 \\
\hline
\end{array}
\qquad
\begin{array}{r}
6 \\
+\ 271 \\
\hline
\end{array}
$$

Things to Remember

Call on students to **add** to the Things to Remember list on the board. **Read** the list.

Help students summarize and record two important Things to Remember.

> **Things to Remember List (sample)**
> 1. The 2 in 328 means 2 tens or 20. It doesn't mean 2.
> 2. You can add 30 more by adding 3 more tens to the tens place. You can add 3 more by adding 3 more ones to the ones place.

Reflection

Ask students to reflect on the discussion process using one of the sample prompts.

> **Reflection Prompts (sample)**
> - Name a *Discussion Builder* that we used today. How did it help the discussion?
> - What *Discussion Builder* could we use next time to make the discussion even better?
> - What did someone do or say today that helped you understand the math?

Review and Practice

Review

Ask students to review page 2 to jog their memory.

Read the statement marked OK. **Call on** a student to explain how the problem was solved.

Read the statement marked Oops. **Call on** a student to explain why it is incorrect or doesn't make sense.

Call on two or three students to read an item on their Things to Remember list.

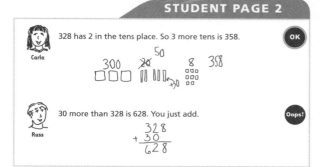

STUDENT PAGE 2

Carla: 328 has 2 in the tens place. So 3 more tens is 358. **OK**

300   20   8   358
           50
          +30

Russ: 30 more than 328 is 628. You just add. **Oops!**

328
+ 30
628

Our Turn

Ask students to refer to page 3.

Use the procedure below and the Clipboard Prompts to discuss students' solutions. **Discuss** the problems one at a time.

> **Read** the problem.
>
> **Ask** students to work with a neighbor to solve it.
>
> **Discuss** one or two students' solutions.

Answer Key	1. 591
	2. 209
	3. 623

STUDENT PAGE 3

Our Turn
Write the answer.

1. What number is 20 more than 571? _____

2. What number is 3 more than 206? _____

3. 613 + 10 = _____

My Turn

Ask students to solve the problems on page 4. **Remind** them to watch out for pitfalls!

After allowing time to work, **read** the answers. **Have** students mark and revise their papers using ink or crayon.

Answer Key	1. 652
	2. 457
	3. 331

STUDENT PAGE 4

My Turn
Write the answer.

1. What number is 40 more than 612? _____

2. What number is 4 more than 453? _____

3. 10 + 321 = _____

Mini Lessons
(2–3 Days Later)

Assess and Reinforce

Multiple Choice Mini Lesson

Distribute Student Page 5.

Problem 1

 Please read problem 1.

Talk with your neighbor about which choices don't make sense. **WAIT**

Who can explain why 693 is the correct choice?

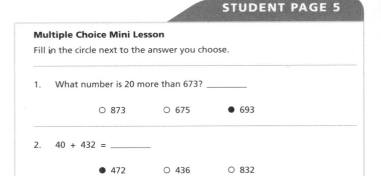

Multiple Choice Mini Lesson

Fill in the circle next to the answer you choose.

1. What number is 20 more than 673? _____

    ○ 873   ○ 675   ● 693

2. 40 + 432 = _____

    ● 472   ○ 436   ○ 832

 Prompt students to articulate why they can add 20 more by increasing the digit in the tens place by 2. Explain that they could also add 20 using the algorithm, although this method may be less efficient.

Problem 2

 Read the problem and find the correct choice. **WAIT**

Which response is correct? Explain why.

Who can describe why 40 + 432 is like adding 4 tens to 432? Explain.

Writing Task Mini Lesson

Distribute Student Page 6.

Ask a student to read the task. **Call on** students to respond with their ideas.

Jot the ideas on the board.

Write an explanation together using their ideas. **Read** it aloud.

Ask students to write an explanation on their page.

Writing Task Mini Lesson

Explain how you know that 10 more than 368 is 378. You may draw a picture on the back to help you explain.

Sample Explanation: I know that 10 more than 368 is 378 because when you add 10 more, the number in the tens place goes up 1 ten. So, the 6 in the tens place changes to 7. That makes 378.

Mathematical Discussion Support

When generating ideas, invite students to use drawings or materials, such as base ten blocks, to help them describe their ideas.

Encourage the use of both standard notation and expanded notation so that students see that 368 is the same as 300 + 60 + 8.

Ask students to explain what the ones place, the tens place, and the hundreds place mean. They should develop flexibility in using terms that have the same meanings, such as 2 tens, 2 groups of ten, twenty, and 20 ones.

What Goes in the Blank?

Lesson at a Glance

Prior Learning Needed

- Have facility with basic addition and subtraction facts
- Understand addition concepts

Lesson Preparation

- Study Lesson Foundation
- Review Teaching Guide and Student Pages
- Prepare stapled packet of Student Pages 1–4 for each student
- Copy and cut in half Student Pages 5 and 6
- Post *Discussion Builders* poster

Mathematical goals

✳ Use number sense to solve missing addend equations

✳ Understand that both sides of an equation show the same amount

Mathematical language and reasoning goals

✳ Read equations with missing addends

✳ Make a drawing to represent an equation

LESSON ROADMAP	GROUPING	TIME	MATERIALS
CORE LESSON: DAY 1			○ *Discussion Builders* poster
Opener			○ Projector (optional)
Discussion Builders Purpose Math Words	👥	🕐	○ Student Page 1
			○ Student Page 2
Starter Problem	👤	🕐	○ Teaching Guide
Discussion			○ Linking cubes or colored chips and a paper cup (suggested)
Student Thinking	👤 👥 👥	🕐	
Things to Remember Reflection	👥	🕐	
CORE LESSON: DAY 2			○ Clipboard Prompts, page 37
Review and Practice			○ Student Page 2 (completed day 1)
Review Day 1 Lesson	👥	🕐	
Our Turn	👥 👥	🕐	○ Student Pages 3 and 4
My Turn	👤	🕐	○ Teaching Guide
			○ Linking cubes or colored chips and a paper cup (suggested)
MINI LESSONS: 2–3 DAYS LATER			○ Student Pages 5 and 6
Assess and Reinforce			○ Teaching Guide
Multiple Choice Mini Lesson	👤 👥 👥	🕐	○ Beans or cubes and a paper cup (suggested)
Writing Task Mini Lesson	👤 👥	🕐	

Lesson Foundation

·Starter Problem·

Copy and complete this equation.
Think about the meaning.

$$5 + 2 = \underline{\hspace{2cm}} + 1$$

Student Thinking

James

I asked myself, "What number is missing so both sides have the same amount?" It's 6. Both sides equal 7. It checks.

OK

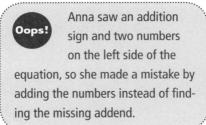

$$5 + 2 = \underline{6} + 1$$

Anna

It says to add, so 5 plus 2 is 7.

Oops!

$$5 + 2 = \underline{7} + 1$$

MATHEMATICAL INSIGHTS & TEACHING TIPS

Modeling Equations

James understood that his goal was to find the missing number so that the amounts on each side of the equals sign would be the same. He drew 5 squares plus 2 squares on the left side, and he drew an upside-down cup (for the missing number) and 1 square on the right side. Since the sum on the left side of the equals sign was 7, he had to think about how many more to add to 1 to have 7 on the right side. He figured out that 6 squares were missing, or hiding under the cup.

Oops! Anna saw an addition sign and two numbers on the left side of the equation, so she made a mistake by adding the numbers instead of finding the missing addend.

He also could have thought about the difference in the number of squares on the left and right sides of the equation. By matching one square on each side, he could see that the difference is 6, which is how many should be under the cup. Later, students will use this idea to solve more complicated algebraic equations.

 Ask students to model, write, and solve equations for word problems such as "I have 5 cents in my left hand and 2 cents in my right. My friend has the same amount of money, but has only 1 cent in his right hand. How many cents are in his left hand?"

Lesson Foundation
(continued)

MATHEMATICAL INSIGHTS & TEACHING TIPS (CONTINUED)

Reading Equations

Anna looked at the two numbers on the left side of the equation, added them, and wrote the answer in the blank. She ignored the 1 after the blank since she already had an (incorrect) answer to put in the blank. By learning to read $5 + 2 = \underline{\quad} + 1$ as "5 plus 2 is the same amount as what number plus 1," students develop a more meaningful understanding of the equals sign.

 Ask students to read equations aloud using the words "a missing number" or "what number" for the blank and "is the same as" for the equals sign.

Checking Equations

Both sides of an equation represent exactly the same amount. This understanding of a balance in value is pivotal to students' future understanding of algebraic equations. Anna must learn to see that her solution is incorrect because the left side represents the amount 7, whereas the right side represents 8. James was able to use his understanding of equality both to solve the problem and to check his answer.

 It is helpful to discuss true and not true number sentences, such as $7 + \underline{3} = 10$ and $7 + 3 = \underline{10} + 6$, in order to emphasize that an equals sign represents equality and always involves a relationship between two amounts that are equal in true equations.

MATHEMATICAL DISCUSSION SUPPORT

Ask students to explain what it means to say that both sides of the equals sign, or both sides of the equation, have the same amount. Provide example equations, such as: $7 = 3 + 4$, $5 + 5 = 10$, and $3 + 2 + 1 = 5 + 1$.

Model how to read equations by saying "a missing number" or "what number" for the blank and "is the same amount as" for the equals sign. Have students read equations aloud using similar language and explain how this helps them solve the problem. Encourage flexibility by including a variety of equation forms for them to read, such as: $\underline{\quad} = 20 + 3$, $30 = \underline{\quad} + 5$, and $7 + 2 = \underline{\quad} + 4$.

Use a balance-scale model, drawn or real, to give meaning to the phrases left side, right side, and equal amounts. Have students identify when the balance scale has equal amounts and when there is more or less on the left side or the right side of the scale.

Core Lesson Day 1

Opener

Review *Discussion Builders*

Read the poster. **Suggest** a section to focus on today:
Presenting Our Ideas, Adding to Others' Ideas, or *Asking More Questions.*

Purpose

Distribute stapled packets of Student Pages 1–4. **Project** an image of page 1 (optional).

Call on a student to read the purpose.

Math Words

Point to and say the first math word. **Ask** students to repeat it aloud or silently.

Read the sentence containing the word.

Give an example using objects or drawings.

Repeat for the other math words.

Starter Problem

Read the Starter Problem. **Call on** a student to restate it in his/her own words.

 Please use what you already know to help you solve this problem on your own. This will prepare you to talk about the math and how to avoid pitfalls in our discussion later on.

I'll walk around and make notes about things we need to discuss. Look out for oops, or pitfalls! (WAIT)

Look at your work. It's easy to have an oops, or pitfall, in this type of problem. You might also have made a pitfall if your answer is 7.

Don't worry. Next we'll discuss how two imaginary students solved this problem. One has a pitfall! You may keep your solution private, but bring up your ideas in the discussion.

STUDENT PAGE 1

Purpose

To understand and solve addition equations that have missing numbers

Math Words

equation	An equation like $5 + 3 = 8$ shows that $5 + 3$ and 8 are equal amounts.
equals sign	An equals sign means "is the same amount as."
both sides	The amounts on both sides of the equals sign in this equation are equal to 4. $$3 + 1 = 2 + 2$$

Starter Problem

Copy and complete this equation.
Think about the meaning.

$$5 + 2 = \underline{\hspace{1cm}} + 1$$

Discussion

Student Thinking

 James I asked myself, "What number is missing so both sides have the same amount?" It's 6. Both sides equal 7. It checks.

$5 + 2 = \underline{6} + 1$

Ask students to refer to page 2. **Read** the statement marked OK.

Explain that this statement is about the same problem students worked on earlier.

 We can learn a lot about the math by studying what this student did.

Read each sentence silently and look at the drawing. Think about what they mean. WAIT

Now talk with a partner about what each sentence and each part of the drawing means.

Listen in, ask questions, and observe. **Note** potential contributions for the discussion.

 Who can come up to show where the 5 is in James' drawing? the 2? the 1? What does the cup stand for?

James drew 2 boxes to show the 2 sides of the equation. Which box is on the left side of the equals sign? the right side? What is the sum in the box on the left side?

The equals sign means that the left side of the equation is the same amount as the right side. What is the amount that we should have on the right side?

Talk to your neighbor about how James might have figured out that there must be 6 under the cup. You can use drawings or materials to share your ideas. WAIT

Since the amounts on both sides of the equals sign have to be equal, explain how James knew that 6 was the missing number. How could he check?

Call on students to state things to remember about solving problems like this.

Start a Things to Remember list on the board.

 MORE DAY 1

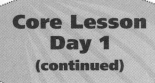

Core Lesson Day 1
(continued)

Discussion

Student Thinking, continued

 It says to add, so 5 plus 2 is 7.

Anna

$$5 + 2 = \underline{7} + 1$$

Oops!

Read the statement marked Oops. **Remind** students that this is a common pitfall.

 Anna made a pitfall when she wrote the sum of 5 plus 2 in the blank. Talk with your neighbor about why this answer doesn't make sense. WAIT

How do you know 7 is not the missing number? Explain.

Who would like to come up and explain why this is a pitfall?

Why does putting 6 in the blank make sense for this equation?

Write the following problems on the board. **Ask** students to talk with a neighbor about which equation has 4 as the missing number. **Remind** them to look out for pitfalls. **Call on** students to show why their answers make sense.

$$3 + 1 = \underline{} + 2 \qquad\qquad 2 + 5 = \underline{} + 3$$

Things to Remember

Call on students to **add** to the Things to Remember list on the board. **Read** the list.

Help students summarize and record two important Things to Remember.

> **Things to Remember List (sample)**
> 1. To read an equation, say "a missing number" for a blank and "is the same amount as" for the equals sign.
> 2. Check to see if both sides of the equation have the same amount.

Reflection

Ask students to reflect on the discussion process using one of the sample prompts.

> **Reflection Prompts (sample)**
> - Name a *Discussion Builder* that we used today. How did it help the discussion?
> - What *Discussion Builder* could we use next time to make the discussion even better?
> - What did someone do or say today that helped you understand the math?

**Core Lesson
Day 2**

Review and Practice

Review

Ask students to review page 2 to jog their memory.

Read the statement marked OK. **Call on** a student to explain how the problem was solved.

Read the statement marked Oops. **Call on** a student to explain why it is incorrect or doesn't make sense.

Call on two or three students to read an item on their Things to Remember list.

James

I asked myself, "What number is missing so both sides have the same amount?" It's 6. Both sides equal 7. It checks.

OK

$$5 + 2 = \underline{6} + 1$$

Anna

It says to add, so 5 plus 2 is 7.

Oops!

$$5 + 2 = \underline{7} + 1$$

Our Turn

Ask students to refer to page 3.

Use the procedure below and the Clipboard Prompts to discuss students' solutions. **Discuss** the problems one at a time.

> **Read** the problem.
>
> **Ask** students to work with a neighbor to solve it.
>
> **Discuss** one or two students' solutions.

> **Answer Key**
> 1. 4
> 2. 3
> 3. 11

STUDENT PAGE 3

Our Turn

Complete each equation.

1. $3 + 7 = \underline{\hspace{1cm}} + 6$

2. $8 + \underline{\hspace{1cm}} = 9 + 2$

3. $4 + \underline{\hspace{1cm}} = 15$

My Turn

Ask students to solve the problems on page 4. **Remind** them to watch out for pitfalls!

After allowing time to work, **read** the answers. **Have** students mark and revise their papers using ink or crayon.

> **Answer Key**
> 1. 7
> 2. 15
> 3. 6

STUDENT PAGE 4

My Turn

Complete each equation.

1. $6 + 6 = \underline{\hspace{1cm}} + 5$

2. $\underline{\hspace{1cm}} + 1 = 8 + 8$

3. $9 + \underline{\hspace{1cm}} = 15$

Mini Lessons
(2–3 Days Later)

Assess and Reinforce

Multiple Choice Mini Lesson

Distribute Student Page 5.

Problem 1

 Please read problem 1.

Talk with your neighbor about which choices don't make sense. [WAIT]

Who can explain why 1 is the missing number?

Encourage students to check for equality by mentally putting the number in the blank and checking whether the total amounts on each side are the same.

Problem 2

 Read the problem and find the correct choice. [WAIT]

Which response is correct? Explain why.

What is the amount we need on both sides of the equals sign?

Writing Task Mini Lesson

Distribute Student Page 6.

Ask a student to read the task. **Call on** students to respond with their ideas.

Jot the ideas on the board.

Write an explanation together using their ideas. **Read** it aloud.

Ask students to write an explanation on their page.

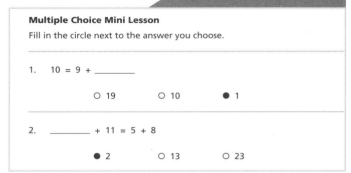

STUDENT PAGE 5

Multiple Choice Mini Lesson
Fill in the circle next to the answer you choose.

1.   10 = 9 + _____
     ○ 19   ○ 10   ● 1

2.   _____ + 11 = 5 + 8
     ● 2   ○ 13   ○ 23

STUDENT PAGE 6

Writing Task Mini Lesson
Explain how you know that 2 is the correct number to put in the blank. You may draw a picture on the back to help you explain.

9 + _____ = 5 + 6

Sample Explanation: The equation says, "9 plus a missing number is the same amount as 5 plus 6." I put 9 counters and a cup on the left side. I put 11 on the right side. The left side needs 2 more in the cup to be the same as the right side. 2 goes in the blank. It checks because both sides have 11.

Mathematical Discussion Support

When generating ideas, invite students to use drawings or materials (such as beans and a cup) to help them represent the equation and the missing number.

Ask students to explain what the equals sign means. Review how to read equations, saying "a missing number" or "what number" for the blank and "is the same as" for the equals sign. Emphasize that the way we read an equation to ourselves helps us know how to solve it.

Place Value Hints

Lesson at a Glance

Prior Learning Needed

- Facility with place value ideas
- Familiarity with missing addend concepts

Lesson Preparation

- Study Lesson Foundation
- Review Teaching Guide and Student Pages
- Prepare stapled packet of Student Pages 1–4 for each student
- Copy and cut in half Student Pages 5 and 6
- Post *Discussion Builders* poster

Mathematical goals

✳ Understand the value of each digit in a numeral

✳ Solve addition equations with missing numbers

Mathematical language and reasoning goals

✳ Understand hundreds, tens, and ones

✳ Write three-digit numerals in an expanded form

LESSON ROADMAP	GROUPING	TIME	MATERIALS
CORE LESSON: DAY 1			○ *Discussion Builders* poster
Opener			○ Projector (optional)
Discussion Builders			○ Student Page 1
Purpose	👥	🕐	○ Student Page 2
Math Words			○ Teaching Guide
Starter Problem	👤	🕐	○ Graph paper, base ten blocks (suggested)
Discussion			
Student Thinking	👤 👥 👥	🕜	
Things to Remember	👥	🕑	
Reflection			
CORE LESSON: DAY 2			○ Clipboard Prompts, page 37
Review and Practice			○ Student Page 2 (completed day 1)
Review Day 1 Lesson	👥	🕐	○ Student Pages 3 and 4
Our Turn	👥 👥	🕜	○ Teaching Guide
My Turn	👤	🕜	○ Graph paper, base ten blocks (suggested)
MINI LESSONS: 2–3 DAYS LATER			○ Student Pages 5 and 6
Assess and Reinforce			○ Teaching Guide
Multiple Choice Mini Lesson	👤 👥 👥	🕜	○ Counters, base ten blocks (suggested)
Writing Task Mini Lesson	👤 👥	🕜	

Lesson Foundation

Starter Problem

Copy and complete this equation.
Think about the meaning.

$$400 + \underline{\hspace{2cm}} + 3 = 453$$

Student Thinking

Daisy

"Four hundred **fifty** three." That's 4 hundreds, 5 tens, and 3 ones. So the 5 tens, or 50, is missing. I checked by adding another way.

OK

$$400 + \underline{50} + 3 = 453$$

$$\begin{array}{r} 400 \\ 50 \\ + \quad 3 \\ \hline 453 \end{array}$$

AJ

I saw a pattern. 453 is 400, then 5, then 3. The 5 is missing.

Oops!

$$400 + \underline{5} + 3 = 453$$

MATHEMATICAL INSIGHTS & TEACHING TIPS

Relating Digits to Values

By reading the number aloud, Daisy connected the digits 4 and 3 to the values 400 and 3 and decided fifty was missing. She correctly wrote 50, for fifty, in the equation. When faced with less straightforward equations such as $3 + 400 + \underline{\hspace{1cm}} = 453$, students should match given values such as the digit 4 and the 400 rather than depending on having the same order on both sides, as happens with standard expanded notation problems. Eventually, students should be able to solve more complicated problems, such as $200 + \underline{\hspace{1cm}} + 80 + 1 = 581$, using their understanding of place value. Working with base ten blocks or graph paper squares can help students learn the values of the ones, tens, and hundreds digits.

Oops! AJ incorrectly wrote a 5 as the missing quantity in the equation $400 + \underline{\hspace{1cm}} + 3 = 453$. He did not think of the missing quantity as 5 tens, or 50.

Lesson Foundation
(continued)

MATHEMATICAL INSIGHTS & TEACHING TIPS (CONTINUED)

Place Value System

AJ may have emerging awareness of the base ten place value system, but incorrectly writes a 5, rather than 5 tens or 50. During the primary grades, students learn the ones, tens, and hundreds place value names for three-digit numbers. This is only a first step in understanding that the digit in the second place stands for that number times ten. The 5 in 453 stands for 5 tens, is equal to the amount "fifty," and can be written as 50.

 Ask students to explain and write their answers in several different ways. Many children develop only a superficial understanding of place value when doing standard expanded notation worksheets and simply follow common patterns.

Horizontal and Vertical Work

Daisy's vertical problem clearly shows the 3 ones lined up in the ones place, the 5 from 50 lined up in the tens place, and the 4 from 400 lined up in the hundreds place. This connection between place names and vertical problems is especially important to children who struggle when they rewrite horizontal problems to make calculation easier. Students don't necessarily think of a vertical problem as being the same as a horizontal equation. Help them see that in the horizontal format, both sides of the equals sign have the same amount, whereas in the vertical format, the amount above and below the line have the same amount.

MATHEMATICAL DISCUSSION SUPPORT

Ask students questions that prompt them to use place value ideas to explain how a number such as 34 is different from 304. They may use materials, pictures, or numbers to help communicate.

Help students develop flexibility in writing numbers in a standard format (453) and in an expanded format (400 + 50 + 3). They also need to be equally comfortable writing addition problems in a horizontal and a vertical format.

Provide opportunities for students to use language, both oral and written, by asking questions such as: "What is another way to say 2 tens? How do we write it?" Ask them to identify which digit means 3 tens in a numeral like 432.

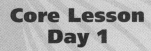

**Core Lesson
Day 1**

Opener

Review *Discussion Builders*

Read the poster. **Suggest** a section to focus on today:
Presenting Our Ideas, Adding to Others' Ideas, or *Asking More Questions.*

Purpose

Distribute stapled packets of
Student Pages 1–4. **Project** an image
of page 1 (optional).

Call on a student to read the purpose.

Math Words

Point to and say the first math word.
Ask students to repeat it aloud or
silently.

Read the sentence containing the word.

Give an example using objects or
drawings.

Repeat for the other math words.

Starter Problem

Read the Starter Problem. **Call on** a student to restate it in his/her own words.

> **STUDENT PAGE 1**
>
> **Purpose**
> To understand place value and solve addition equations
>
> **Math Words**
>
> | | |
> |---|---|
> | **place** | The number 645 has 6 in the hundreds place, 4 in the tens place, and 5 in the ones place. |
> | **hundreds, tens, and ones** | 6 hundreds, 4 tens, and 5 ones is the same as 600 + 40 + 5, or 645. |
>
> **Starter Problem**
>
> Copy and complete this equation.
> Think about the meaning.
>
> $$400 + \underline{} + 3 = 453$$

 Please use what you already know to help you solve this problem on your own. This will prepare
you to talk about the math and how to avoid pitfalls in our discussion later on.

I'll walk around and make notes about things we need to discuss. Look out for oops, or pitfalls! (WAIT)

Look at your work. It's easy to have an oops, or pitfall, in this type of problem. You might also have
made a pitfall if you only wrote a 5.

Don't worry. Next we'll discuss how two imaginary students solved this problem. One has a pitfall!
You may keep your solution private, but bring up your ideas in the discussion.

Discussion

Student Thinking

Daisy

"Four hundred **fifty** three." That's 4 hundreds, 5 tens, and 3 ones. So the 5 tens, or 50, is missing. I checked by adding another way.

$$400 + \underline{50} + 3 = 453$$

$$\begin{array}{r} 400 \\ 50 \\ +\ \ 3 \\ \hline 453 \end{array}$$

Ask students to refer to page 2. **Read** the statement marked OK.

Explain that this statement is about the same problem students worked on earlier.

 We can learn a lot about the math by studying what this student did.

Read each sentence silently and look at Daisy's work. Think about what they mean. WAIT

Now talk with a partner about what each sentence and each part of Daisy's work means.

Listen in, ask questions, and observe. **Note** potential contributions for the discussion.

 Daisy put 50 in the blank. How do you think reading 453 out loud gave Daisy a hint that 50 was the missing number? What does the 5 in 453 stand for?

Talk to your neighbor about how Daisy knows that 453 is the same as 4 hundreds, 5 tens, and 3 ones. WAIT

What does the 4 in 453 mean? How do we know it doesn't mean 4 or 40?

What does the 3 in 453 mean? How do we know it doesn't mean 300?

Why did Daisy line up the numbers the way she did to check her answer?

Call on students to state things to remember about solving problems like this.

Start a Things to Remember list on the board.

MORE DAY 1

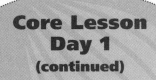

Core Lesson Day 1 (continued)

Discussion

Student Thinking, continued

STUDENT PAGE 2

AJ

I saw a pattern. 453 is 400, then 5, then 3. The 5 is missing.

 Oops!

$$400 + \underline{5} + 3 = 453$$

Read the statement marked Oops. **Remind** students that this is a common pitfall.

 AJ made a pitfall by writing 5 instead of 50. Talk with your neighbor about why this is incorrect. WAIT

Who would like to come up and explain why this is a pitfall?

Who can explain why 50 is the number that goes in the blank?

Write the following problems on the board. **Ask** students to talk with a neighbor about whether 5 or 50 is the missing number in these equations. **Remind** students to look out for pitfalls. **Call on** students to explain.

$$400 + \underline{\hspace{1cm}} + 30 = 435 \qquad 400 + 3 + \underline{\hspace{1cm}} = 453$$

Things to Remember

Call on students to **add** to the Things to Remember list on the board. **Read** the list.

Help students summarize and record two important Things to Remember.

> **Things to Remember List (sample)**
> 1. Read a number out loud and think about what each digit means.
> 2. I know 50 + 400 + 3 is equal to 453, not 543. The first digit on the left is the hundreds place, then the tens place, then the ones place.

Reflection

Ask students to reflect on the discussion process using one of the sample prompts.

> **Reflection Prompts (sample)**
> • Name a *Discussion Builder* that we used today. How did it help the discussion?
> • What *Discussion Builder* could we use next time to make the discussion even better?
> • What did someone do or say today that helped you understand the math?

**Core Lesson
Day 2**

Review and Practice

Review

Ask students to review page 2 to jog their memory.

Read the statement marked OK. **Call on** a student to explain how the problem was solved.

Read the statement marked Oops. **Call on** a student to explain why it is incorrect or doesn't make sense.

Call on two or three students to read an item on their Things to Remember list.

STUDENT PAGE 2

 "Four hundred **fifty** three." That's 4 hundreds, 5 tens, and 3 ones. So the 5 tens, or 50, is missing. I checked by adding another way.

Daisy

$400 + \underline{50} + 3 = 453$

$$\begin{array}{r} 400 \\ 50 \\ + 3 \\ \hline 453 \end{array}$$

 I saw a pattern. 453 is 400, then 5, then 3. The 5 is missing.

AJ

$400 + \underline{5} + 3 = 453$

Our Turn

Ask students to refer to page 3.

Use the procedure below and the Clipboard Prompts to discuss students' solutions. **Discuss** the problems one at a time.

> **Read** the problem.
>
> **Ask** students to work with a neighbor to solve it.
>
> **Discuss** one or two students' solutions.

Answer Key	1. 600
	2. 300
	3. 200

STUDENT PAGE 3

Our Turn

Complete each equation.

1. _____ + 40 + 5 = 645

2. 40 + 7 + _____ = 347

3. 207 = 7 + _____

My Turn

Ask students to solve the problems on page 4. **Remind** them to watch out for pitfalls!

After allowing time to work, **read** the answers. **Have** students mark and revise their papers using ink or crayon.

Answer Key	1. 600
	2. 900
	3. 200

STUDENT PAGE 4

My Turn

Complete each equation.

1. _____ + 50 + 2 = 652

2. 30 + 1 + _____ = 931

3. 205 = 5 + _____

Mini Lessons
(2–3 Days Later)

Assess and Reinforce

Multiple Choice Mini Lesson

Distribute Student Page 5.

Problem 1

 Please read problem 1.

Talk with your neighbor about which choices don't make sense. **WAIT**

What is the correct choice?

Who can explain why 4 is the missing number?

 Some students may add 700 and 20 and write 720 in the blank. Reemphasize that a blank stands for a missing number and that both sides of the equation must total the same amount. 724 is not equal to 720 + 20 + 700.

Problem 2

 Read the problem and find the correct choice. **WAIT**

Which response is correct? Explain why.

Why is it a pitfall to choose the first answer? Explain.

Multiple Choice Mini Lesson

Fill in the circle next to the answer you choose.

1. $724 = $ _____ $ + 20 + 700$

   ○ 720   ○ 400   ● 4

2. $724 = $ _____ hundreds + 2 tens + 4 ones

   ○ 700   ○ 72   ● 7

Writing Task Mini Lesson

Distribute Student Page 6.

Ask a student to read the task. **Call on** students to respond with their ideas.

Jot the ideas on the board.

Write an explanation together using their ideas. **Read** it aloud.

Ask students to write an explanation on their page.

Writing Task Mini Lesson

Explain how you know that 2 is the correct number to put in the blank. Draw a picture on the back or use numbers to help show your ideas.

$527 = $ _____ tens + 7 ones + 5 hundreds

Sample Explanation: 527 means 500 plus 20 plus 7. On the right side of the equals sign, the number sentence has 5 hundred plus 7. It needs 20, or 2 tens, more, so 2 is the missing number.

 Mathematical Discussion Support

When generating ideas, invite students to use drawings or materials, such as counters or base ten blocks, to help them describe their thinking.

Ask students to explain what it means to write or say 2 tens. Ask them to explain how they know the 5 in 527 means 500.

Minus a Few

Lesson at a Glance

- Count and group objects in tens and ones
- Understand place value
- Have facility with basic addition and subtraction facts

Lesson Preparation

- Study Lesson Foundation
- Review Teaching Guide and Student Pages
- Prepare stapled packet of Student Pages 1–4 for each student
- Copy and cut in half Student Pages 5 and 6
- Post *Discussion Builders* poster

Mathematical goals

✱ Use understanding of digit values to subtract with regrouping

✱ Understand that addition and subtraction are related operations

Mathematical language and reasoning goals

✱ Use mathematical language to explain regrouping

✱ Use addition to check a subtraction problem

LESSON ROADMAP			MATERIALS
CORE LESSON: DAY 1	GROUPING	TIME	○ *Discussion Builders* poster
Opener			○ Projector (optional)
Discussion Builders Purpose Math Words			○ Student Page 1 ○ Student Page 2
Starter Problem			○ Teaching Guide ○ Place value materials for trading tens and ones (suggested)
Discussion			
Student Thinking			
Things to Remember Reflection			
CORE LESSON: DAY 2			○ Clipboard Prompts, page 37
Review and Practice			○ Student Page 2 (completed day 1)
Review Day 1 Lesson			○ Student Pages 3 and 4
Our Turn			○ Teaching Guide
My Turn			○ Place value materials for trading tens and ones (suggested)
MINI LESSONS: 2–3 DAYS LATER			○ Student Pages 5 and 6
Assess and Reinforce			○ Teaching Guide
Multiple Choice Mini Lesson			○ Place value materials for trading tens and ones (suggested)
Writing Task Mini Lesson			

Lesson Foundation

·Starter Problem·

Think about the meaning.   42
Solve.   − 7

Student Thinking

Conner

I needed more ones. I got a ten to put with the 2 ones to make 12 ones. Then I subtracted 7. It's 35. It checks.

OK

$$\begin{array}{r} 3\overset{12}{\cancel{4}\cancel{2}} \\ -\ 7 \\ \hline 35 \end{array}$$

check

$35 + 7 = 42$

Zina

It's easier if I turn the ones upside down. 7 take away 2 is 5, and 4 take away 0 is 4. That's 45.

Oops!

$$\begin{array}{r} 42 \\ -\ 7 \\ \hline 45 \end{array}$$

MATHEMATICAL INSIGHTS & TEACHING TIPS

Regrouped Quantities Are Equivalent

Conner chose to use the standard subtraction algorithm found in textbooks, even though this problem can also be efficiently solved using mental math. Either method is correct, and it is helpful to have students share other methods for solving this problem.

Oops! Zina subtracted 2 from 7 in the ones column, which is incorrect because the 2 is part of the minuend and 7 is the subtrahend.

Conner started with the ones column, and since he couldn't subtract 7 from 2 (without getting a negative number), he said he needed more ones. So he "got a ten and put it with the 2 ones to make 12 ones." Decomposing 42 into the equivalent amount of 3 tens plus 1 ten and 2 ones and then regrouping to make 3 tens and 12 ones are fundamental understandings underlying this algorithm. It is equally important to understand that the quantity 4 tens and 2 ones and the quantity 3 tens and 12 ones are both equivalent to 42. Conner should understand that subtracting 7 from 3 tens and 12 ones is mathematically equivalent to subtracting 7 from 4 tens and 2 ones. An incomplete understanding of this idea often leads to errors.

Lesson Foundation
(continued)

MATHEMATICAL INSIGHTS & TEACHING TIPS (CONTINUED)

 Students can practice regrouping the same amount several ways. For example, they might show 42 as 4 tens and 2 ones, as 3 tens and 12 ones, as 42 ones, or as 2 tens and 22 ones. The critical understanding is that all of these quantities are equivalent.

Subtracting Quantities, Not Digits

Zina has learned one important aspect of the standard subtraction procedure: start with the ones and then move to the tens. However, the algorithm often leads students to think of two separate problems (subtracting the ones to get one "answer" and then subtracting the tens to get another "answer"). Instead of reversing the digits in the ones column when she couldn't subtract 7 from 2, Zina needed to think about regrouping the quantity 42 into 3 tens and 12 ones. She also needed to call on her number sense to see that the difference has to be smaller than the starting number.

Relating Addition and Subtraction Through a Family of Facts

Some students think of subtraction as finding the missing part of a related addition number sentence. This works well for problems such as $7 - 2 = \_\_$, but it is more difficult for primary grade students to interpret when they encounter $2 - 7 = \_\_$, as Zina did when subtracting in the ones column. In fact, an incomplete understanding of the fact family 7, 5, and 2 may underlie the tendency to make the same pitfall as Zina and think that $2 - 7 = 5$. They simply associate the numbers 7, 2, and 5 and may not pay attention to whether the problem is $7 - 2$ or $2 - 7$. Later, when students learn that $2 - 7$ is negative 5, they can examine subtraction algorithms that do not require regrouping.

MATHEMATICAL DISCUSSION SUPPORT

Ask students to give a variety of ways to read the problem and to distinguish correct ways of reading from incorrect ways. For example, in the ones column, it is correct to say 2 minus 7, 2 subtract 7, 2 take away 7, and 7 from 2; however, it is incorrect to say 7 minus 2, 7 take away 2, 7 subtract 2, or 2 from 7.

Encourage and model the use of language that supports the concept of trading 1 ten for 10 ones and of thinking of 4 tens as equal to 3 tens and 10 ones. For example, you might say: "4 tens is equal to 3 tens and 10 ones. It is also equal to 40. What can you tell us about 6 tens? 20 ones?"

**Core Lesson
Day 1**

Opener

Review *Discussion Builders*

Read the poster. **Suggest** a section to focus on today:
Presenting Our Ideas, Adding to Others' Ideas, or *Asking More Questions.*

Purpose

Distribute stapled packets of Student Pages 1–4. **Project** an image of page 1 (optional).

Call on a student to read the purpose.

Math Words

Point to and say the first math word. **Ask** students to repeat it aloud or silently.

Read the sentence containing the word.

Give an example using objects or drawings.

Repeat for the other math words.

Starter Problem

Read the Starter Problem. **Call on** a student to restate it in his/her own words.

STUDENT PAGE 1

Purpose
To know when and how to regroup when subtracting

Math Words

ones	The 4 in the number 24 is in the ones place, so it means 4 ones.
tens	The 4 in 42 is in the tens place, so it means 4 tens, or 40, not 4.
regroup	One way to regroup 2 tens and 3 ones is into 1 ten and 13 ones. These amounts are equal.

Starter Problem

Think about the meaning.
Solve.

$$\begin{array}{r} 42 \\ -\ 7 \\ \hline \end{array}$$

 Please use what you already know to help you solve this problem on your own. This will prepare you to talk about the math and how to avoid pitfalls in our discussion later on.

I'll walk around and make notes about things we need to discuss. Look out for oops, or pitfalls!

Look at your work. It's easy to have an oops, or pitfall, in this type of problem. You might also have made a pitfall if your answer is more than 40.

Don't worry. Next we'll discuss how two imaginary students solved this problem. One has a pitfall! You may keep your solution private, but bring up your ideas in the discussion.

Discussion

Student Thinking

Conner

I needed more ones. I got a ten to put with the 2 ones to make 12 ones. Then I subtracted 7. It's 35. It checks.

 OK

3 12
4̶2̶
− 7
35

check
35 + 7 = 42

Ask students to refer to page 2. **Read** the statement marked OK.

Explain that this statement is about the same problem students worked on earlier.

 We can learn a lot about the math by studying what this student did.

Read each sentence silently and look at Conner's work. Think about what they mean. **WAIT**

Now talk with a partner about what each sentence and each part of Conner's work means.

Listen in, ask questions, and observe. **Note** potential contributions for the discussion.

 Who can show us why Conner got a 10 to put with the 2 ones? How can you tell by just looking whether or not Conner needed to regroup?

Why did he cross out the 4 tens and write a 3 above? What does the little 1 by the 2 mean?

Talk to your neighbor about how you know the starting amount is still 42, even if it's regrouped into 3 tens and 12 ones. **WAIT**

Who can explain how Conner checked by adding? What is another way to solve the problem?

How could you use Conner's method to subtract 61 − 8?

Call on students to state things to remember about solving problems like this.

Start a Things to Remember list on the board.

MORE DAY 1

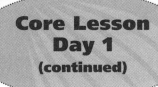

Core Lesson Day 1 (continued)

Discussion

Student Thinking, continued

Zina

It's easier if I turn the ones upside down. 7 take away 2 is 5, and 4 take away 0 is 4. That's 45.

 Oops!

$$\begin{array}{r} 42 \\ -\ 7 \\ \hline 45 \end{array}$$

Read the statement marked Oops. **Remind** students that this is a common pitfall.

 Zina made a pitfall when she turned the numbers in the ones column upside down to subtract. Talk with your neighbor about why her answer is incorrect. WAIT

Who would like to come up and explain why this is a pitfall?

Who can explain why 45 doesn't make sense as the answer?

Write the following problems on the board. **Ask** students to talk with a neighbor about whether it makes sense to regroup or not on these problems. **Remind** students to look out for pitfalls. **Call on** students to explain.

$$\begin{array}{r} 43 \\ -\ 7 \\ \hline \end{array} \qquad \begin{array}{r} 47 \\ -\ 3 \\ \hline \end{array}$$

Things to Remember

Call on students to **add** to the Things to Remember list on the board. **Read** the list.

Help students summarize and record two important Things to Remember.

Things to Remember List (sample)
1. If you need more ones, regroup instead of subtracting upside down.
2. If you regroup 4 tens and 2 ones into 3 tens and 12 ones, the amounts are the same.

Reflection

Ask students to reflect on the discussion process using one of the sample prompts.

Reflection Prompts (sample)
- Name a *Discussion Builder* that we used today. How did it help the discussion?
- What *Discussion Builder* could we use next time to make the discussion even better?
- What did someone do or say today that helped you understand the math?

Review and Practice

Review

Ask students to review page 2 to jog their memory.

Read the statement marked OK. **Call on** a student to explain how the problem was solved.

Read the statement marked Oops. **Call on** a student to explain why it is incorrect or doesn't make sense.

Call on two or three students to read an item on their Things to Remember list.

 Conner: I needed more ones. I got a ten to put with the 2 ones to make 12 ones. Then I subtracted 7. It's 35. It checks. **OK**

$$\begin{array}{r} 3\,\overset{12}{\cancel{4}\cancel{2}} \\ -\ 7 \\ \hline 35 \end{array}$$

check
$$\overset{1}{35} + 7 = 42$$

 Zina: It's easier if I turn the ones upside down. 7 take away 2 is 5, and 4 take away 0 is 4. That's 45. **Oops!**

$$\begin{array}{r} 42 \\ -\ 7 \\ \hline 45 \end{array}$$

Our Turn

Ask students to refer to page 3.

Use the procedure below and the Clipboard Prompts to discuss students' solutions. **Discuss** the problems one at a time.

> **Read** the problem.
>
> **Ask** students to work with a neighbor to solve it.
>
> **Discuss** one or two students' solutions.

Answer Key	1. 15
	2. 59
	3. 11

Our Turn

Write the answer for each problem.

1. $\begin{array}{r} 23 \\ -\ 8 \\ \hline \end{array}$

2. $65 - 6 =$ _____

3. $\begin{array}{r} 20 \\ -\ 9 \\ \hline \end{array}$

My Turn

Ask students to solve the problems on page 4. **Remind** them to watch out for pitfalls!

After allowing time to work, **read** the answers. **Have** students mark and revise their papers using ink or crayon.

Answer Key	1. 36
	2. 22
	3. 32

My Turn

Write the answer for each problem.

1. $\begin{array}{r} 42 \\ -\ 6 \\ \hline \end{array}$

2. $\begin{array}{r} 30 \\ -\ 8 \\ \hline \end{array}$

3. $37 - 5 =$ _____

Mini Lessons
(2–3 Days Later)

Assess and Reinforce

Multiple Choice Mini Lesson

Distribute Student Page 5.

Problem 1

 Please read problem 1.

Talk with your neighbor about which choices don't make sense. (WAIT)

How could you know that 27 is the correct choice without even doing the problem?

▶ *Help students see that taking 7 from 34 cannot give an answer greater than 34. It must be less because they are subtracting 7.*

Problem 2

 Read the problem and find the correct choice. (WAIT)

Which response is correct? Explain why.

What are some ways to prove that 48 is the correct choice? Explain.

Multiple Choice Mini Lesson

Fill in the circle next to the answer you choose.

1. 34 − 7 = _____

    ○ 37   ○ 33   ● 27

2.   56
      − 8

    ● 48   ○ 52   ○ 42

Writing Task Mini Lesson

Distribute Student Page 6.

Ask a student to read the task. **Call on** students to respond with their ideas.

Jot the ideas on the board.

Write an explanation together using their ideas. **Read** it aloud.

Ask students to write an explanation on their page.

Writing Task Mini Lesson

Explain how you could regroup to solve this problem.

25 − 8 = _____

Sample Explanation: 25 is the same as 2 tens and 5 ones. I need to subtract 8 ones, but that's more than 5 ones. If I take apart a ten, I will have 10 more ones. That's 15 ones. Then I can subtract 8. I have 7 ones left. 1 ten minus 0 tens is 1 ten. The final answer is 1 ten and 7 ones, or 17.

Mathematical Discussion Support

When generating ideas, encourage students to explain what regrouping means. Support their explanations and mathematical language by asking specific questions such as: "What could you regroup 25 into? What about 15?" Write some of their ideas on the board to keep a written record of mathematical words used.

Regroup and Subtract

Prior Learning Needed

- Count and group objects in tens and ones
- Understand place value
- Have facility with basic addition and subtraction facts

Lesson Preparation

- Study Lesson Foundation
- Review Teaching Guide and Student Pages
- Prepare stapled packet of Student Pages 1–4 for each student
- Copy and cut in half Student Pages 5 and 6
- Post *Discussion Builders* poster

Mathematical goals

✳ Use understanding of digit values to subtract with regrouping

✳ Understand that a number can be regrouped in more than one way

Mathematical language and reasoning goals

✳ Use mathematical language to explain regrouping

✳ Understand that addition and subtraction are related operations

LESSON ROADMAP			MATERIALS
CORE LESSON: DAY 1	GROUPING	TIME	○ *Discussion Builders* poster
Opener			○ Projector (optional)
Discussion Builders			○ Student Page 1
Purpose	👥	🕐	○ Student Page 2
Math Words			○ Teaching Guide
Starter Problem	👤	🕐	○ Base ten blocks or other place value materials (suggested)
Discussion			
Student Thinking	👤 👥 👥	🕐	
Things to Remember	👥	🕐	
Reflection			
CORE LESSON: DAY 2			○ Clipboard Prompts, page 37
Review and Practice			○ Student Page 2 (completed day 1)
Review Day 1 Lesson	👥	🕐	○ Student Pages 3 and 4
Our Turn	👥 👥	🕐	○ Teaching Guide
My Turn	👤	🕐	○ Base ten blocks or other place value materials (suggested)
MINI LESSONS: 2–3 DAYS LATER			○ Student Pages 5 and 6
Assess and Reinforce			○ Teaching Guide
Multiple Choice Mini Lesson	👤 👥 👥	🕐	○ Base ten blocks or other place value materials (suggested)
Writing Task Mini Lesson	👤 👥	🕐	

Lesson Foundation

Starter Problem

Think about the meaning. 64
Find the difference. − 25

Student Thinking

Megan

5 is more than 4, so I needed more ones. I regrouped a ten and put it with the 4 to make 14. I got 39. It checks.

OK

$$\begin{array}{r} {}^{5}\!\!\!\not{6}\,{}^{14}\!\!\!\not{4} \\ -\ 2\ 5 \\ \hline 3\ 9 \end{array}$$

check
$$\begin{array}{r} {}^{1}2\ 5 \\ +\ 3\ 9 \\ \hline 6\ 4 \end{array}$$

Luke

I borrowed 1 and put it with the 4. Then, I subtracted.

Oops!

$$\begin{array}{r} 6\,{}^{14}\!\!\!\not{4} \\ -\ 2\ 5 \\ \hline 4\ 9 \end{array}$$

MATHEMATICAL INSIGHTS & TEACHING TIPS

Using Algorithms

Megan correctly applied the commonly used standard algorithm to subtract a two-digit number. She also verified that her answer is correct by adding. Working with two-digit numbers is the foundation for success with the subtraction of any multidigit numbers. For many problems, especially those with larger numbers, standard algorithms are the most efficient procedures for calculating. For example, it makes sense to use the algorithm for 64 – 25 and 648 – 152, but not for 64 – 63. Students should look at the problem and purposefully decide what method to use.

 Oops! Using the standard algorithm to subtract, Luke incorrectly put 10 more ones in the ones column without diminishing the tens column by 1 ten.

Relating Addition and Subtraction

Subtraction can be thought of as "a whole minus a part equals the other part." In other words, the sum of the two parts (the difference and the amount subtracted) should always equal the whole or starting amount. Megan used this idea to check her work. So, 39 (the difference) plus 25 (the amount subtracted) equals 64 (the starting amount).

**Lesson
Foundation**
(continued)

MATHEMATICAL INSIGHTS & TEACHING TIPS (CONTINUED)

 Students can examine simple subtraction problems, such as 4 – 1 = 3 and 6 – 4 = 2, to help them understand the relationship between addition and subtraction. They can see that adding the difference to the amount subtracted always gives the starting amount.

What Does That Little 1 Mean?

Luke seems to have only a partial understanding of the standard algorithm. Some clues to his understanding lie in the way he talks about what he did. He said that he borrowed 1 (not 1 ten) and put it with the 4. It is unclear what borrow means to him since he did not diminish the number of tens by 1. Students need to understand that the starting amount (6 tens and 4 ones) needs to be regrouped into 5 tens and 14 ones. Luke regrouped 64 into 6 tens and 14 ones, which is actually 74. When algorithms are learned in conjunction with understanding and number sense, there is less likelihood that they will be misinterpreted, misused, or misremembered.

 Caution should be used when talking about the regrouping process. It is confusing to say, "Trade (or regroup) 1 from the 6 and put it with the 4 to make 14." It is more accurate to say, "Trade (or regroup) 1 ten from 6 tens and put it with the 4 ones to make 14 ones." Also, using the term "borrow," rather than "trade" or "regroup," may confuse students who associate borrowing with owing and paying back something.

MATHEMATICAL DISCUSSION SUPPORT

Encourage students to explain why it is necessary to regroup for the ones place in problems like 75 – 28. Use place value terms, such as "regroup a ten" and "move 10 ones over to the ones place." Help students rephrase inaccurate language, such as "borrow 1 and put it with the 5."

 Model the language attached to subtraction problems for the students. Occasionally ask them to identify and label the parts of a subtraction problem using phrases such as: starting amount (or minuend), amount taken away (subtrahend), and amount left (difference).

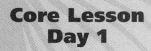

Core Lesson Day 1

Opener

Review *Discussion Builders*

Read the poster. **Suggest** a section to focus on today:
Presenting Our Ideas, Adding to Others' Ideas, or *Asking More Questions.*

Purpose

Distribute stapled packets of Student Pages 1–4. **Project** an image of page 1 (optional).

Call on a student to read the purpose.

Math Words

Point to and say the first math words. **Ask** students to repeat them aloud or silently.

Read the sentence containing the words.

Give an example using objects or drawings.

Repeat for the other math word.

Starter Problem

Read the Starter Problem. **Call on** a student to restate it in his/her own words.

STUDENT PAGE 1

Purpose

To practice regrouping when subtracting and to check by adding

Math Words

tens and ones	6 tens and 4 ones is the same amount as 60 + 4, or 64.
regroup	One way to regroup 6 tens and 4 ones is 5 tens and 14 ones. They are both equal to 64.

Starter Problem

Think about the meaning.
Find the difference.

$$\begin{array}{r} 64 \\ -\ 25 \\ \hline \end{array}$$

 Please use what you already know to help you solve this problem on your own. This will prepare you to talk about the math and how to avoid pitfalls in our discussion later on.

I'll walk around and make notes about things we need to discuss. Look out for oops, or pitfalls!

Look at your work. It's easy to have an oops, or pitfall, in this type of problem. You might also have made a pitfall if your answer is more than 40.

Don't worry. Next we'll discuss how two imaginary students solved this problem. One has a pitfall! You may keep your solution private, but bring up your ideas in the discussion.

Discussion

Student Thinking

5 is more than 4, so I needed more ones. I regrouped a ten and put it with the 4 to make 14. I got 39. It checks.

OK

Megan

Ask students to refer to page 2. **Read** the statement marked OK.

Explain that this statement is about the same problem students worked on earlier.

We can learn a lot about the math by studying what this student did.

Read each sentence silently and look at Megan's work. Think about what they mean. **WAIT**

Now talk with a partner about what each sentence and each part of Megan's work means.

Listen in, ask questions, and observe. **Note** potential contributions for the discussion.

Who can come to the board to explain how Megan solved the problem by regrouping? You may use pictures or blocks to show us.

Why did Megan say that she needed more ones? Why did she cross out the 6 and write a 5? Why did she write 14 above the 4?

Megan regrouped 6 tens and 4 ones to make 5 tens and 14 ones. Are these the same amounts? Who can explain why?

Talk to your neighbor about how Megan knew her answer was correct when she said, "It checks."

What do you add together to check a subtraction problem? How do you know if your answer is incorrect? What do we call the answer when you subtract?

How could we subtract 80 – 24? How could we check the answer?

Call on students to state things to remember about solving problems like this.

Start a Things to Remember list on the board.

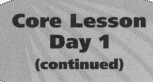

**Core Lesson
Day 1**
(continued)

Discussion

Student Thinking, continued

 I borrowed 1 and put it with the 4. Then, I subtracted.

Luke

$$\begin{array}{r} 6\overset{14}{\cancel{4}} \\ -\ 25 \\ \hline 4\ 9 \end{array}$$

Oops!

Read the statement marked Oops. **Remind** students that this is a common pitfall.

 Luke made a pitfall when he got more ones to put with the 4, but didn't regroup a ten to get them. Talk with your neighbor about why his answer doesn't make sense. **WAIT**

Who would like to come up and explain why the answer 49 doesn't make sense?

Why is this a pitfall? What is a correct way to solve the problem?

Write the following problems on the board. **Ask** students to talk with a neighbor about why the middle example is the only one that makes sense and is correct. **Remind** students to look out for pitfalls. **Call on** students to explain their thinking.

$$74 - 25 = 51 \qquad\qquad 74 - 25 = 49 \qquad\qquad 74 - 25 = 59$$

Things to Remember

Call on students to **add** to the Things to Remember list on the board. **Read** the list.

Help students summarize and record two important Things to Remember.

> **Things to Remember List (sample)**
> 1. To get more ones, you can regroup a ten into 10 ones.
> 2. If you regroup, remember to show that you moved a ten from the tens column.

Reflection

Ask students to reflect on the discussion process using one of the sample prompts.

> **Reflection Prompts (sample)**
> • Name a *Discussion Builder* that we used today. How did it help the discussion?
> • What *Discussion Builder* could we use next time to make the discussion even better?
> • What did someone do or say today that helped you understand the math?

**Core Lesson
Day 2**

Review and Practice

Review

Ask students to review page 2 to jog their memory.

Read the statement marked OK. **Call on** a student to explain how the problem was solved.

Read the statement marked Oops. **Call on** a student to explain why it is incorrect or doesn't make sense.

Call on two or three students to read an item on their Things to Remember list.

> **STUDENT PAGE 2**
>
> Megan
>
> 5 is more than 4, so I needed more ones. I regrouped a ten and put it with the 4 to make 14. I got 39. It checks. **OK**
>
> $$\begin{array}{r} 5\overset{1}{\cancel{6}}\overset{14}{\cancel{4}} \\ -25 \\ \hline 39 \end{array} \qquad \begin{array}{r} \text{check} \\ \overset{1}{2}5 \\ +39 \\ \hline 64 \end{array}$$
>
> Luke
>
> I borrowed 1 and put it with the 4. Then, I subtracted. **Oops!**
>
> $$\begin{array}{r} 6\overset{14}{\cancel{4}} \\ -25 \\ \hline 49 \end{array}$$

Our Turn

Ask students to refer to page 3.

Use the procedure below and the Clipboard Prompts to discuss students' solutions. **Discuss** the problems one at a time.

> **Read** the problem.
>
> **Ask** students to work with a neighbor to solve it.
>
> **Discuss** one or two students' solutions.

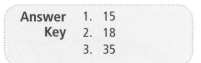

Answer Key
1. 15
2. 18
3. 35

> **STUDENT PAGE 3**
>
> **Our Turn**
>
> Write the answer for each problem. Check your work.
>
> 1. $\begin{array}{r} 42 \\ -27 \\ \hline \end{array}$ Check
>
> 2. $\begin{array}{r} 60 \\ -42 \\ \hline \end{array}$ Check
>
> 3. 54 – 19 = _____   Check

My Turn

Ask students to solve the problems on page 4. **Remind** them to watch out for pitfalls!

After allowing time to work, **read** the answers. **Have** students mark and revise their papers using ink or crayon.

Answer Key
1. 19
2. 51
3. 46

> **STUDENT PAGE 4**
>
> **My Turn**
>
> Write the answer for each problem. Check your work.
>
> 1. $\begin{array}{r} 46 \\ -27 \\ \hline \end{array}$ Check
>
> 2. $\begin{array}{r} 90 \\ -39 \\ \hline \end{array}$ Check
>
> 3. 74 – 28 = _____   Check

Mini Lessons
(2–3 Days Later)

Assess and Reinforce

Multiple Choice Mini Lesson

Distribute Student Page 5.

Problem 1

 Please read problem 1.

Talk with your neighbor about which choices don't make sense. (WAIT)

Who can show why 26 is the missing number?

 Watch for students who regroup incorrectly. Other students may not notice regrouping is necessary and may subtract the smaller number from the larger in the ones column.

Problem 2

 Read the problem and find the correct choice. (WAIT)

Which response is correct? Explain why.

Who can prove that 77 is the correct answer?

STUDENT PAGE 5

Multiple Choice Mini Lesson
Fill in the circle next to the answer you choose.

1.   53 – 27 = _____

   ○ 34   ○ 36   ● 26

2.   83 – 6 = _____

   ○ 23   ● 77   ○ 87

Writing Task Mini Lesson

Distribute Student Page 6.

Ask a student to read the task. **Call on** students to respond with their ideas.

Jot the ideas on the board.

Write an explanation together using their ideas. **Read** it aloud.

Ask students to write an explanation on their page.

STUDENT PAGE 6

Writing Task Mini Lesson
Explain how you know the answer to this subtraction problem is 14.

$$\begin{array}{r} 32 \\ -18 \\ \hline \end{array}$$

Sample Explanation: There are only 2 ones. I need more ones so I can subtract 8 ones. I took a ten from the 3 tens and regrouped it into 10 ones to go with the 2 ones. That made 12 ones. I had 2 tens left, and when I subtracted the ones and the tens, I got 14 for my answer.

Mathematical Discussion Support

Invite students to use drawings or materials, such as base ten blocks, to help them describe their ideas.

Ask students to identify the digits in the ones place and the tens place in the problem. Remind them what regrouping means and ask them to explain why regrouping is helpful in problems like these.

Teaching Guides

Number Line Sense

Lesson at a Glance

Prior Learning Needed

- Use a number line
- Understand the relative magnitude of whole numbers
- Use place value sense to work with benchmark numbers in multiples of 10

Lesson Preparation

- Study Lesson Foundation
- Review Teaching Guide and Student Pages
- Prepare stapled packet of Student Pages 1–4 for each student
- Copy and cut in half Student Pages 5 and 6
- Post *Discussion Builders* poster

Mathematical goals

✳ Name a point by estimating its distance from 0

✳ Name a point halfway between two other points on a number line

Mathematical language and reasoning goals

✳ Use reasoning to estimate the location of points on a number line

✳ Use the term "point" for a location of a number on a number line

LESSON ROADMAP			MATERIALS
CORE LESSON: DAY 1	GROUPING	TIME	○ *Discussion Builders* poster
Opener			○ Projector (optional)
Discussion Builders Purpose Math Words	👥	🕐	○ Student Page 1
			○ Student Page 2
Starter Problem	🧑	🕐	○ Teaching Guide
Discussion			○ Paper strips of equal length for making number lines (suggested)
Student Thinking	🧑 👥 👥	🕐	
Things to Remember Reflection	👥	🕐	
CORE LESSON: DAY 2			○ Clipboard Prompts, page 37
Review and Practice			○ Student Page 2 (completed day 1)
Review Day 1 Lesson	👥	🕐	○ Student Pages 3 and 4
Our Turn	👥 👥	🕐	○ Teaching Guide
My Turn	🧑	🕐	○ Paper strips of equal length for making number lines (suggested)
MINI LESSONS: 2–3 DAYS LATER			○ Student Pages 5 and 6
Assess and Reinforce			○ Teaching Guide
Multiple Choice Mini Lesson	🧑 👥 👥	🕐	○ Paper strips of equal length for making number lines (suggested)
Writing Task Mini Lesson	🧑 👥	🕐	

Lesson Foundation

LESSON SNAPSHOT

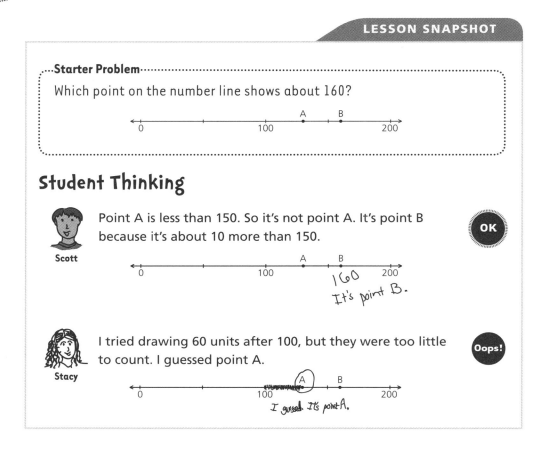

Starter Problem

Which point on the number line shows about 160?

Student Thinking

Scott

Point A is less than 150. So it's not point A. It's point B because it's about 10 more than 150.

OK

160
It's point B.

Stacy

I tried drawing 60 units after 100, but they were too little to count. I guessed point A.

Oops!

I guessed. It's point A.

MATHEMATICAL INSIGHTS & TEACHING TIPS

Using Reasoning to Locate Points

One can use any known distance on the number line to determine other values. Scott knew the distance from 100 to 200. Then he used reasoning to find 150, which is the halfway point. He knew that 160 had to be more than 150, so he knew that point A was incorrect. Using the same reasoning process, he could have found the location of 125 by marking the halfway point between 100 and 150.

 To find the point for 160, Stacy tried drawing 60 single units after 100, but she didn't use reasoning to correctly estimate either the size of 1 unit or a group of 10 units. Also, she didn't use half the distance between 100 and 200 as a starting point.

Iterating Equal-Sized "Chunks" to Locate Points

The name of a point on a number line is determined by how far it is from 0. This distance is measured in equal-sized whole units or parts of whole units (as with fractions and decimals). Scott realized that the distance from 150 to 160 was 10 units and estimated that point B was about 10 units more than the mark for 150. He could iterate this distance as a chunk of 10 to check his estimate for the size of 10 units. If 5 chunks

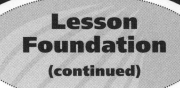

Lesson Foundation
(continued)

MATHEMATICAL INSIGHTS & TEACHING TIPS (CONTINUED)

of 10 units fit between 150 and 200, his estimate for the size of 10 units should be correct. He could use this chunk of 10 units to estimate the location of other numbers.

 Students may be confused about whether 160 is a point on the number line or a line 160 units long. Point B represents 160 on the number line; however, the location of that point is determined by how many units it is to the right of 0.

Number Lines Are Infinite

Stacy realized that the point for 160 would be 60 units after 100 and tried unsuccessfully to draw each unit. She will need to learn how to use benchmark numbers, such as multiples of 10 and halfway points, to estimate the location of a point.

A number line has an infinite number of points and represents all kinds of numbers. For example, the name of a point that is half of the distance from 0 to 1 is 1/2 or 0.5. The point halfway between 0 and 1/2 is 1/4 or 0.25. The distance between any two numbers can always be split to locate a new number. The numbers on a number line increase from left to right, regardless of whether they are positive or negative.

 Plant a seed for the idea that numbers, other than the counting numbers, can be represented on a number line. Ask, "What number do you think would go halfway between 0 and 1? between 5 and 6? between 25 and 26?"

MATHEMATICAL DISCUSSION SUPPORT

Ask students to explain how to name the point that is halfway between two other points. Encourage the use of if-then statements, such as: "If this distance is 5 units long, then 1 unit would be about this long"; "If the distance between 100 and 150 is 50 units long, then half of that distance would be 25 units long." Make the connection between the words "about" and "estimate."

Draw a large number line on the board and mark intervals on the number line as shown in the Starter Problem. Explain that the phrase *name a point* means assigning a number to that point. The point represents a number on the number line, as determined by the point's distance from 0. Ask students to name points that you indicate on the number line.

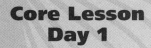

Core Lesson Day 1

Opener

Review *Discussion Builders*

Read the poster. **Suggest** a section to focus on today:
Presenting Our Ideas, Adding to Others' Ideas, or *Asking More Questions.*

Purpose

Distribute stapled packets of Student Pages 1–4. **Project** an image of page 1 (optional).

Call on a student to read the purpose.

Math Words

Point to and say the first math words. **Ask** students to repeat them aloud or silently.

Read the sentence containing the words.

Give an example using objects or drawings.

Repeat for the other math words.

Starter Problem

Read the Starter Problem. **Call on** a student to restate it in his/her own words.

 Please use what you already know to help you solve this problem on your own. This will prepare you to talk about the math and how to avoid pitfalls in our discussion later on.

I'll walk around and make notes about things we need to discuss. Look out for oops, or pitfalls! [WAIT]

Look at your work. It's easy to have an oops, or pitfall, in this type of problem. You might also have made a pitfall if you chose point A.

Don't worry. Next we'll discuss how two imaginary students solved this problem. One has a pitfall! You may keep your solution private, but bring up your ideas in the discussion.

STUDENT PAGE 1

Purpose
To name a number for a point on a number line

Math Words

number line	A number line shows numbers in order along a line.
point	A dot on a number line shows where the point for a number is.
unit	A unit has a length of 1.

Starter Problem

Which point on the number line shows about 160?

```
        A   B
←---+-------•---•---→
0       100      200
```

Discussion

Student Thinking

STUDENT PAGE 2

Scott

Point A is less than 150. So it's not point A. It's point B because it's about 10 more than 150.

OK

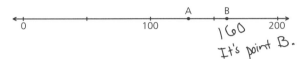

Ask students to refer to page 2. **Read** the statement marked OK.

Explain that this statement is about the same problem students worked on earlier.

We can learn a lot about the math by studying what this student did.

Read each sentence silently and look at Scott's work. Think about what they mean. **WAIT**

Now talk with a partner about what each sentence and each part of Scott's work means.

Listen in, ask questions, and observe. **Note** potential contributions for the discussion.

Who can come up to show where 150 would be on this number line? Explain.

Would the point for 160 be before or after 150? Explain why point A cannot be 160.

Talk to your neighbor about what distance on Scott's number line shows 10 units.

Who can show what distance shows about 10 units? What distance shows 50 units? How could Scott check to make sure his estimate for 10 units is about right?

What number would be 1 unit past 150? 10 units past 150? Explain. Who can come up and prove that point B is about 160?

Call on students to state things to remember about solving problems like this.

Start a Things to Remember list on the board.

MORE DAY 1

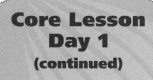

**Core Lesson
Day 1**
(continued)

Discussion

Student Thinking, continued

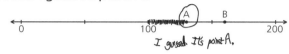

STUDENT PAGE 2

Stacy

I tried drawing 60 units after 100, but they were too little to count. I guessed point A.

Oops!

0 ——————— 100 ——Ⓐ— B ——— 200

I guessed. It's point A.

Read the statement marked Oops. **Remind** students that this is a common pitfall.

 Stacy made a pitfall when she tried to draw 60 tiny little units. Talk with your neighbor about why this method isn't practical. **WAIT**

Who can explain in their own words how to use halfway marks to estimate what number a point shows?

Who can use Scott's method to show why point A is about 130?

Draw a number line like in the Starter Problem and show points for about 140 and about 190. **Ask** students to talk with a neighbor about how to use benchmarks to decide which point shows about 190. **Remind** them to look out for pitfalls. **Call on** students to explain.

Things to Remember

Call on students to **add** to the Things to Remember list on the board. **Read** the list.

Help students summarize and record two important Things to Remember.

Things to Remember List (sample)
1. It helps to think about the halfway point between numbers like 100 and 200.
2. Sometimes it helps to estimate the length of 10 units when the units are so tiny.

Reflection

Ask students to reflect on the discussion process using one of the sample prompts.

Reflection Prompts (sample)
- Name a *Discussion Builder* that we used today. How did it help the discussion?
- What *Discussion Builder* could we use next time to make the discussion even better?
- What did someone do or say today that helped you understand the math?

**Core Lesson
Day 2**

Review and Practice

Review

Ask students to review page 2 to jog their memory.

Read the statement marked OK. **Call on** a student to explain how the problem was solved.

Read the statement marked Oops. **Call on** a student to explain why it is incorrect or doesn't make sense.

Call on two or three students to read an item on their Things to Remember list.

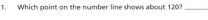

Our Turn

Ask students to refer to page 3.

Use the procedure below and the Clipboard Prompts to discuss students' solutions. **Discuss** the problems one at a time.

> **Read** the problem.
>
> **Ask** students to work with a neighbor to solve it.
>
> **Discuss** one or two students' solutions.

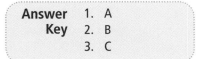

Answer Key
1. A
2. B
3. C

Our Turn

Write the letter for the point that shows the number.

1. Which point on the number line shows about 120? _____

2. Which point on the number line shows about 180? _____

3. Which point on the number line shows about 90? _____

My Turn

Ask students to solve the problems on page 4. **Remind** them to watch out for pitfalls!

After allowing time to work, **read** the answers. **Have** students mark and revise their papers using ink or crayon.

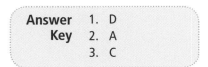

Answer Key
1. D
2. A
3. C

My Turn

Write the letter for the point that shows the number.

1. Which point on the number line shows about 80? _____

2. Which point on the number line shows about 170? _____

3. Which point on the number line shows about 175? _____

Mini Lessons
(2–3 Days Later)

Assess and Reinforce

Multiple Choice Mini Lesson

Distribute Student Page 5.

Problem 1

 Please read problem 1.

Talk with your neighbor about which choices don't make sense. WAIT

Why might someone make an oops and choose 41?

What is the correct choice?

Multiple Choice Mini Lesson

Fill in the circle next to the answer you choose.

1. What number is the best estimate for point X?

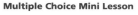

   X

   | 0 | 10 | 20 | 30 | 40 | 50 | 60 |

   ○ 55   ● 45   ○ 41

2. What number is the best estimate for point X?

   X

   | 0 | 50 | 100 | 150 | 200 |

   ○ 110   ○ 105   ● 125

 Students may count a single unit and think the mark after 40 should be 41. Help them understand that the distance between 40 and point X is halfway between 40 and 50.

Problem 2

 Read the problem and find the correct choice. WAIT

Which response is correct? Explain why.

How can you know that 125 is halfway between 100 and 150? Explain.

Writing Task Mini Lesson

Distribute Student Page 6.

Ask a student to read the task. **Call on** students to respond with their ideas.

Jot the ideas on the board.

Write an explanation together using their ideas. **Read** it aloud.

Ask students to write an explanation on their page.

Writing Task Mini Lesson

Explain how you know that a good estimate for point X is 150. You may draw a picture on the back to help explain.

   X

   | 0 | 100 | 200 | 300 |

Sample Explanation: Point X is about halfway between 100 and 200. There are 100 units between 100 and 200. Half of 100 is 50, so there would be 50 units more after 100 to get to the halfway point. That's 150.

Mathematical Discussion Support

When generating ideas, invite students to use materials such as paper strips or drawings of number lines.

Ask students to explain what a "good estimate" means. Remind them that when they are using benchmarks and number sense to think about where a number may be located on a number line, they are estimating.

Have them practice estimating the location of different points on number lines drawn on the board, using benchmarks to help them. Reinforce the use of the terms "unit" and "halfway."

Marking Points for Numbers

Lesson at a Glance

Prior Learning Needed

- Use a number line
- Understand the relative magnitude of whole numbers

Lesson Preparation

- Study Lesson Foundation
- Review Teaching Guide and Student Pages
- Prepare stapled packet of Student Pages 1–4 for each student
- Copy and cut in half Student Pages 5 and 6
- Post *Discussion Builders* poster

Mathematical goals

✷ Locate numbers on a number line

✷ Estimate distances on a number line

Mathematical language and reasoning goals

✷ Use halfway points and benchmarks to locate points on a number line

✷ Use reasoning to compare the relative magnitude of numbers

LESSON ROADMAP			MATERIALS
CORE LESSON: DAY 1	GROUPING	TIME	○ *Discussion Builders* poster
Opener			○ Projector (optional)
Discussion Builders Purpose Math Words	👥	🕐	○ Student Page 1 ○ Student Page 2
Starter Problem	👤	🕐	○ Teaching Guide ○ Paper strips of equal
Discussion			length for making number lines (suggested)
Student Thinking	👤 👥 👥	🕐	
Things to Remember Reflection	👥	🕐	
CORE LESSON: DAY 2			○ Clipboard Prompts, page 37
Review and Practice			○ Student Page 2 (completed day 1)
Review Day 1 Lesson	👥	🕐	○ Student Pages 3 and 4
Our Turn	👥 👥	🕐	○ Teaching Guide
My Turn	👤	🕐	○ Paper strips of equal length for making number lines (suggested)
MINI LESSONS: 2–3 DAYS LATER			○ Student Pages 5 and 6
Assess and Reinforce			○ Teaching Guide
Multiple Choice Mini Lesson	👤 👥 👥	🕐	○ Paper strips of equal length for making
Writing Task Mini Lesson	👤 👥	🕐	number lines (suggested)

Lesson Foundation

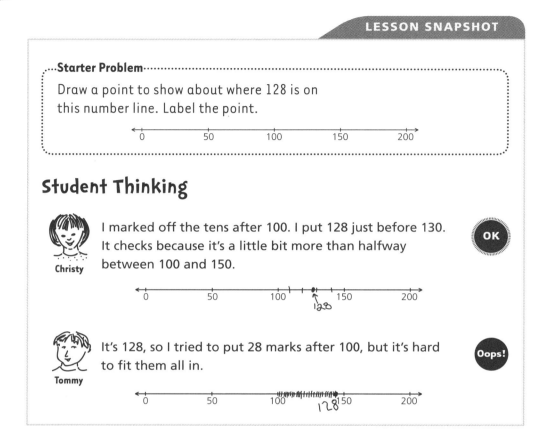

LESSON SNAPSHOT

Starter Problem

Draw a point to show about where 128 is on this number line. Label the point.

Student Thinking

Christy

I marked off the tens after 100. I put 128 just before 130. It checks because it's a little bit more than halfway between 100 and 150.

OK

Tommy

It's 128, so I tried to put 28 marks after 100, but it's hard to fit them all in.

Oops!

MATHEMATICAL INSIGHTS & TEACHING TIPS

Benchmarks on the Number Line

Christy realized that it wasn't practical to draw every whole unit between 100 and 128 accurately on this number line. So she estimated the length of 10 units and used that distance to figure out about where to locate 128. She checked her estimate by seeing that 128 was a little more than halfway between 100 and 150 (halfway would be 125). Students should be encouraged to go beyond counting marks or units and use place value and number sense.

Oops! Tommy made 28 marks after 100 to locate the point for 128, but because the size of the units needed to be so small, he couldn't draw them the right size on his number line.

Mathematicians use arrows to emphasize that number lines continue in both directions, with positive numbers to the right of 0 and negative numbers to the left of 0. Number lines contain an infinite number of points, no matter which points are labeled.

 Use students' previous classroom experience with a number line on which every whole unit is marked to transition to other labeling systems, such as those in which every 10 units or 50 units are marked. Point out that the in-between numbers exist but are not labeled.

MATHEMATICAL INSIGHTS & TEACHING TIPS (CONTINUED)

Estimating the Size of 1 Unit or 10 Units

Tommy didn't realize that it isn't practical to fit 50 units of equal length between 100 and 150 on his number line, or he didn't have an alternate strategy. Instead of trying to squeeze in little marks for individual units, Tommy could have estimated the length of 10 units, as Christy did, and used that length to estimate where to locate 128 on the number line.

Number Lines and Rulers

Both number lines and rulers are geometric representations that have marks showing a number of units of length. Rulers are designed to measure lengths, so they have labels to show where each unit (such as 0 units, 1 unit, 2 units) ends. Rulers use standardized units, such as centimeters or inches. Number lines show points, both as a distance from 0 and as a location in comparison to other numbers. A number line uses any conveniently sized unit, depending upon the purpose. Although the size of a unit on a number line is arbitrary, every unit on a given number line must be equal.

 A number line does not have to start at 0. For example, one could draw a number line from 100 up to 130, fold it into 3 segments of equal lengths, and label it in units of 10. Once the distance from 100 to 110 is set, all other distances of 10 units must be made the same length.

MATHEMATICAL DISCUSSION SUPPORT

Ask students to explain why it isn't practical to mark off every whole unit between 100 and 150 on the number line given. Explain that if the number line were enlarged, then it might be possible, but still not very practical with so many units to mark off.

Develop counting flexibility by starting with a number such as 100 or 250 and counting by tens (100, 110, 120; 250, 260, 270).

Help students understand that a unit describes the length of the space between the points for two consecutive whole numbers on the number line (e.g., between 8 and 9 or 50 and 51).

Model the use of phrases such as "about," "a bit less than 130," and "closer to 130 than to 120" when referring to a point drawn on a number line. Explain that using information to figure out about where a number goes means that we are estimating where the number is.

Core Lesson Day 1

Opener

Review *Discussion Builders*

Read the poster. **Suggest** a section to focus on today:
Presenting Our Ideas, Adding to Others' Ideas, or *Asking More Questions.*

Purpose

Distribute stapled packets of Student Pages 1–4. **Project** an image of page 1 (optional).

Call on a student to read the purpose.

Math Words

Point to and say the first math word. **Ask** students to repeat it aloud or silently.

Read the sentence containing the word.

Give an example using objects or drawings.

Repeat for the other math words.

Starter Problem

Read the Starter Problem. **Call on** a student to restate it in his/her own words.

 Please use what you already know to help you solve this problem on your own. This will prepare you to talk about the math and how to avoid pitfalls in our discussion later on.

I'll walk around and make notes about things we need to discuss. Look out for oops, or pitfalls! (WAIT)

Look at your work. It's easy to have an oops, or pitfall, in this type of problem. You might also have made a pitfall if your point is not about halfway between 100 and 150.

Don't worry. Next we'll discuss how two imaginary students solved this problem. One has a pitfall! You may keep your solution private, but bring up your ideas in the discussion.

STUDENT PAGE 1

Purpose
To use estimation to mark and label a point on a number line

Math Words

units	The space between 0 and 10 on a number line is 10 units long.

10 units

0 ———————— 10

halfway between	25 is halfway between 0 and 50 on a number line.
benchmarks	Benchmark numbers, like 10, 50, and 100, help you estimate.

Starter Problem

Draw a point to show about where 128 is on this number line. Label the point.

0   50   100   150   200

Discussion

Student Thinking

 Christy I marked off the tens after 100. I put 128 just before 130. It checks because it's a little bit more than halfway between 100 and 150. **OK**

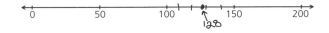

0   50   100   125   150   200

128

Ask students to refer to page 2. **Read** the statement marked OK.

Explain that this statement is about the same problem students worked on earlier.

 We can learn a lot about the math by studying what this student did.

Read each sentence silently and look at Christy's work. Think about what they mean. **WAIT**

Now talk with a partner about what each sentence and each part of Christy's work means.

Listen in, ask questions, and observe. **Note** potential contributions for the discussion.

 Who can come up to show how Christy marked off the tens between 100 and 150? How many groups of 10 units are between 100 and 150? How could Christy estimate the length of 10 units on the number line?

What number does the first mark after 100 represent? Where is 130 on Christy's number line?

What might she mean by "I put 128 just before 130"? How much before 130?

Talk to your neighbor about why Christy said, "It checks because it's a little bit more than halfway between 100 and 150." **WAIT**

Which number is halfway between 100 and 150? How does knowing where 125 is on the number line help you mark the point for 128? About where would you mark a point for 80?

Call on students to state things to remember about solving problems like this.

Start a Things to Remember list on the board.

 MORE DAY 1

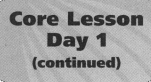

**Core Lesson
Day 1
(continued)**

Discussion

Student Thinking, continued

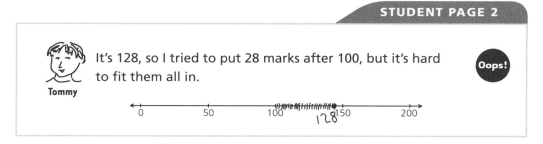

STUDENT PAGE 2

It's 128, so I tried to put 28 marks after 100, but it's hard to fit them all in.

Tommy

Oops!

Read the statement marked Oops. **Remind** students that this is a common pitfall.

Tommy made a pitfall by using the wrong size of units. Talk with your neighbor about why his method doesn't make sense. WAIT

Why isn't it practical for Tommy to mark off 28 units? Why does it make sense to use benchmarks like 150 and 125 when marking points on a number line?

Who can show a correct way to mark the point for 128 on the number line?

Ask students to talk with a neighbor about where to draw a point on the Starter Problem number line to show 175. **Remind** them to look out for pitfalls. **Call on** students to show why their answer makes sense.

Things to Remember

Call on students to **add** to the Things to Remember list on the board. **Read** the list.

Help students summarize and record two important Things to Remember.

> **Things to Remember List (sample)**
> 1. Estimating and marking every 10 units instead of every unit is sometimes helpful.
> 2. It helps to know what number is halfway between two other numbers.

Reflection

Ask students to reflect on the discussion process using one of the sample prompts.

> **Reflection Prompts (sample)**
> • Name a *Discussion Builder* that we used today. How did it help the discussion?
> • What *Discussion Builder* could we use next time to make the discussion even better?
> • What did someone do or say today that helped you understand the math?

Review and Practice

Review

Ask students to review page 2 to jog their memory.

Read the statement marked OK. **Call on** a student to explain how the problem was solved.

Read the statement marked Oops. **Call on** a student to explain why it is incorrect or doesn't make sense.

Call on two or three students to read an item on their Things to Remember list.

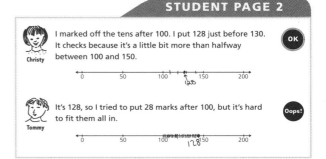

Christy: I marked off the tens after 100. I put 128 just before 130. It checks because it's a little bit more than halfway between 100 and 150. **OK**

Tommy: It's 128, so I tried to put 28 marks after 100, but it's hard to fit them all in. **Oops!**

Our Turn

Ask students to refer to page 3.

Use the procedure below and the Clipboard Prompts to discuss students' solutions. **Discuss** the problems one at a time.

> **Read** the problem.
>
> **Ask** students to work with a neighbor to solve it.
>
> **Discuss** one or two students' solutions.

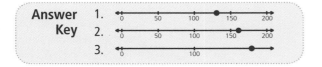

Answer Key
1.
2.
3.

Our Turn

Draw a point to show about where the number is on each number line. Label the point.

1. 131

2. 162

3. 180

My Turn

Ask students to solve the problems on page 4. **Remind** them to watch out for pitfalls!

After allowing time to work, **read** the answers. **Have** students mark and revise their papers using ink or crayon.

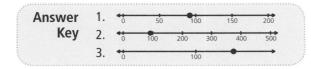

Answer Key
1.
2.
3.

My Turn

Draw a point to show about where the number is on each number line. Label the point.

1. 92

2. 92

3. 152

Mini Lessons
(2–3 Days Later)

Assess and Reinforce

Multiple Choice Mini Lesson

Distribute Student Page 5.

Problem 1

 Please read problem 1.

Talk with your neighbor about which choices don't make sense. **WAIT**

How could you know that 137 is marked correctly on the last number line?

 Encourage students to use number sense to see that the first number line is incorrect. Since 137 is less than 150, 137 must be to the left of 150 on the number line.

Problem 2

 Read the problem and find the correct choice. **WAIT**

Which response is correct? Explain why.

How can you check that a point is in about the right place if all the numbers are not written on a number line? Explain.

Multiple Choice Mini Lesson

Fill in the circle next to the answer you choose.

1. Which number line correctly shows the number 137?

2. Which number line correctly shows the number 121?

Writing Task Mini Lesson

Distribute Student Page 6.

Ask a student to read the task. **Call on** students to respond with their ideas.

Jot the ideas on the board.

Write an explanation together using their ideas. **Read** it aloud.

Ask students to write an explanation on their page.

Writing Task Mini Lesson

Explain how you know about where to mark and label the number 70 on this number line.

Sample Explanation: I found 50 halfway between 0 and 100. Then, I found 75 halfway between 50 and 100. Then, I went back just a little to find 5 less than 75.

Mathematical Discussion Support

It may be helpful to provide students with materials such as a large copy of the number line and a paper strip to represent 200 units. Ask them to fold the paper strips to find equal parts and to explain which numbers are at the fold lines.

Ensure students understand that they are estimating where the point for 70 is on the number line. They are using number sense and benchmarks to approximate the location of the point on the number line.

Add On a Bit More

Prior Learning Needed

- Use a number line
- Use place value understanding
- Understand addition concepts

Lesson Preparation

- Study Lesson Foundation
- Review Teaching Guide and Student Pages
- Prepare stapled packet of Student Pages 1–4 for each student
- Copy and cut in half Student Pages 5 and 6
- Post *Discussion Builders* poster

Mathematical goals

✳ Increase a number by a specific amount

✳ Add on across a multiple of 10

Mathematical language and reasoning goals

✳ Use a mental number line to add

✳ Use benchmarks to add on in easy steps

LESSON ROADMAP			MATERIALS
CORE LESSON: DAY 1	GROUPING	TIME	
Opener			○ *Discussion Builders* poster
Discussion Builders Purpose Math Words			○ Projector (optional)
			○ Student Page 1
Starter Problem			○ Student Page 2
			○ Teaching Guide
Discussion			○ Paper strips of equal length for making number lines, place value materials (suggested)
Student Thinking			
Things to Remember Reflection			
CORE LESSON: DAY 2			
Review and Practice			○ Clipboard Prompts, page 37
Review Day 1 Lesson			○ Student Page 2 (completed day 1)
Our Turn			○ Student Pages 3 and 4
My Turn			○ Teaching Guide
			○ Paper strips of equal length for making number lines, place value materials (suggested)
MINI LESSONS: 2–3 DAYS LATER			
Assess and Reinforce			○ Student Pages 5 and 6
Multiple Choice Mini Lesson			○ Teaching Guide
Writing Task Mini Lesson			

Lesson Foundation

····Starter Problem····

Think about the meaning. Solve.

$$285 + 7 = \underline{\hspace{2cm}}$$

Student Thinking

Jackson

I added in my head with easy steps. First, I added on 5 to get to 290. Then, I needed to add on 2 more. It's 292. I could add using paper to check.

OK

Alika

I rewrote the numbers up and down on paper. It's 985.

Oops!

$$
\begin{array}{r}
285 \\
+\ 7 \\
\hline
985
\end{array}
$$

MATHEMATICAL INSIGHTS & TEACHING TIPS

Using a Mental Number Line to Add On

Jackson thought of a number line in his head to visualize adding 285 + 7. He started with the larger addend, 285, and he added 7 in two parts. First, he added 5 to 285 to get to 290, the next benchmark number ending in a 0. Then, he used place value understanding to add the second part, 2, to 290.

Oops! Alika rewrote the problem vertically using the addition algorithm to add 285 and 7, but she made an error by recording and adding the 7 in the hundreds column.

Jackson also could have used other combinations of "hops" on the number line (even though they might be less efficient or more open to pitfalls), such as 285 + 2 + 5 or 285 + 1 + 1 + 1 + 2 + 2. It is important for students to understand that since the addition operation is commutative, the order of the hops doesn't matter as long as the total added on is 7. A mental number line is a powerful model that helps students visualize addition, strengthen their number sense, and use benchmark numbers, whether they are computing with whole numbers, fractions, or decimals.

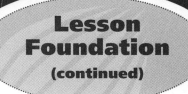

MATHEMATICAL INSIGHTS & TEACHING TIPS (CONTINUED)

 Jackson's number line shows a long hop for 285 and two short hops for +5 and +2. Encourage students to make the hops somewhat proportional to the size of the numbers but not to worry about being exact. In this lesson, the drawing is being used as a tool to help students visualize and support their reasoning. Students may also simply make a dot for 285, the starting amount, rather than showing a hop from 0 to 285.

Addition Algorithm Pitfalls

Both Jackson and Alika knew that the traditional paper-and-pencil addition algorithm could be used to add 285 and 7. However, as in Alika's case, students often don't align the place values correctly when the two addends have different numbers of digits. When she wrote a vertical problem, she lined up the numbers on the left. She also didn't notice that 985 didn't make sense when adding just 7 more to 285.

Choosing When to Use the Paper-and-Pencil Algorithm

Jackson said, "I could add using paper to check." Encourage students to make a deliberate choice about whether to compute mentally or use the algorithm. Although both approaches are appropriate, Jackson's mental number line method may be more efficient and less susceptible to pitfalls when adding on a small amount.

 Students need to be convinced that using a mental number line to add on will result in the same sum as using the paper-and-pencil algorithm. Ask them to prove it (perhaps by using base ten blocks or expanded notation) and to explain why.

MATHEMATICAL DISCUSSION SUPPORT

Ask students questions that prompt them to explain and use the terms "increasing" or "adding on." Also, have students explain and show how they break, or decompose, a number such as 7 into smaller parts so they can add on in easy steps.

Help students use place value ideas and reasonableness to explain why it doesn't make sense to get 985 as the sum of 285 and 7. Encourage students to draw their own number lines to show how to add on using easy steps.

Help students make the connection between the size of the "hops" on the number line and what Jackson calls "easy steps." Explicitly show that Jackson's goal was to get to a multiple of 10 and then add on from there.

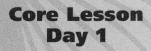
Opener

Review *Discussion Builders*

Read the poster. **Suggest** a section to focus on today:
Presenting Our Ideas, Adding to Others' Ideas, or *Asking More Questions.*

Purpose

Distribute stapled packets of Student Pages 1–4. **Project** an image of page 1 (optional).

Call on a student to read the purpose.

Math Words

Point to and say the first math word. **Ask** students to repeat it aloud or silently.

Read the sentence containing the word.

Give an example using objects or drawings.

Repeat for the other math words.

Starter Problem

Read the Starter Problem. **Call on** a student to restate it in his/her own words.

 Please use what you already know to help you solve this problem on your own. This will prepare you to talk about the math and how to avoid pitfalls in our discussion later on.

I'll walk around and make notes about things we need to discuss. Look out for oops, or pitfalls! **WAIT**

Look at your work. It's easy to have an oops, or pitfall, in this type of problem. You might also have made a pitfall if your answer is more than 300.

Don't worry. Next we'll discuss how two imaginary students solved this problem. One has a pitfall! You may keep your solution private, but bring up your ideas in the discussion.

> **STUDENT PAGE 1**
>
> **Purpose**
> To add a few more to a large number
>
> **Math Words**
>
> | | |
> |---|---|
> | **sum** | When I add 55 + 2, the sum is 57. |
> | **add on** | I can start with 55 beads and add on 2 more to make 57 beads. |
>
> **Starter Problem**
> Think about the meaning. Solve.
>
> $$285 + 7 = \text{\_\_\_\_\_}$$

Discussion

Student Thinking

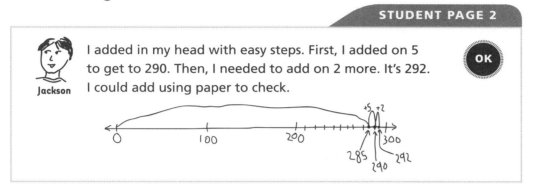

Jackson: I added in my head with easy steps. First, I added on 5 to get to 290. Then, I needed to add on 2 more. It's 292. I could add using paper to check.

OK

Ask students to refer to page 2. **Read** the statement marked OK.

Explain that this statement is about the same problem students worked on earlier.

 We can learn a lot about the math by studying what this student did.

Read each sentence silently and look at the drawing. Think about what they mean. **WAIT**

Now talk with a partner about what each sentence and each part of the drawing means.

Listen in, ask questions, and observe. **Note** potential contributions for the discussion.

 Who can come up to explain how Jackson showed 285 on his number line? How did he show "plus 7"?

Jackson said he "added in my head with easy steps." Why do you think he added 5 first? How did he know he needed to add 2 more? Why is it easy to know the sum of 290 + 2?

Talk to your neighbor about what would happen if Jackson used different hops. What if he made a hop for 3 more and another hop for 4 more? Would he still get 292? **WAIT**

Who can show some other hops Jackson could use to add 7 more? Which seem easiest to use? How could you add 126 + 8 in easy steps?

Call on students to state things to remember about solving problems like this.

Start a Things to Remember list on the board.

MORE DAY 1

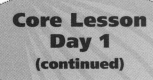

**Core Lesson
Day 1
(continued)**

Discussion

Student Thinking, continued

 I rewrote the numbers up and down on paper. It's 985. **Oops!**

Alika

$$\begin{array}{r} 285 \\ +\ 7 \\ \hline 985 \end{array}$$

Read the statement marked Oops. **Remind** students that this is a common pitfall.

 Alika made a pitfall when she wrote the digit 7 below the digit 2. Talk with your neighbor about why her answer doesn't make sense and is a pitfall. **WAIT**

Why doesn't Alika's answer make sense? Is it too high or too low?

Did she line up the 7 with the hundreds place or the ones place? Explain how she mistakenly added 700 instead of 7.

Write the following problems on the board. **Ask** students to talk with a neighbor about which problem shows how to add 428 + 4 by lining up the digits with the same place values. **Remind** them to look out for pitfalls. **Call on** students to explain.

$$\begin{array}{r} 428 \\ +\ 4 \\ \hline \end{array} \qquad \begin{array}{r} 428 \\ +\ 4 \\ \hline \end{array}$$

Things to Remember

Call on students to **add** to the Things to Remember list on the board. **Read** the list.

Help students summarize and record two important Things to Remember.

> **Things to Remember List (sample)**
> 1. To add on a bit more, think of a number line so you can add in your head using easy steps.
> 2. Think about the value of digits when you write an addition problem so that you add ones to ones, tens to tens, and hundreds to hundreds.

Reflection

Ask students to reflect on the discussion process using one of the sample prompts.

> **Reflection Prompts (sample)**
> • Name a *Discussion Builder* that we used today. How did it help the discussion?
> • What *Discussion Builder* could we use next time to make the discussion even better?
> • What did someone do or say today that helped you understand the math?

**Core Lesson
Day 2**

Review and Practice

Review

Ask students to review page 2 to jog their memory.

Read the statement marked OK. **Call on** a student to explain how the problem was solved.

Read the statement marked Oops. **Call on** a student to explain why it is incorrect or doesn't make sense.

Call on two or three students to read an item on their Things to Remember list.

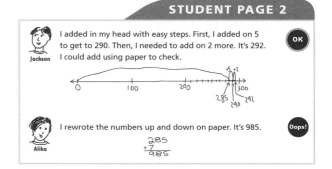

STUDENT PAGE 2

Jackson: I added in my head with easy steps. First, I added on 5 to get to 290. Then, I needed to add on 2 more. It's 292. I could add using paper to check. **OK**

Alika: I rewrote the numbers up and down on paper. It's 985. **Oops!**

285
+ 7
985

Our Turn

Ask students to refer to page 3.

Use the procedure below and the Clipboard Prompts to discuss students' solutions. **Discuss** the problems one at a time.

> **Read** the problem.
>
> **Ask** students to work with a neighbor to solve it.
>
> **Discuss** one or two students' solutions.

Answer Key	1. 143
	2. 432
	3. 216

STUDENT PAGE 3

Our Turn

Write the answer for each problem on the line.

1. $135 + 8 =$ _____

2. $427 + 5 =$ _____

3. $209 + 7 =$ _____

My Turn

Ask students to solve the problems on page 4. **Remind** them to watch out for pitfalls!

After allowing time to work, **read** the answers. **Have** students mark and revise their papers using ink or crayon.

Answer Key	1. 243
	2. 441
	3. 160

STUDENT PAGE 4

My Turn

Write the answer for each problem on the line.

1. $239 + 4 =$ _____

2. $432 + 9 =$ _____

3. $152 + 8 =$ _____

Mini Lessons
(2–3 Days Later)

Assess and Reinforce

Multiple Choice Mini Lesson

Distribute Student Page 5.

Problem 1

 Please read problem 1.

Talk with your neighbor about which choices don't make sense. WAIT

How could you check to see if 233 is the missing number?

(i) *Remind students to start with the larger addend (226) and add on the smaller amount (7) in easy steps. It would not make sense to start with 7 and add on 226.*

Problem 2

 Read the problem and find the correct choice. WAIT

Which response is correct? Explain why.

What benchmark number(s) could you use to help you find the right answer of 262? Explain.

> **STUDENT PAGE 5**
>
> **Multiple Choice Mini Lesson**
> Fill in the circle next to the answer you choose.
>
> 1. $7 + 226 =$ _____
>   ○ 926   ○ 230   ● 233
>
> 2. $8 + 254 =$ _____
>   ○ 252   ○ 260   ● 262

Writing Task Mini Lesson

Distribute Student Page 6.

Ask a student to read the task. **Call on** students to respond with their ideas.

Jot the ideas on the board.

Write an explanation together using their ideas. **Read** it aloud.

Ask students to write an explanation on their page.

> **STUDENT PAGE 6**
>
> **Writing Task Mini Lesson**
> Explain how you know how to add 7 + 156 in easy steps. You may draw a picture on the back to help explain.

> **Sample Explanation:** It's easier to start with 156 than 7. 156 and 4 more is 160. 160 and 3 more is 163. I added 7 by adding 4 more and then 3 more.

Mathematical Discussion Support

Ask students to explain what benchmark numbers are, give examples, and explain why they are easy numbers to add on to. For example, it is easy to add a one-digit number to numbers that end in 0. Review what it means to add on in easy steps. Talk about why it is okay to start with 156 even when 7 is the first addend listed.

A Little Less

Prior Learning Needed

- Count back from a number
- Use a number line
- Understand subtraction concepts

Lesson Preparation

- Study Lesson Foundation
- Review Teaching Guide and Student Pages
- Prepare stapled packet of Student Pages 1–4 for each student
- Copy and cut in half Student Pages 5 and 6
- Post *Discussion Builders* poster

Mathematical goals

✳ Decrease a number by a specific amount

✳ Count forward or backward across a decade mark or century mark

Mathematical language and reasoning goals

✳ Represent subtraction on a number line

✳ Relate decreasing to subtraction

LESSON ROADMAP			MATERIALS
CORE LESSON: DAY 1	GROUPING	TIME	○ *Discussion Builders* poster
Opener *Discussion Builders* Purpose Math Words			○ Projector (optional) ○ Student Page 1 ○ Student Page 2
Starter Problem			○ Teaching Guide ○ Paper for drawing number lines (suggested)
Discussion Student Thinking			
Things to Remember Reflection			
CORE LESSON: DAY 2			○ Clipboard Prompts, page 37
Review and Practice Review Day 1 Lesson			○ Student Page 2 (completed day 1)
Our Turn			○ Student Pages 3 and 4 ○ Teaching Guide
My Turn			○ Paper for drawing number lines (suggested)
MINI LESSONS: 2–3 DAYS LATER			○ Student Pages 5 and 6
Assess and Reinforce Multiple Choice Mini Lesson			○ Teaching Guide ○ Paper for drawing number lines (suggested)
Writing Task Mini Lesson			

Lesson Foundation

LESSON SNAPSHOT

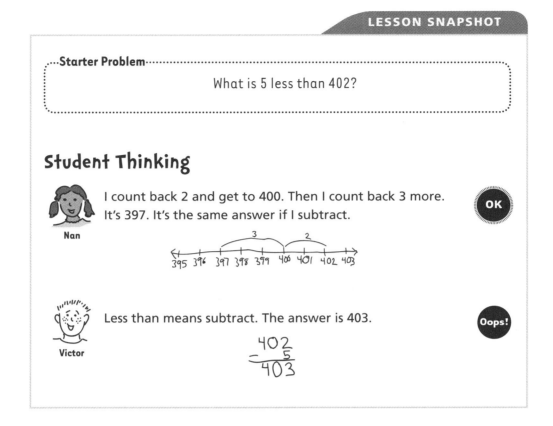

·····Starter Problem·····

What is 5 less than 402?

Student Thinking

Nan

I count back 2 and get to 400. Then I count back 3 more. It's 397. It's the same answer if I subtract.

OK

Victor

Less than means subtract. The answer is 403.

$$\begin{array}{r} 402 \\ -5 \\ \hline 403 \end{array}$$

Oops!

MATHEMATICAL INSIGHTS & TEACHING TIPS

Decreasing a Number Using a Number Line

It is often easier to count back to decrease a number by a specific amount than to use the subtraction algorithm. Nan used a number line to help her visualize counting back 5 from 402. Notice that she made two hops on the number line. First, she hopped back 2 units to get to 400. Then, she hopped back 3 more units to get to 397.

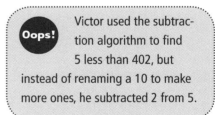

Oops! Victor used the subtraction algorithm to find 5 less than 402, but instead of renaming a 10 to make more ones, he subtracted 2 from 5.

 Students often make errors counting back when they have to cross a multiple of 10 or 100. Working with number lines helps students develop a mental number line and draws their attention to easy steps during mental computation. Help students think about counting units or groups of units, not interval marks on the number line.

MATHEMATICAL INSIGHTS & TEACHING TIPS (CONTINUED)

Subtraction Algorithm Pitfalls

Victor knew that the subtraction algorithm could be used to decrease 402 by 5; however, as in Victor's case, the common subtraction algorithm is often subject to pitfalls. Perhaps he thought, "I can't take the 5 from 2, so I'll take 2 from 5." This is a common error. More important, Victor failed to notice that his answer didn't make sense. His answer, 403, is more than the amount he started with, 402.

For this problem, Victor is correct that "less than means subtract." But notice that it would not mean subtract if the question were something like "Is 40 less than 38?"

 Remind students to look back at their answers to make sure that they make sense. They should also be aware of the pitfalls to watch out for in using the algorithm. When it makes sense, they should compute mentally, rather than use the algorithm.

Crossing Multiples of 100 When Counting

When subtracting a small amount, it is efficient to count up or count back to find the difference. When the numbers are relatively close in value, it is efficient to count up to find the difference. Alert students that they must be extra careful when crossing a multiple of 10 or 100. They should become fluent in solving problems that involve increases, decreases, and differences like the following:

How much less is 397 than 402?   What is 5 less than 402?

How much more is 402 than 397?   What is 5 more than 397?

MATHEMATICAL DISCUSSION SUPPORT

When students are using a number line to subtract, encourage them to talk about the number of units that they are moving, or hops they are making. For example, "I went 2 units to the left to stop at 400 and then 3 more units to land at 397." Also, encourage them to use the phrases "less than" and "count back."

The following questions use similar language but mean very different things. Help students clarify the differences by relating them to concrete situations that use money or distances.

• How much less is 397 than 402?
• What is 5 less than 402?
• Which is less, 5 or 402?

Core Lesson Day 1

Opener

Review *Discussion Builders*

Read the poster. **Suggest** a section to focus on today:
Presenting Our Ideas, Adding to Others' Ideas, or *Asking More Questions.*

Purpose

Distribute stapled packets of Student Pages 1–4. **Project** an image of page 1 (optional).

Call on a student to read the purpose.

Math Words

Point to and say the first math words. **Ask** students to repeat them aloud or silently.

Read the sentence containing the words.

Give an example using objects or drawings.

Repeat for the other math words.

Starter Problem

Read the Starter Problem. **Call on** a student to restate it in his/her own words.

 Please use what you already know to help you solve this problem on your own. This will prepare you to talk about the math and how to avoid pitfalls in our discussion later on.

I'll walk around and make notes about things we need to discuss. Look out for oops, or pitfalls! (WAIT)

Look at your work. It's easy to have an oops, or pitfall, in this type of problem. You might also have made a pitfall if your answer is more than 400.

Don't worry. Next we'll discuss how two imaginary students solved this problem. One has a pitfall! You may keep your solution private, but bring up your ideas in the discussion.

STUDENT PAGE 1

Purpose
To find an amount less than a number

Math Words

less than	A penny is 4 cents less than a nickel.
count back	To count back from 100, you say "99, 98, 97, . . ."

Starter Problem

What is 5 less than 402?

Discussion

Student Thinking

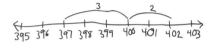

STUDENT PAGE 2

 Nan

I count back 2 and get to 400. Then I count back 3 more. It's 397. It's the same answer if I subtract.

 OK

Ask students to refer to page 2. **Read** the statement marked OK.

Explain that this statement is about the same problem students worked on earlier.

 We can learn a lot about the math by studying what this student did.

Read each sentence silently and look at the drawing. Think about what they mean. **WAIT**

Now talk with a partner about what each sentence and each part of the drawing means.

Listen in, ask questions, and observe. **Note** potential contributions for the discussion.

 What number do you think Nan started with on her number line, 5 or 402? Why?

Who can come up to show how Nan's number line shows that she counted back 2 and then counted back 3 more? What do the hops mean?

Why did Nan start by counting back 2 and then 3 instead of counting back 5 all at once?

Nan said, "It's the same answer if I subtract." Talk to your neighbor about why counting back is the same as subtracting. **WAIT**

Is it easier to count back or to subtract for this problem? Explain.

Who can use a number line or counting back to find 6 less than 105?

Call on students to state things to remember about solving problems like this.

Start a Things to Remember list on the board.

MORE DAY 1

Core Lesson Day 1
(continued)

Discussion

Student Thinking, continued

Less than means subtract. The answer is 403.

Victor

$$\begin{array}{r} 402 \\ -5 \\ \hline 403 \end{array}$$

 Oops!

Read the statement marked Oops. **Remind** students that this is a common pitfall.

 Victor made a pitfall when he subtracted the digits in the ones place incorrectly. Talk with your neighbor about why his answer doesn't make sense. **WAIT**

Who would like to come up and explain how you know Victor's answer doesn't make sense? Is it too high or too low? Why is it easy to make this pitfall?

Write the following problems on the board. **Ask** students to talk with a neighbor about which of these has an answer of 403. **Remind** students to look out for pitfalls. **Call on** students to explain why their answers make sense.

$$\begin{array}{r} 402 \\ -5 \\ \hline \end{array} \qquad\qquad \begin{array}{r} 405 \\ -2 \\ \hline \end{array}$$

Things to Remember

Call on students to **add** to the Things to Remember list on the board. **Read** the list.

Help students summarize and record two important Things to Remember.

> **Things to Remember List (sample)**
> 1. To find a little less than a number, count back, use a number line, or subtract.
> 2. It may be easier to count back or use mental math than to subtract on paper.

Reflection

Ask students to reflect on the discussion process using one of the sample prompts.

> **Reflection Prompts (sample)**
> • Name a *Discussion Builder* that we used today. How did it help the discussion?
> • What *Discussion Builder* could we use next time to make the discussion even better?
> • What did someone do or say today that helped you understand the math?

Core Lesson Day 2

Review and Practice

Review

Ask students to review page 2 to jog their memory.

Read the statement marked OK. **Call on** a student to explain how the problem was solved.

Read the statement marked Oops. **Call on** a student to explain why it is incorrect or doesn't make sense.

Call on two or three students to read an item on their Things to Remember list.

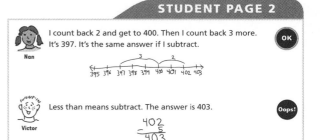

STUDENT PAGE 2

Nan: I count back 2 and get to 400. Then I count back 3 more. It's 397. It's the same answer if I subtract. **OK**

395 396 397 398 399 400 401 402 403

Victor: Less than means subtract. The answer is 403. **Oops!**

402
- 5
403

Our Turn

Ask students to refer to page 3.

Use the procedure below and the Clipboard Prompts to discuss students' solutions. **Discuss** the problems one at a time.

> **Read** the problem.
>
> **Ask** students to work with a neighbor to solve it.
>
> **Discuss** one or two students' solutions.

Answer Key
1. 49
2. 198
3. 501

STUDENT PAGE 3

Our Turn

Write the answer for each problem on the line.

1. What is 3 less than 52? _____

2. What is 7 less than 205? _____

3. 510 – 9 = _____

My Turn

Ask students to solve the problems on page 4. **Remind** them to watch out for pitfalls!

After allowing time to work, **read** the answers. **Have** students mark and revise their papers using ink or crayon.

Answer Key
1. 199
2. 399
3. 294

STUDENT PAGE 4

My Turn

Write the answer for each problem on the line.

1. What is 6 less than 205? _____

2. What is 1 less than 400? _____

3. 302 – 8 = _____

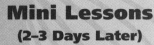

Mini Lessons
(2–3 Days Later)

Assess and Reinforce

Multiple Choice Mini Lesson

Distribute Student Page 5.

Problem 1

 Please read problem 1.
Talk with your neighbor about which choices don't make sense. WAIT
How could you know that 8 less than 305 is 297?

 Help students realize they can quickly count back using a mental number line. For example, 5 less than 305 is 300. Then students can count back 3 more to 297.

Problem 2

 Read the problem and find the correct choice. WAIT
Which response is correct? Explain why.
How can you check to make sure that the correct choice is 199? Explain.

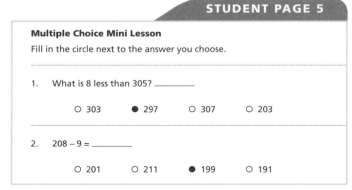

STUDENT PAGE 5

Multiple Choice Mini Lesson
Fill in the circle next to the answer you choose.

1. What is 8 less than 305? _____
    ○ 303 ● 297 ○ 307 ○ 203

2. 208 – 9 = _____
    ○ 201 ○ 211 ● 199 ○ 191

Writing Task Mini Lesson

Distribute Student Page 6.

Ask a student to read the task. **Call on** students to respond with their ideas.

Jot the ideas on the board.

Write an explanation together using their ideas. **Read** it aloud.

Ask students to write an explanation on their page.

STUDENT PAGE 6

Writing Task Mini Lesson
Explain how you know that 7 less than 403 is 396. Draw a picture or a number line on the back to show how you know.

Sample Explanation: I can count back 3 to get to 400 and then count back 4 more to get to 396. So, 7 less than 403 is 396. I can also subtract 403 – 7 to get 396.

English Learner Access

Mathematical Discussion Support

Ask students to explain what "less than" means in each of these situations:

7 is less than 9   7 less than 9 is 2

Posing questions and situations such as these encourages flexibility in mathematical language and requires students to read mathematical situations more critically.

Finding the Difference

Prior Learning Needed

- Use a number line
- Use mental math and basic addition facts
- Subtract using an algorithm

Lesson Preparation

- Study Lesson Foundation
- Review Teaching Guide and Student Pages
- Prepare stapled packet of Student Pages 1–4 for each student
- Copy and cut in half Student Pages 5 and 6
- Post *Discussion Builders* poster

Mathematical goals

✷ Find the difference between two numbers by counting up and by subtracting

✷ Regroup across 0 when using the subtraction algorithm

Mathematical language and reasoning goals

✷ Recognize and solve word problems that require finding the difference

✷ Count up in easy steps using benchmarks, such as multiples of 10

LESSON ROADMAP			MATERIALS
CORE LESSON: DAY 1	GROUPING	TIME	○ *Discussion Builders* poster
Opener			○ Projector (optional)
Discussion Builders			○ Student Page 1
Purpose	👥	🕐	○ Student Page 2
Math Words			○ Teaching Guide
Starter Problem	👤	🕐	○ Paper for drawing number lines, rulers (suggested)
Discussion			
Student Thinking	👤 👥 👥	🕐	
Things to Remember Reflection	👥	🕐	
CORE LESSON: DAY 2			○ Clipboard Prompts, page 37
Review and Practice			○ Student Page 2 (completed day 1)
Review Day 1 Lesson	👥	🕐	○ Student Pages 3 and 4
Our Turn	👥 👥	🕐	○ Teaching Guide
My Turn	👤	🕐	○ Paper for drawing number lines, rulers (suggested)
MINI LESSONS: 2–3 DAYS LATER			○ Student Pages 5 and 6
Assess and Reinforce			○ Teaching Guide
Multiple Choice Mini Lesson	👤 👥 👥	🕐	○ Paper for drawing number lines, rulers (suggested)
Writing Task Mini Lesson	👤 👥	🕐	

Lesson Foundation

····Starter Problem····

Alisha read to page 198 the first week. Then, she read to page 304 the second week. How many pages did she read the second week? _____

Student Thinking

Yolanda

To find the difference, I started at 198 and added on to make 304. It's 106 pages. I can subtract to check.

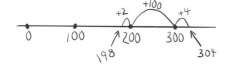

OK

Raymond

I subtracted to find the difference.

$$\begin{array}{r} \overset{2}{3}0^{1}4 \\ -198 \\ \hline 196 \end{array}$$

Oops!

MATHEMATICAL INSIGHTS & TEACHING TIPS

Adding On to Find the Difference

Yolanda added on using a number line to find the difference between 198 and 304. She started at 198 and then added 2 more to get to 200, 100 more to get to 300, and 4 more to get to 304. The benchmark numbers 200 and 300 helped her add on in easy steps. She understood that 2 + 100 + 4 is equal to 106, the number of pages Alisha read the second week. Many students develop a mental image of a number line to help them visualize the adding-on process. This strategy can be used to find exact answers and estimates.

Oops! Raymond realized that he could subtract to find the difference, but he regrouped across 0 incorrectly. He also didn't notice that his answer was unreasonable.

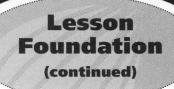

MATHEMATICAL INSIGHTS & TEACHING TIPS (CONTINUED)

Finding the Difference or Missing Addend

This problem can be viewed either as a difference (304 – 198 = ___) or a missing addend problem (198 + ____ = 304). In other words, one way to think about the problem is to find the difference between reading 304 pages and 198 pages. Or you can think about starting with 198 pages (the first addend) and reading some more (the missing addend) to get to 304 pages (the total). Yolanda added on to find the difference, or missing addend, a method that follows the structure of the problem situation. Both Yolanda and Raymond realized that subtraction could be used to find the difference between 304 and 198. However, Raymond made a regrouping error when subtracting.

 Take-away, the most common model for subtraction and the one usually associated with the standard algorithm, does not fit well with this problem. Nothing is being taken away. Most students will need explicit instruction to help them relate a difference or missing addend situation with subtraction.

Regrouping Across 0

Students often make errors when using the standard subtraction algorithm and regrouping with a number that has a 0. Raymond knew the sequence of steps for regrouping but skipped over the tens place, which has 0 tens. Although the long-term goal is to automatically carry out the steps, during the learning phase Raymond should think about the values of the digits and the meaning of regrouping. Regrouping is a special form of breaking numbers apart; we take a unit such as 1 hundred and break it into 10 units of ten. In fact, some students with a robust understanding of place value are able to think of the 30 in 304 as representing 30 tens, which can be regrouped into 29 tens and 1 more ten. Regardless of the method and skill, it is important for all students to pause and make sense of an answer and self-correct if necessary.

MATHEMATICAL DISCUSSION SUPPORT

Students commonly associate subtraction with taking something away. However, it is also important for them to associate subtraction with comparing two numbers to find a difference and with finding how much is added on to one number to get a total (missing addend). Ask students to verbalize the situation in the word problem in different ways.

Promote flexibility in the way students think about and talk about subtraction. Use terms and phrases such as "compare," "find the difference," "subtract," and "add on to find the difference" when you talk about subtraction problems. This provides students a variety of words and ideas to use when they deal with subtraction.

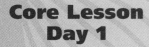

**Core Lesson
Day 1**

Opener

Review *Discussion Builders*

Read the poster. **Suggest** a section to focus on today:
Presenting Our Ideas, Adding to Others' Ideas, or *Asking More Questions.*

Purpose

Distribute stapled packets of Student Pages 1–4. **Project** an image of page 1 (optional).

Call on a student to read the purpose.

Math Words

Point to and say the first math word. **Ask** students to repeat it aloud or silently.

Read the sentence containing the word.

Give an example using objects or drawings.

Repeat for the other math words.

Starter Problem

Read the Starter Problem. **Call on** a student to restate it in his/her own words.

 Please use what you already know to help you solve this problem on your own. This will prepare you to talk about the math and how to avoid pitfalls in our discussion later on.

I'll walk around and make notes about things we need to discuss. Look out for oops, or pitfalls! **WAIT**

STUDENT PAGE 1

Purpose
To find a difference using counting strategies or subtraction

Math Words

difference	The difference between two numbers can be found by subtracting.
find the difference	To find the difference between 15 and 10, you can count the units from 10 up to 15 on the number line.

5 units

0   5   10   15

benchmark numbers	Numbers that are easy to use, like 10, 50, 100, and 200, are benchmark numbers.

Starter Problem

Alisha read to page 198 the first week. Then, she read to page 304 the second week. How many pages did she read the second week? _____

Look at your work. It's easy to have an oops, or pitfall, in this type of problem. You might also have made a pitfall if your answer is not between 100 and 110.

Don't worry. Next we'll discuss how two imaginary students solved this problem. One has a pitfall! You may keep your solution private, but bring up your ideas in the discussion.

Discussion

Student Thinking

To find the difference, I started at 198 and added on to make 304. It's 106 pages. I can subtract to check.

OK

Yolanda

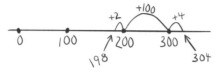

Ask students to refer to page 2. **Read** the statement marked OK.

Explain that this statement is about the same problem students worked on earlier.

We can learn a lot about the math by studying what this student did.

Read each sentence silently and look at the drawing. Think about what they mean.

Now talk with a partner about what each sentence and each part of the drawing means.

Listen in, ask questions, and observe. **Note** potential contributions for the discussion.

Who can come up to explain how Yolanda showed how many pages were read the first week? How did she show the total number of pages read in two weeks?

Why could she add on from 198 to 304 to solve the problem? Why did she make hops of 2, 100, and 4 to find how many pages from 198 to 304? If she made just one hop, how long would it be? What other hops could she have made to find the number of pages between 198 and 304?

Will Yolanda get the same answer if she subtracts? Explain why.

Talk to your neighbor about what Yolanda meant by "find the difference."

How does the number line picture show the difference between 304 and 198?

How could you use Yolanda's method to subtract 402 – 299?

Call on students to state things to remember about solving problems like this.

Start a Things to Remember list on the board.

MORE DAY 1

**Core Lesson
Day 1**
(continued)

Discussion

Student Thinking, continued

 Raymond

I subtracted to find the difference.

 Oops!

$$\begin{array}{r} \overset{2}{\cancel{3}}0^{1}4 \\ -198 \\ \hline 196 \end{array}$$

Read the statement marked Oops. **Remind** students that this is a common pitfall.

 Raymond made a pitfall when he regrouped across the 0 incorrectly. Talk with your neighbor about why this is incorrect. **WAIT**

Who would like to come up and explain how Raymond regrouped incorrectly? Explain why his answer should be closer to 100 than 200.

Why is it easy to have a pitfall in this problem?

Who can show a correct way to subtract? How could we check by adding?

Write the following problem on the board. **Ask** students to solve it at least two different ways. **Remind** them to look out for pitfalls. **Call on** students to explain why their answer makes sense.

$$\begin{array}{r} 105 \\ - 98 \\ \hline \end{array}$$

Things to Remember

Call on students to **add** to the Things to Remember list on the board. **Read** the list.

Help students summarize and record two important Things to Remember.

Things to Remember List (sample)
1. Adding on can help you find the difference between two numbers.
2. Check your answer when there are zeros in subtraction problems, especially if you need to regroup.

Reflection

Ask students to reflect on the discussion process using one of the sample prompts.

Reflection Prompts (sample)
- Name a *Discussion Builder* that we used today. How did it help the discussion?
- What *Discussion Builder* could we use next time to make the discussion even better?
- What did someone do or say today that helped you understand the math?

**Core Lesson
Day 2**

Review and Practice

Review

Ask students to review page 2 to jog their memory.

Read the statement marked OK. **Call on** a student to explain how the problem was solved.

Read the statement marked Oops. **Call on** a student to explain why it is incorrect or doesn't make sense.

Call on two or three students to read an item on their Things to Remember list.

 Yolanda: To find the difference, I started at 198 and added on to make 304. It's 106 pages. I can subtract to check. **OK**

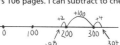

Raymond: I subtracted to find the difference. **Oops!**

Our Turn

Ask students to refer to page 3.

Use the procedure below and the Clipboard Prompts to discuss students' solutions. **Discuss** the problems one at a time.

> **Read** the problem.
>
> **Ask** students to work with a neighbor to solve it.
>
> **Discuss** one or two students' solutions.

Answer Key	1. 208
	2. 126
	3. 117

Our Turn

Solve each problem. Write the answer.

1. Kelly's team made 197 paper flowers in the morning and the rest in the afternoon. At the end of the day, they had 405 flowers. How many flowers did they make in the afternoon? _____

2. Sarah made a chain with 86 paper clips. Then, her friend put on more to make a chain with 212 paper clips. How many did the friend put on? _____

3. 302
   − 185

My Turn

Ask students to solve the problems on page 4. **Remind** them to watch out for pitfalls!

After allowing time to work, **read** the answers. **Have** students mark and revise their papers using ink or crayon.

Answer Key	1. 122
	2. 238
	3. 327

My Turn

Solve each problem. Write the answer.

1. J.R. had 280 pennies last year. Now, he has 402 pennies. How many pennies did he get this year? _____

2. John made a chain with 77 paper clips. Then, his friends put on more to make a chain with 315 paper clips. How many did the friends put on? _____

3. 502
   − 175

Mini Lessons
(2–3 Days Later)

Assess and Reinforce

Multiple Choice Mini Lesson

Distribute Student Page 5.

Problem 1

Please read problem 1.

Talk with your neighbor about which choices don't make sense. WAIT

How could you prove that 64 is the missing number?

 Suggest students count up using a number line or benchmarks like 40 and 100 to find the difference.

Problem 2

Read the problem and find the correct choice. WAIT

Which response is correct? Explain why.

Is it easier to subtract on paper or count up on a number line for this problem? Explain.

Multiple Choice Mini Lesson

Fill in the circle next to the answer you choose.

1. Alice baked 36 cookies. She needs 100 for the bake sale. How many cookies does she still need to bake?

   ○ 136   ● 64   ○ 74

2. Allen had 280 trading cards last year. Now he has 410. How many more trading cards did he get this year?

   ○ 410   ● 130   ○ 270

Writing Task Mini Lesson

Distribute Student Page 6.

Ask a student to read the task. **Call on** students to respond with their ideas.

Jot the ideas on the board.

Write an explanation together using their ideas. **Read** it aloud.

Ask students to write an explanation on their page.

Writing Task Mini Lesson

Explain how you know that the difference between 405 and 296 is 109. Draw a picture on the back to show how you know.

Sample Explanation: I can use 300 and 400 as benchmarks. I start at 296 and count up to 300. Then I count to 400. Then I count to 405. It's 4 + 100 + 5, or 109.

Mathematical Discussion Support

Ask students to explain the special meaning of the term "difference" in this problem and how the term might be used another way outside of math class. For example, we might say the difference between two shirts is their color.

Add On Using Place Value

Lesson at a Glance

Prior Learning Needed

- Understand place value
- Use mental math and basic addition facts
- Understand addition concepts

Lesson Preparation

- Study Lesson Foundation
- Review Teaching Guide and Student Pages
- Prepare stapled packet of Student Pages 1–4 for each student
- Copy and cut in half Student Pages 5 and 6
- Post *Discussion Builders* poster

Mathematical goals

✳ Use place value understanding to compute mentally

✳ Use place value knowledge to increase a three- or four-digit number

Mathematical language and reasoning goals

✳ Add multiples of 10 or 100 mentally

✳ Understand standard and expanded notation

LESSON ROADMAP			MATERIALS
CORE LESSON: DAY 1	GROUPING	TIME	○ *Discussion Builders* poster
Opener			○ Projector (optional)
Discussion Builders			○ Student Page 1
Purpose	👥	🕐	○ Student Page 2
Math Words			○ Teaching Guide
Starter Problem	👤	🕐	○ Place value materials (suggested)
Discussion			
Student Thinking	👤 👥 👥	🕐	
Things to Remember Reflection	👥	🕐	
CORE LESSON: DAY 2			○ Clipboard Prompts, page 37
Review and Practice			○ Student Page 2 (completed day 1)
Review Day 1 Lesson	👥	🕐	○ Student Pages 3 and 4
Our Turn	👥 👥	🕐	○ Teaching Guide
My Turn	👤	🕐	○ Place value materials (suggested)
MINI LESSONS: 2–3 DAYS LATER			○ Student Pages 5 and 6
Assess and Reinforce			○ Teaching Guide
Multiple Choice Mini Lesson	👤 👥 👥	🕐	○ Place value materials (suggested)
Writing Task Mini Lesson	👤 👥	🕐	

Lesson Foundation

·····Starter Problem·····

What number is 100 more than 1,357? _____

Student Thinking

Ernesto

1,357 has 3 in the hundreds place. So, 1 more hundred is 1,457. It's the short way to write 1,000 + 400 + 50 + 7.

OK

1,000   400
         300   50   7   {1,457}

          ←+100

Kendra

100 more than 1,357 is 2,357. I added.

Oops!

$$1,357$$
$$+\ 100$$
$$\overline{2,357}$$

MATHEMATICAL INSIGHTS & TEACHING TIPS

Place Value and Mental Computation

Ernesto added 100 more simply by increasing the digit in the hundreds place by 1. This is a key place value concept because it enables students to perform mental calculations and judge the reasonableness of their answers. An extension of this idea is to add any multiple of 100, such as adding 600 more by increasing the hundreds digit by 6.

Oops! Kendra wrote down the addends, incorrectly lining up the digits beginning on the left so that the place values were mismatched.

 Students will soon catch on to the pattern of adding on to the hundreds digit to add multiples of 100 and may forget why. Therefore, it is important to ask them to explain their reasoning and to prove their answers.

MATHEMATICAL INSIGHTS & TEACHING TIPS (CONTINUED)

Choosing When to Use the Paper-and-Pencil Algorithm

Kendra saw the words "100 more" in the problem and, without thinking, added 100 using the paper-and-pencil algorithm. Although this is a viable method to use, it is not the most efficient method for this problem. Students who are stuck on paper-and-pencil algorithms are often not confident in their abilities to compute mentally using place value concepts or to use reasoning to solve a problem. This also means that if they use the algorithm incorrectly, they may not detect their errors. Developing their flexibility, confidence, and competence to compute both mentally and with paper and pencil is important.

Kendra's incorrect method provides an opportunity to discuss several important ideas: Why is it important to line up the digits so that like place values are added together? Why is it important to look back to see if an answer is reasonable or not? Why is it important to make a conscious choice about the methods we use?

Relating to Expanded Notation

Notice that Ernesto's drawing relates place value representations to expanded notation. His drawing shows that the 1 in 1,357 means 1,000; the 3 in 1,357 means 300; the 5 means 50; and the 7 means 7. He also seems to understand that 1,000 + 400 + 50 + 7 (the expanded form) is 1,457 (standard form). Part of understanding place value is knowing that the 3 in the hundreds place means both 3 hundreds and 300, and that 100 more is 4 hundreds or 400.

 Some students incorrectly think that the 3 in 1,357 means 3, or 3 ones. Have them represent numbers using base ten blocks or sketch pictures of the numbers. Help them become fluent in writing the represented number in both expanded form and standard form.

MATHEMATICAL DISCUSSION SUPPORT

Reinforce the use of phrases such as "value of the place" and "hundreds place."

Students should practice writing numbers both in standard notation (for example, 9,827) and in expanded notation (for example, 9,000 + 800 + 20 + 7).

Model the use of language that reinforces the value of each digit. For example, call 3 in the hundreds place 3 hundreds or 300, but not 3. Elicit similar language from the students by pointing to each digit in a number like 457 and asking what it represents.

Core Lesson
Day 1

Opener

Review *Discussion Builders*

Read the poster. **Suggest** a section to focus on today:
Presenting Our Ideas, Adding to Others' Ideas, or *Asking More Questions.*

Purpose

Distribute stapled packets of Student Pages 1–4. **Project** an image of page 1 (optional).

Call on a student to read the purpose.

Math Words

Point to and say the first math word. **Ask** students to repeat it aloud or silently.

Read the sentence containing the word.

Give an example using objects or drawings.

Repeat for the other math words.

Starter Problem

Read the Starter Problem. **Call on** a student to restate it in his/her own words.

 Please use what you already know to help you solve this problem on your own. This will prepare you to talk about the math and how to avoid pitfalls in our discussion later on.

I'll walk around and make notes about things we need to discuss. Look out for oops, or pitfalls! (WAIT)

STUDENT PAGE 1

Purpose
To use place value to understand how to add on to a number

Math Words

thousands	The 5 in the number 5,382 has a value of 5 thousands, or 5,000.
hundreds	The 3 in the number 5,382 has a value of 3 hundreds, or 300.
tens	The 8 in the number 5,382 has a value of 8 tens, or 80.
ones	The 2 in the number 5,382 has a value of 2 ones, or 2.

Starter Problem

What number is 100 more than 1,357? _____

Look at your work. It's easy to have an oops, or pitfall, in this type of problem. You might also have made a pitfall if your number is more than 1,500.

Don't worry. Next we'll discuss how two imaginary students solved this problem. One has a pitfall! You may keep your solution private, but bring up your ideas in the discussion.

Discussion

Student Thinking

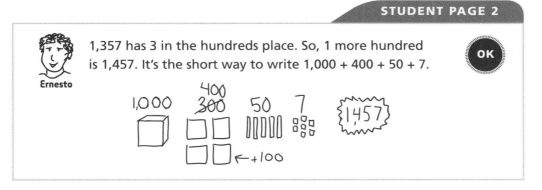

STUDENT PAGE 2

Ernesto

1,357 has 3 in the hundreds place. So, 1 more hundred is 1,457. It's the short way to write 1,000 + 400 + 50 + 7.

OK

Ask students to refer to page 2. **Read** the statement marked OK.

Explain that this statement is about the same problem students worked on earlier.

 We can learn a lot about the math by studying what this student did.

Read each sentence silently and look at the drawing. Think about what they mean. WAIT

Now talk with a partner about what each sentence and each part of the drawing means.

Listen in, ask questions, and observe. **Note** potential contributions for the discussion.

 Who can read the second digit in the Starter Problem aloud? How would reading the number help Ernesto know what blocks to draw for 1,357?

Who can come up and show what blocks Ernesto used to stand for hundreds? What do the other blocks represent? What number does his drawing show?

Talk to your neighbor about how Ernesto showed 100 more than 1,357. WAIT

Ernesto said that 1,357 has a 3 in the hundreds place. What did he mean? How does he show that 100 more than 1,357 is 1,457? Is 1,000 + 400 + 50 + 7 equal to 1,457? Explain how you know.

Who can show how to find 40 + 1,357? How many tens do you add?

Call on students to state things to remember about solving problems like this.

Start a Things to Remember list on the board.

 MORE DAY 1

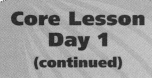

**Core Lesson
Day 1**
(continued)

Discussion

Student Thinking, continued

STUDENT PAGE 2

100 more than 1,357 is 2,357. I added.

Kendra

Oops!

$$1,357$$
$$+\ 100$$
$$\overline{2,357}$$

Read the statement marked Oops. **Remind** students that this is a common pitfall.

Kendra made a pitfall when she didn't line up the digits with the same place values. Talk with your neighbor about why this is incorrect. **WAIT**

Who would like to come up and explain a correct way to line up the digits?

How did it help Ernesto to think about the place value of each digit in 1,357?

Write the following problem on the board. **Ask** students to solve it at least two different ways. **Remind** them to look out for pitfalls. **Call on** students to explain why their answer makes sense.

What number is 60 more than 2,308?

Things to Remember

Call on students to **add** to the Things to Remember list on the board. **Read** the list.

Help students summarize and record two important Things to Remember.

Things to Remember List (sample)
1. The 3 in 1,357 means 3 hundreds, or 300. It doesn't mean 3.
2. Find 200 more by adding 2 more to the digit in the hundreds place.

Reflection

Ask students to reflect on the discussion process using one of the sample prompts.

Reflection Prompts (sample)
- Name a *Discussion Builder* that we used today. How did it help the discussion?
- What *Discussion Builder* could we use next time to make the discussion even better?
- What did someone do or say today that helped you understand the math?

**Core Lesson
Day 2**

Review and Practice

Review

Ask students to review page 2 to jog their memory.

Read the statement marked OK. **Call on** a student to explain how the problem was solved.

Read the statement marked Oops. **Call on** a student to explain why it is incorrect or doesn't make sense.

Call on two or three students to read an item on their Things to Remember list.

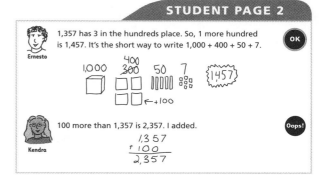

STUDENT PAGE 2

1,357 has 3 in the hundreds place. So, 1 more hundred is 1,457. It's the short way to write 1,000 + 400 + 50 + 7.   **OK**

Ernesto

1,000   400   50   7   {1457}
                    300
                    ←+100

100 more than 1,357 is 2,357. I added.   **Oops!**

Kendra

    1,357
    +100
    2,357

Our Turn

Ask students to refer to page 3.

Use the procedure below and the Clipboard Prompts to discuss students' solutions. **Discuss** the problems one at a time.

> **Read** the problem.
>
> **Ask** students to work with a neighbor to solve it.
>
> **Discuss** one or two students' solutions.

Answer Key	
1.	8,762
2.	3,951
3.	4,970

STUDENT PAGE 3

Our Turn

Solve each problem. Write the answer on the line.

1. What number is 20 more than 8,742? _____

2. What number is 900 more than 3,051? _____

3. 300 + 4,670 = _____

My Turn

Ask students to solve the problems on page 4. **Remind** them to watch out for pitfalls!

After allowing time to work, **read** the answers. **Have** students mark and revise their papers using ink or crayon.

Answer Key	
1.	7,968
2.	254
3.	5,650

STUDENT PAGE 4

My Turn

Solve each problem. Write the answer on the line.

1. What number is 400 more than 7,568? _____

2. What number is 50 more than 204? _____

3. 10 + 5,640 = _____

Mini Lessons
(2–3 Days Later)

Assess and Reinforce

Multiple Choice Mini Lesson

Distribute Student Page 5.

Problem 1

 Please read problem 1.
Talk with your neighbor about which choices don't make sense. WAIT
Who can show why 5,338 is the correct choice?

 Ask students to articulate that they can add on 100 by increasing the digit in the hundreds place by 1. They can also add on 100 using the algorithm, although this method is less efficient.

Problem 2

 Read the problem and find the correct choice. WAIT
Which response is correct? Explain why.
How does knowing how to find 100 more help you find 600 more? Explain.

Writing Task Mini Lesson

Distribute Student Page 6.

Ask a student to read the task. **Call on** students to respond with their ideas.

Jot the ideas on the board.

Write an explanation together using their ideas. **Read** it aloud.

Ask students to write an explanation on their page.

Multiple Choice Mini Lesson
Fill in the circle next to the answer you choose.

1. What number is 100 more than 5,238?
   ○ 6,238   ○ 52,138   ● 5,338

2. 8,092 + 600 = _____
   ○ 80,692   ● 8,692   ○ 1,492

Writing Task Mini Lesson
Explain how you know that 300 more than 4,205 is 4,505. Draw a picture on the back to show how you know.

Sample Explanation: I know that 100 more than 4,205 is 4,305, and 200 more is 4,405, so 300 more is 4,505. I can also add 300 to 4,205. Either way, the digit in the hundreds place changes to 5.

Mathematical Discussion Support
Ask students to explain what the hundreds place (ones place, tens place, thousands place) means. They should be flexible in explaining that 2 in the hundreds place also means 200. Model how to read the numbers and call on students to read them.
Ask them to listen for clues about the place values of the digits as they read. They might also write the number using expanded notation (4,000 + 200 + 5) and then show 300 more.

What Number Is Missing?

Prior Learning Needed

- Understand place value
- Facility with basic addition and subtraction facts
- Understand addition and subtraction concepts

Lesson Preparation

- Study Lesson Foundation
- Review Teaching Guide and Student Pages
- Prepare stapled packet of Student Pages 1–4 for each student
- Copy and cut in half Student Pages 5 and 6
- Post *Discussion Builders* poster

Mathematical goals

✳ Use number sense to solve missing addend equations

✳ Understand that both sides of an equation show the same amount

Mathematical language and reasoning goals

✳ Read equations with missing addends

✳ Make a drawing to represent an equation

LESSON ROADMAP			MATERIALS
CORE LESSON: DAY 1	GROUPING	TIME	
Opener			○ *Discussion Builders* poster
Discussion Builders			○ Projector (optional)
Purpose	👥	🕐	○ Student Page 1
Math Words			○ Student Page 2
Starter Problem	👤	🕐	○ Teaching Guide
Discussion			○ Place value materials such as base ten blocks, paper bags (suggested)
Student Thinking	👤 👥 👥	🕐	
Things to Remember Reflection	👥	🕐	
CORE LESSON: DAY 2			○ Clipboard Prompts, page 37
Review and Practice			○ Student Page 2 (completed day 1)
Review Day 1 Lesson	👥	🕐	○ Student Pages 3 and 4
Our Turn	👥 👥	🕐	○ Teaching Guide
My Turn	👤	🕐	○ Place value materials such as base ten blocks, paper bags (suggested)
MINI LESSONS: 2–3 DAYS LATER			○ Student Pages 5 and 6
Assess and Reinforce			○ Teaching Guide
Multiple Choice Mini Lesson	👤 👥 👥	🕐	○ Place value materials, paper bags, number lines (suggested)
Writing Task Mini Lesson	👤 👥	🕐	

Lesson Foundation

···Starter Problem···

Copy and complete this equation.
Think about the meaning.

$$20 + \underline{\hspace{1cm}} = 54$$

Student Thinking

Anita

I read it to myself: "20 plus a missing number is equal to 54." Both sides of the equals sign need to be the same amount. The left side needs 34 more. It checks.

 OK

$$20 + \underline{34} = 54$$

Joel

It says to add, so 20 plus 54 is 74.

$$20 + \underline{74} = 54$$

Oops!

MATHEMATICAL INSIGHTS & TEACHING TIPS

Reading Equations

Anita read the equation to herself, saying "a missing number" for the blank in the equation and "is equal to" for the equals sign. This allowed her to use number sense to determine what went in the blank. Joel may not know how to put the symbols into words. Instead, he may have seen the symbols as individual objects: two numbers, an addition sign, and a blank. He may have seen the blank merely as a place for the answer, rather than a missing number in an equation.

Oops! Joel saw an addition sign and two numbers, so he incorrectly added the numbers to find the sum rather than finding the missing addend.

 Ask students to read equations aloud, interpreting the blank as "what number" and the equals sign as "is the same amount as." For example, it is helpful to read 9 + 3 = 5 + ___ as "9 and 3 is the same amount as 5 and what number."

MATHEMATICAL INSIGHTS & TEACHING TIPS (CONTINUED)

Modeling Equations

Anita drew a model showing two amounts, one on each side of the equals sign. To solve the equation, she needs to find the missing number on the left side so that the amounts are equal. One way is to match 2 tens from the left side with 2 tens on the right side to find the difference in the two amounts. Another way is to count up from 20 to 54 to find out how many more are needed to make both sides equal. Either way, the missing number on the left side is 34.

 ▶ *Ask students to demonstrate what an equation means with materials or drawings. They may also make up word problems to model the equation. An example of a word problem is: "I had 20 cents and wanted to buy something for 54 cents. How much more money did I need?"*

Checking for Equality

Both sides of an equation represent exactly the same amount. This understanding is pivotal to students' future understanding of algebraic equations. Joel should see that his solution is incorrect because 94, or 20 + 74, is not equal to 54. Anita's equation is correct since both sides of the equation are equal to 54.

MATHEMATICAL DISCUSSION SUPPORT

It may be helpful for students to model the equation using base ten blocks for each known number and a paper bag for the missing number. 20 plus a number of blocks in the bag will equal 54. Students figure out how many blocks to put in the bag so that the amounts on both sides of the equation (or both sides of the equals sign) are equal.

Model how to read equations by saying "a missing number" for the blank and "is equal to" or "is the same amount as" for the equals sign. Have students read equations aloud using similar language. Notice that knowing how to read the equation is a first step to solving it.

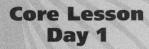

**Core Lesson
Day 1**

Opener

Review *Discussion Builders*

Read the poster. **Suggest** a section to focus on today:
Presenting Our Ideas, Adding to Others' Ideas, or *Asking More Questions.*

Purpose

Distribute stapled packets of Student Pages 1–4. **Project** an image of page 1 (optional).

Call on a student to read the purpose.

Math Words

Point to and say the first math word. **Ask** students to repeat it aloud or silently.

Read the sentence containing the word.

Give an example using objects or drawings.

Repeat for the other math words.

Starter Problem

Read the Starter Problem. **Call on** a student to restate it in his/her own words.

 Please use what you already know to help you solve this problem on your own. This will prepare you to talk about the math and how to avoid pitfalls in our discussion later on.

I'll walk around and make notes about things we need to discuss. Look out for oops, or pitfalls! ⬡WAIT

Look at your work. It's easy to have an oops, or pitfall, in this type of problem. You might also have made a pitfall if the number you wrote in the blank is greater than 54.

Don't worry. Next we'll discuss how two imaginary students solved this problem. One has a pitfall! You may keep your solution private, but bring up your ideas in the discussion.

STUDENT PAGE 1

Purpose
To understand and solve addition equations with missing numbers

Math Words

equation	An equation like 5 + 30 = 35 shows that 5 + 30 and 35 are equal.
equals sign	An equals sign means "is the same amount as."
both sides	The amounts on both sides of the equals sign in this equation are equal to 20. 10 + 10 = 19 + 1

Starter Problem

Copy and complete this equation. Think about the meaning.

20 + _____ = 54

Discussion

Student Thinking

 I read it to myself: "20 plus a missing number is equal to 54." Both sides of the equals sign need to be the same amount. The left side needs 34 more. It checks.

Anita

 OK

Ask students to refer to page 2. **Read** the statement marked OK.

Explain that this statement is about the same problem students worked on earlier.

 We can learn a lot about the math by studying what this student did.

Read each sentence silently and look at the drawing. Think about what they mean. WAIT

Now talk with a partner about what each sentence and each part of the drawing means.

Listen in, ask questions, and observe. **Note** potential contributions for the discussion.

 What words did Anita say for the blank? for the equals sign?

Who can come up and show how Anita's drawing is like the equation in the Starter Problem? How does her drawing show the 20? the 54? the blank?

Talk with your neighbor about what Anita meant when she said, "Both sides of the equals sign need to be the same amount." WAIT

What parts of Anita's drawing have to show the same amounts? Why?

How could she figure out that the left side needs 34 more to be the same amount as 54? How could she check to see if 34 is the correct missing number?

Call on students to state things to remember about solving problems like this.

Start a Things to Remember list on the board.

 MORE DAY 1

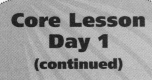

Discussion

Student Thinking, continued

Joel

It says to add, so 20 plus 54 is 74.

$20 + \underline{74} = 54$

Oops!

Read the statement marked Oops. **Remind** students that this is a common pitfall.

 Joel made a pitfall when he added the two numbers and wrote the sum in the blank. Talk with your neighbor about why this answer doesn't make sense. WAIT

How do you know Joel's equation is incorrect?

How could Joel have checked to make sure his answer made sense?

Write the following problems on the board. **Ask** students to talk with a neighbor about what number is missing for these equations. **Remind** students to look out for pitfalls. **Call on** students to show why their equations make sense.

$$20 + \underline{\hphantom{00}} = 54 \qquad 20 + 34 = \underline{\hphantom{00}}$$

Things to Remember

Call on students to **add** to the Things to Remember list on the board. **Read** the list.

Help students summarize and record two important Things to Remember.

Things to Remember List (sample)
1. To read an equation, say "a missing number" for a blank and "is equal to" for the equals sign.
2. Check to see if both sides of the equation are the same amount.

Reflection

Ask students to reflect on the discussion process using one of the sample prompts.

Reflection Prompts (sample)
- Name a *Discussion Builder* that we used today. How did it help the discussion?
- What *Discussion Builder* could we use next time to make the discussion even better?
- What did someone do or say today that helped you understand the math?

**Core Lesson
Day 2**

Review and Practice

Review

Ask students to review page 2 to jog their memory.

Read the statement marked OK. **Call on** a student to explain how the problem was solved.

Read the statement marked Oops. **Call on** a student to explain why it is incorrect or doesn't make sense.

Call on two or three students to read an item on their Things to Remember list.

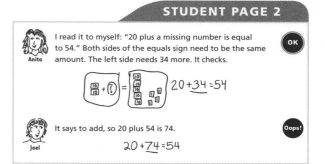

STUDENT PAGE 2

Anita — I read it to myself: "20 plus a missing number is equal to 54." Both sides of the equals sign need to be the same amount. The left side needs 34 more. It checks. **OK**

$20 + \underline{34} = 54$

Joel — It says to add, so 20 plus 54 is 74. **Oops!**

$20 + \underline{74} = 54$

Our Turn

Ask students to refer to page 3.

Use the procedure below and the Clipboard Prompts to discuss students' solutions. **Discuss** the problems one at a time.

> **Read** the problem.
>
> **Ask** students to work with a neighbor to solve it.
>
> **Discuss** one or two students' solutions.

Answer Key
1. 20
2. 6
3. 71

STUDENT PAGE 3

Our Turn

Write a number on the line to complete each equation. You may use drawings to help you.

1. $30 + \underline{\hspace{1cm}} = 50$

2. $68 = 62 + \underline{\hspace{1cm}}$

3. $4 + \underline{\hspace{1cm}} = 75$

My Turn

Ask students to solve the problems on page 4. **Remind** them to watch out for pitfalls!

After allowing time to work, **read** the answers. **Have** students mark and revise their papers using ink or crayon.

Answer Key
1. 10
2. 65
3. 4

STUDENT PAGE 4

My Turn

Write a number on the line to complete each equation. You may use drawings to help you.

1. $15 + \underline{\hspace{1cm}} = 25$

2. $20 + \underline{\hspace{1cm}} = 85$

3. $53 = 49 + \underline{\hspace{1cm}}$

Assess and Reinforce

Multiple Choice Mini Lesson

Distribute Student Page 5.

Problem 1

 Please read problem 1.

Talk with your neighbor about which choices don't make sense. **WAIT**

How could you prove that 26 is the missing number?

 One strategy is to try out different choices for the missing number. Students can check to see whether the total amounts on each side of the equation are the same.

Multiple Choice Mini Lesson

Fill in the circle next to the answer you choose.

1. $4 + \underline{\hspace{1cm}} = 30$

   ○ 34   ● 26   ○ 24   ○ 30

2. $40 + 10 + \underline{\hspace{1cm}} = 60$

   ○ 110   ○ 50   ● 10   ○ 0

Problem 2

 Read the problem and find the correct choice. **WAIT**

Which response is correct? Explain why.

How do you know that 50 is not the correct answer? Explain.

Writing Task Mini Lesson

Distribute Student Page 6.

Ask a student to read the task. **Call on** students to respond with their ideas.

Jot the ideas on the board.

Write an explanation together using their ideas. **Read** it aloud.

Ask students to write an explanation on their page.

Writing Task Mini Lesson

Explain how you know that 32 is the correct number to write in the blank to complete the equation.

$$8 + \underline{\hspace{1cm}} = 40$$

Sample Explanation: I know that I need to have equal amounts on both sides of the equals sign. That means I need to add something to 8 to make it equal to 40. I could use a number line to count up from 8 to 40, or I could count back 8 from 40. Either way, I get 32. I can check my answer by adding 32 and 8, which is the same as 40.

 Mathematical Discussion Support

Ask students to explain what the blank and the equals sign mean. Encourage students to verbalize what has to be true about both sides of an equals sign for the equation to make sense and be correct. Model and elicit the use of synonymous mathematical words and phrases, such as "equals," "equivalent," and "the same amount as."

Values of Digits

Lesson at a Glance

Prior Learning Needed

- Understand place value
- Understand addition and missing addend concepts

Lesson Preparation

- Study Lesson Foundation
- Review Teaching Guide and Student Pages
- Prepare stapled packet of Student Pages 1–4 for each student
- Copy and cut in half Student Pages 5 and 6
- Post *Discussion Builders* poster

Mathematical goals

✳ Understand the value of each digit in a numeral

✳ Understand the equivalence of numbers written different ways

Mathematical language and reasoning goals

✳ Use hundreds place, tens place, and so on when explaining ideas

✳ Write four-digit numerals in expanded form

LESSON ROADMAP			MATERIALS
CORE LESSON: DAY 1	GROUPING	TIME	○ *Discussion Builders* poster
Opener			○ Projector (optional)
Discussion Builders			○ Student Page 1
Purpose	👥	🕐	○ Student Page 2
Math Words			○ Teaching Guide
Starter Problem	👤	🕐	○ Graph paper, base ten blocks (suggested)
Discussion			
Student Thinking	👤 👥 👥	🕐	
Things to Remember Reflection	👥	🕐	
CORE LESSON: DAY 2			○ Clipboard Prompts, page 37
Review and Practice			○ Student Page 2 (completed day 1)
Review Day 1 Lesson	👥	🕐	○ Student Pages 3 and 4
Our Turn	👥 👥	🕐	○ Teaching Guide
My Turn	👤	🕐	○ Graph paper, base ten blocks (suggested)
MINI LESSONS: 2–3 DAYS LATER			○ Student Pages 5 and 6
Assess and Reinforce			○ Teaching Guide
Multiple Choice Mini Lesson	👤 👥 👥	🕐	○ Graph paper, base ten blocks (suggested)
Writing Task Mini Lesson	👤 👥	🕐	

Lesson Foundation

····Starter Problem····

Copy and complete this equation.
Think about the meaning.

$$2,409 = 2,000 + \underline{\hspace{2cm}} + 9$$

Student Thinking

John

I read 2,409 out loud: "Two thousand, **four hundred** nine." The 4 means 4 hundreds. I checked by adding another way.

$$2,409 = 2,000 + \underline{400} + 9$$

$$\begin{array}{r} 2,000 \\ 400 \\ + \quad 9 \\ \hline 2,409 \end{array}$$

OK

Trina

I added the numbers and got 2,009. Then I wrote the answer in the blank.

$$2,409 = 2,000 + \underline{2,009} + 9$$

Oops!

MATHEMATICAL INSIGHTS & TEACHING TIPS

Relating Digits to Values

By reading the number 2,409 aloud, John figured out that the digit 4, for 400, was missing on the right side of the equation. When faced with less straightforward equations, such as 2,453 = 3 + 400 + 2,000 + ____ , students should match given values, such as the digit 4 and the 400, rather than depending on having the same order on both sides. Many children develop only a superficial understanding of place value when doing standard expanded notation worksheets and simply follow a rote pattern. Eventually, students should be able to solve equations such as 5,681 = 5,000 + ____ + 200 + 80 + 1 by using place value knowledge to know that 400 is the missing number.

 Oops! Trina incorrectly interpreted the equation when she added the numbers on the right side of the equation and wrote the sum in the blank.

John's vertical problem serves as a check of his work, and it shows that he understands that the 9 ones line up in the ones place, the 4 from the 400 lines up in the hundreds place, and so on. This connection between place names and vertical problems is especially important when students are learning to rewrite horizontal problems to make calculation easier.

MATHEMATICAL INSIGHTS & TEACHING TIPS (CONTINUED)

 Ask students to explain their answers in several different ways and use base ten blocks or graph paper squares to illustrate their understanding of place value.

Place Value System

Trina translated this as a simple addition problem, so she added 2,000 plus 9 and wrote the answer in the blank. She needed to interpret the problem as an equation with a missing number and to realize that she could use place value concepts to solve it. During the primary grades, students learn the ones, tens, hundreds, and thousands place value names for the digits in order. This is only a first step in understanding that in the base ten place value system, each place to the left has a value of ten times the previous place. For example, 726 means $(7 \times 100) + (2 \times 10) + (6 \times 1)$.

Reading Numbers with Zero

John read the number correctly as "two thousand, four hundred nine." Students may need explicit practice reading numbers that have a zero digit. They may also have difficulty finding the missing number in an equation such as _____ = 6,000 + 30 + 5. Because they think the sum will have only three digits, they write 635 instead of 6,035.

 Students need practice reading and writing numbers with zeros. Point out that although a number such as 2,409 means there is a zero in the tens place, it doesn't mean that there are 0 tens in 2,409. In fact, there are almost 241 tens in 2,409.

MATHEMATICAL DISCUSSION SUPPORT

Ask students questions that prompt them to explain the value of specific digits and the correct way to write numbers that represent specific digits. They may use materials, pictures, or numbers to help communicate. Ask students to read numbers aloud. In particular, numbers with a zero digit often cause students to stumble. Provide examples like 2,058 or 6,005 and ask students to read the numbers and explain the value of each digit.

Place value language has subtleties that need to be pointed out explicitly. Note the difference between asking "How many ones are in 4,170?" and "How many ones are in the ones place for 4,170?" There are 4,170 ones in 4,170, but there are 0 ones in the ones place. Consider using base ten blocks to point out that there are 12 hundreds, not just 2 hundreds, in 1,200. Also note that 2 is in the hundreds place and means 2 hundreds or 200.

**Core Lesson
Day 1**

Opener

Review *Discussion Builders*

Read the poster. **Suggest** a section to focus on today:
Presenting Our Ideas, Adding to Others' Ideas, or *Asking More Questions.*

Purpose

Distribute stapled packets of Student Pages 1–4. **Project** an image of page 1 (optional).

Call on a student to read the purpose.

Math Words

Point to and say the first math word.
Ask students to repeat it aloud or
silently.

Read the sentence containing the word.

Give an example using objects or
drawings.

Repeat for the other math words.

Starter Problem

Read the Starter Problem. **Call on** a student to restate it in his/her own words.

 Please use what you already know to
help you solve this problem on your
own. This will prepare you to talk
about the math and how to avoid
pitfalls in our discussion later on.

I'll walk around and make notes
about things we need to discuss.
Look out for oops, or pitfalls! (WAIT)

Look at your work. It's easy to have an oops, or pitfall, in this type of problem. You might also have
made a pitfall if your answer is less than 100 or more than 500.

Don't worry. Next we'll discuss how two imaginary students solved this problem. One has a pitfall!
You may keep your solution private, but bring up your ideas in the discussion.

STUDENT PAGE 1

Purpose
To understand the value of each digit in a number

Math Words

place	The number 3,204 has a 3 in the thousands place, a 2 in the hundreds place, a 0 in the tens place, and a 4 in the ones place.
thousands, hundreds, tens, and ones	3 thousands, 7 hundreds, 4 tens, and 5 ones is the same amount as $3,000 + 700 + 40 + 5$.
digits	The number 3,204 has 4 digits: 3, 2, 0, and 4.

Starter Problem

Copy and complete this equation.
Think about the meaning.

$$2,409 = 2,000 + \underline{\hspace{1cm}} + 9$$

Discussion

Student Thinking

I read 2,409 out loud: "Two thousand, **four hundred** nine." The 4 means 4 hundreds. I checked by adding another way.

John

OK

$$2{,}409 = 2{,}000 + \underline{400} + 9$$

$$\begin{array}{r} 2{,}000 \\ 400 \\ + \quad 9 \\ \hline 2{,}409 \end{array}$$

Ask students to refer to page 2. **Read** the statement marked OK.

Explain that this statement is about the same problem students worked on earlier.

 We can learn a lot about the math by studying what this student did.

Read each sentence silently and look at John's work. Think about what they mean. **WAIT**

Now talk with a partner about what each sentence and each part of John's work means.

Listen in, ask questions, and observe. **Note** potential contributions for the discussion.

 Who can come up to show how John knew that the 4 meant 400?

How do you think reading 2,409 out loud helped John decide that 400 was the number to put in the blank?

What does the 2 in 2,409 stand for? What number is in the tens place? What does that mean?

Talk to your neighbor about how John checked to know for sure that 2,409 is the same as 2,000 + 400 + 9. **WAIT**

Who can explain why John lined up the numbers the way he did?

Could you add up the numbers another way? Explain.

Call on students to state things to remember about solving problems like this.

Start a Things to Remember list on the board.

MORE DAY 1

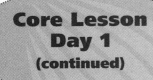

Core Lesson Day 1 (continued)

Discussion

Student Thinking, continued

STUDENT PAGE 2

I added the numbers and got 2,009. Then I wrote the answer in the blank.

Oops!

Trina

$$2,409 = 2,000 + \underline{2,009} + 9$$

Read the statement marked Oops. **Remind** students that this is a common pitfall.

Trina made a pitfall when she added 2,000 plus 9 and wrote the sum in the blank. Talk with your neighbor about why this is incorrect. **WAIT**

Who would like to come up and explain why this is a pitfall?

How could Trina have checked to see if her equation made sense?

Write the following problems on the board. **Ask** students to talk with a neighbor about what number is missing in each of these problems. **Remind** students to look out for pitfalls. **Call on** students to explain why their equations make sense.

$$9,455 = 9,000 + 400 + \underline{\quad} + 50 \qquad 9,055 = 9,000 + 5 + \underline{\quad}$$

Things to Remember

Call on students to **add** to the Things to Remember list on the board. **Read** the list.

Help students summarize and record two important Things to Remember.

> **Things to Remember List (sample)**
> 1. Read a number out loud and think about the value of each digit.
> 2. You can write the values for the digits in 1,253 in different orders, like 1,000 + 200 + 50 + 3, and 200 + 1,000 + 3 + 50.

Reflection

Ask students to reflect on the discussion process using one of the sample prompts.

> **Reflection Prompts (sample)**
> • Name a *Discussion Builder* that we used today. How did it help the discussion?
> • What *Discussion Builder* could we use next time to make the discussion even better?
> • What did someone do or say today that helped you understand the math?

Review and Practice

Review

Ask students to review page 2 to jog their memory.

Read the statement marked OK. **Call on** a student to explain how the problem was solved.

Read the statement marked Oops. **Call on** a student to explain why it is incorrect or doesn't make sense.

Call on two or three students to read an item on their Things to Remember list.

 John
I read 2,409 out loud: "Two thousand, **four hundred** nine." The 4 means 4 hundreds. I checked by adding another way. OK

$2{,}409 = 2{,}000 + \underline{400} + 9$

$$\begin{array}{r} 2{,}000 \\ 400 \\ + \quad 9 \\ \hline 2{,}409 \end{array}$$

 Trina
I added the numbers and got 2,009. Then I wrote the answer in the blank. Oops!

$2{,}409 = 2{,}000 + \underline{2{,}009} + 9$

Our Turn

Ask students to refer to page 3.

Use the procedure below and the Clipboard Prompts to discuss students' solutions. **Discuss** the problems one at a time.

> **Read** the problem.
>
> **Ask** students to work with a neighbor to solve it.
>
> **Discuss** one or two students' solutions.

Answer Key	1. 40
	2. 20
	3. 5,206

Our Turn

Write the answer for each problem on the line.

1. $1{,}345 = 300 + 5 + 1{,}000 + \underline{\hspace{1cm}}$

2. $5{,}027 = 5{,}000 + \underline{\hspace{1cm}} + 7$

3. $200 + 5{,}000 + 6 = \underline{\hspace{1cm}}$

My Turn

Ask students to solve the problems on page 4. **Remind** them to watch out for pitfalls!

After allowing time to work, **read** the answers. **Have** students mark and revise their papers using ink or crayon.

Answer Key	1. 200
	2. 800
	3. 40

My Turn

Write the answer for each problem on the line.

1. $60 + 4 + \underline{\hspace{1cm}} + 1{,}000 = 1{,}264$

2. $5{,}803 = 3 + \underline{\hspace{1cm}} + 5{,}000$

3. $8{,}041 = 8{,}000 + \underline{\hspace{1cm}} + 1$

Mini Lessons
(2–3 Days Later)

Assess and Reinforce

Multiple Choice Mini Lesson

Distribute Student Page 5.

Problem 1

 Please read problem 1.
Talk with your neighbor about which choices don't make sense. (WAIT)
Who can explain why 4 is the missing number?

 Students should think about the values of digits when checking to see that the 3 thousands, 6 hundreds, and 5 tens from 3,654 are represented on the right side of the equation, but the 4 ones are not.

Problem 2

 Read the problem and find the correct choice. (WAIT)
Which response is correct? Explain why.
Why is 600 an incorrect answer? Explain.

Writing Task Mini Lesson

Distribute Student Page 6.

Ask a student to read the task. **Call on** students to respond with their ideas.

Jot the ideas on the board.

Write an explanation together using their ideas. **Read** it aloud.

Ask students to write an explanation on their page.

Multiple Choice Mini Lesson

Fill in the circle next to the answer you choose.

1. $3,654 = \underline{\hphantom{xxx}} + 50 + 600 + 3,000$

   ○ 3000   ○ 3,654   ○ 54   ● 4

2. $3,654 = \underline{\hphantom{xxx}}$ hundreds + 5 tens + 3 thousands + 4 ones

   ○ 600   ○ 654   ● 6   ○ 3

Writing Task Mini Lesson

Explain how you know that 400 is the correct number to put in the blank. Use a picture or numbers on the back to show your ideas.

$$6,405 = 6,000 + \underline{\hphantom{xxx}} + 5$$

Sample Explanation: The place value pattern goes right to left: "ones, tens, hundreds, thousands." 6,405 means 6 thousands + 4 hundreds + 0 tens + 5 ones. The 4 hundreds are missing from the equation, so 400 goes in the blank.

Mathematical Discussion Support

Ask students to explain what each digit in the numeral means. To develop flexibility in the way students think about the value of the digits, ask questions such as: "What number do we write to represent 6 thousands? What about 5 ones?" This will also help develop their ability to understand and use place value language.

Regroup a Ten

Prior Learning Needed

- Solve subtraction word problems
- Use the subtraction algorithm with regrouping

Lesson Preparation

- Study Lesson Foundation
- Review Teaching Guide and Student Pages
- Prepare stapled packet of Student Pages 1–4 for each student
- Copy and cut in half Student Pages 5 and 6
- Post *Discussion Builders* poster

Mathematical goals

✳ Use understanding of digit values to subtract with regrouping

✳ Understand that addition and subtraction are related operations

Mathematical language and reasoning goals

✳ Use mathematical language to explain regrouping

✳ Use addition to check a subtraction problem

LESSON ROADMAP			MATERIALS
CORE LESSON: DAY 1	GROUPING	TIME	○ *Discussion Builders* poster
Opener			○ Projector (optional)
Discussion Builders			○ Student Page 1
Purpose	👥	🕐	○ Student Page 2
Math Words			○ Teaching Guide
Starter Problem	👤	🕐	○ Place value materials (suggested)
Discussion			
Student Thinking	👤 👥 👥	🕜	
Things to Remember Reflection	👥	🕐	
CORE LESSON: DAY 2			○ Clipboard Prompts, page 37
Review and Practice			○ Student Page 2 (completed day 1)
Review Day 1 Lesson	👥	🕐	○ Student Pages 3 and 4
Our Turn	👥 👥	🕜	○ Teaching Guide
My Turn	👤	🕐	○ Place value materials (suggested)
MINI LESSONS: 2–3 DAYS LATER			○ Student Pages 5 and 6
Assess and Reinforce			○ Teaching Guide
Multiple Choice Mini Lesson	👤 👥 👥	🕜	○ Place value materials (suggested)
Writing Task Mini Lesson	👤 👥	🕐	

Lesson Foundation

Starter Problem

Think about the meaning.
Solve.

$$262 - 38$$

Student Thinking

Patty

I needed more ones. I regrouped a ten and put it with the 2 to make 12 ones. Then I subtracted and got 224. It checks.

OK

$$\begin{array}{r} 2\overset{5}{6}\overset{12}{2} \\ -\ 38 \\ \hline 224 \end{array} \qquad \begin{array}{r} \overset{1}{2}24 \\ +\ 38 \\ \hline 262 \end{array}$$

Ray

First, I just subtracted the ones: 8 minus 2 is 6. Then I subtracted the tens: 6 minus 3 is 3. Then I wrote down the 2 from the hundreds. It's 236.

Oops!

$$\begin{array}{r} 262 \\ -\ 38 \\ \hline 236 \end{array}$$

MATHEMATICAL INSIGHTS & TEACHING TIPS

Learning the Standard Subtraction Algorithm

Patty looked at the problem and knew that she needed to regroup before she started calculating. This is an important habit for students to form when they are first learning the standard subtraction algorithm. In the problem 62 – 38, using language such as "2 ones take away 8 ones" makes it more apparent that regrouping is necessary because 8 is greater than 2. Some language, such as "2 minus 8" or "8 from 2," may be less likely to trigger the idea that regrouping is needed, but is also correct. Ray, for example, incorrectly used the language "8 minus 2," rather than "2 minus 8." Perhaps he thinks that minus is like plus and the numbers are interchangeable. It is important for students to learn that, unlike addition, subtraction is not a commutative operation; the numbers in a subtraction problem cannot be interchanged.

Oops! Ray subtracted 2 from 8 in the ones column, which is incorrect because the 2 is part of the minuend and the 8 is part of the subtrahend.

Lesson Foundation
(continued)

MATHEMATICAL INSIGHTS & TEACHING TIPS (CONTINUED)

Understanding Regrouping

Breaking (decomposing) 62 into the equivalent amount of 5 tens plus 1 ten and 2 ones and regrouping 1 ten into 10 ones are some of the fundamental understandings for using algorithms. Patty gave evidence of such understanding.

 Students can practice regrouping the same amount several ways. For example, they might show 42 as 4 tens and 2 ones, 3 tens and 12 ones, 42 ones, or 2 tens and 22 ones. The critical understanding is that all of these quantities are equivalent.

Basic Fact Knowledge

Note that the 12 – 8 is treated like a basic fact, and the difference should be retrieved from memory or quickly computed mentally. Students who have difficulty subtracting numbers in the teens may find it helpful to think about using 10 as a bridge for subtracting 8. So, to subtract 8 from 12, they subtract the 2 ones, then get the rest (6) from the 10, leaving 4.

Some students think of subtraction as finding the missing part of a related known addition number sentence. This works well for problems such as 8 – 2 = __ , but it is more difficult to interpret when encountering 2 – 8 = __ in the ones column. In fact, an incorrect application of the fact family associated with the numbers 8, 6, and 2 (i.e., 8 – 6 = 2, 6 + 2 = 8, and 8 – 2 = 6) may underlie the tendency to reverse numbers, as Ray did when faced with 2 minus 8. He may have also misapplied the fact family when he checked his answer.

MATHEMATICAL DISCUSSION SUPPORT

Make sure students read the entire subtraction problem ("two hundred sixty-two minus thirty-eight," "two hundred sixty-two take away thirty-eight," or "thirty-eight from two hundred sixty-two"). Then, include questions that elicit understanding of breaking 62 into parts. These parts can be 60 and 2, or 5 tens and 1 ten (which will be traded) and 2 ones. They can also break up 38 into 30 and 8.

Encourage use of language, including the term "regroup," that supports the concept of trading 1 ten for 10 ones and placing the 10 ones with any other ones. Use place value materials or drawings that illustrate the action of regrouping a ten for 10 ones.

Core Lesson Day 1

Opener

Review *Discussion Builders*

Read the poster. **Suggest** a section to focus on today:
Presenting Our Ideas, Adding to Others' Ideas, or *Asking More Questions.*

Purpose

Distribute stapled packets of Student Pages 1–4. **Project** an image of page 1 (optional).

Call on a student to read the purpose.

Math Words

Point to and say the first math words. **Ask** students to repeat them aloud or silently.

Read the sentence containing the words.

Give an example using objects or drawings.

Repeat for the other math word.

Starter Problem

Read the Starter Problem. **Call on** a student to restate it in his/her own words.

 Please use what you already know to help you solve this problem on your own. This will prepare you to talk about the math and how to avoid pitfalls in our discussion later on.

I'll walk around and make notes about things we need to discuss. Look out for oops, or pitfalls!

Look at your work. It's easy to have an oops, or pitfall, in this type of problem. You might also have made a pitfall if your answer is more than 224.

Don't worry. Next we'll discuss how two imaginary students solved this problem. One has a pitfall! You may keep your solution private, but bring up your ideas in the discussion.

STUDENT PAGE 1

Purpose
To know when and how to regroup when subtracting

Math Words

hundreds, tens, and ones	235 is the same amount as 2 hundreds, 3 tens, and 5 ones, or 200 + 30 + 5.
regroup	You can regroup 2 hundreds, 3 tens, and 5 ones into 2 hundreds, 2 tens, and 15 ones. Both amounts are equal.

Starter Problem

Think about the meaning.
Solve.

$$\begin{array}{r} 262 \\ -\ 38 \\ \hline \end{array}$$

Discussion

Student Thinking

Patty

I needed more ones. I regrouped a ten and put it with the 2 to make 12 ones. Then I subtracted and got 224. It checks.

OK

$$\begin{array}{r} \overset{5}{\cancel{2}}\overset{12}{\cancel{6}}\cancel{2} \\ -\ 38 \\ \hline 224 \end{array} \qquad \begin{array}{r} \overset{1}{2}24 \\ +\ 38 \\ \hline 262 \end{array}$$

Ask students to refer to page 2. **Read** the statement marked OK.

Explain that this statement is about the same problem students worked on earlier.

We can learn a lot about the math by studying what this student did.

Read each sentence silently and look at Patty's work. Think about what they mean. (WAIT)

Now talk with a partner about what each sentence and each part of Patty's work means.

Listen in, ask questions, and observe. **Note** potential contributions for the discussion.

Who can come to explain how Patty solved the problem? You may use pictures or blocks to show us.

Why did Patty regroup a ten and put it with the 2 ones? How can you tell by just looking whether or not you need to regroup?

Why do you think she crossed out the 6 and wrote a 5 above it? Why did she cross out the 2 and write a little 12 above it?

Talk to your neighbor about how you know the starting amount is still 262, even if it's regrouped into 2 hundreds, 5 tens, and 12 ones. (WAIT)

Explain how Patty checked her answer.

Would you need to regroup to solve the problem 329 − 42? Explain how.

Call on students to state things to remember about solving problems like this.

Start a Things to Remember list on the board.

MORE DAY 1

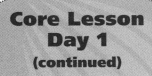

Core Lesson Day 1 (continued)

Discussion

Student Thinking, continued

Ray

First, I just subtracted the ones: 8 minus 2 is 6. Then I subtracted the tens: 6 minus 3 is 3. Then I wrote down the 2 from the hundreds. It's 236.

Oops!

$$\begin{array}{r} 2\,6\,2 \\ -\ 3\,8 \\ \hline 2\,3\,6 \end{array}$$

Read the statement marked Oops. **Remind** students that this is a common pitfall.

 Ray made a pitfall by saying "8 minus 2." Talk with your neighbor about why this is incorrect. **WAIT**

Who would like to come up and explain some correct ways to read the ones column? Is it correct to read the ones column as "8 take away 2" or "2 take away 8"? Is it correct to read it as "2 from 8" or "8 from 2"?

Write the following problems on the board. **Ask** students to talk with a neighbor about whether to regroup or not on these problems. **Remind** students to look out for pitfalls. **Call on** students to explain why their answers make sense.

$$\begin{array}{r} 262 \\ -\ 38 \end{array} \qquad \begin{array}{r} 268 \\ -\ 32 \end{array}$$

Things to Remember

Call on students to **add** to the Things to Remember list on the board. **Read** the list.

Help students summarize and record two important Things to Remember.

> **Things to Remember List (sample)**
> 1. When you need more ones in the starting number, regroup a ten into 10 ones.
> 2. If you regroup 6 tens and 2 ones into 5 tens and 12 ones, they both equal 62.

Reflection

Ask students to reflect on the discussion process using one of the sample prompts.

> **Reflection Prompts (sample)**
> - Name a *Discussion Builder* that we used today. How did it help the discussion?
> - What *Discussion Builder* could we use next time to make the discussion even better?
> - What did someone do or say today that helped you understand the math?

Review and Practice

Review

Ask students to review page 2 to jog their memory.

Read the statement marked OK. **Call on** a student to explain how the problem was solved.

Read the statement marked Oops. **Call on** a student to explain why it is incorrect or doesn't make sense.

Call on two or three students to read an item on their Things to Remember list.

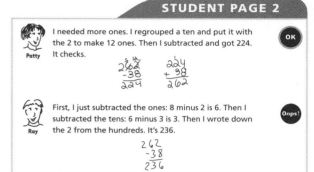

STUDENT PAGE 2

Patty: I needed more ones. I regrouped a ten and put it with the 2 to make 12 ones. Then I subtracted and got 224. It checks. **OK**

$$\begin{array}{r}\overset{5}{\cancel{2}}\overset{12}{\cancel{6}}2\\-\ 38\\\hline 224\end{array}\qquad\begin{array}{r}\overset{1}{2}24\\+\ 38\\\hline 262\end{array}$$

Ray: First, I just subtracted the ones: 8 minus 2 is 6. Then I subtracted the tens: 6 minus 3 is 3. Then I wrote down the 2 from the hundreds. It's 236. **Oops!**

$$\begin{array}{r}262\\-\ 38\\\hline 236\end{array}$$

Our Turn

Ask students to refer to page 3.

Use the procedure below and the Clipboard Prompts to discuss students' solutions. **Discuss** the problems one at a time.

> **Read** the problem.
>
> **Ask** students to work with a neighbor to solve it.
>
> **Discuss** one or two students' solutions.

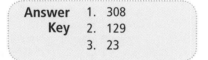

Answer	1.	308
Key	2.	129
	3.	23

STUDENT PAGE 3

Our Turn

Write the answer for each problem. Check your work by adding.

1. 357
    − 49   Check

2. 165
    − 36   Check

3.   50
    − 27   Check

My Turn

Ask students to solve the problems on page 4. **Remind** them to watch out for pitfalls!

After allowing time to work, **read** the answers. **Have** students mark and revise their papers using ink or crayon.

Answer	1.	516
Key	2.	22
	3.	307

STUDENT PAGE 4

My Turn

Write the answer for each problem. Check your work by adding.

1. 542
    − 26   Check

2.   70
    − 48   Check

3. 346
    − 39   Check

Mini Lessons
(2–3 Days Later)

Assess and Reinforce

Multiple Choice Mini Lesson

Distribute Student Page 5.

Problem 1

 Please read problem 1.

Talk with your neighbor about which choices don't make sense. **WAIT**

Who can show or explain why 37 is the correct choice?

 Students should understand the answer cannot be forty-something because, after regrouping, 2 tens taken from 5 tens gives a number in the thirties.

Problem 2

 Read the problem and find the correct choice. **WAIT**

Which response is correct? Explain why.

Why can't the correct answer have an 8 in the ones place? Explain.

>
> **Multiple Choice Mini Lesson**
> Fill in the circle next to the answer you choose.
>
> 1. $64 - 27 =$ _____
>   ○ 33   ● 37   ○ 43   ○ 47
>
> 2. $50 - 38 =$ _____
>   ● 12   ○ 18   ○ 22   ○ 28

Writing Task Mini Lesson

Distribute Student Page 6.

Ask a student to read the task. **Call on** students to respond with their ideas.

Jot the ideas on the board.

Write an explanation together using their ideas. **Read** it aloud.

Ask students to write an explanation on their page.

>
> **Writing Task Mini Lesson**
> Explain how regrouping could be used to solve this problem.
>
> $75 - 48 =$ _____

> **Sample Explanation:** 75 is 70 and 5. You need to take away 4 tens and 8 ones. There aren't enough ones, so you have to use a ten from the 70 to help. Then you have 6 tens and 15 ones take away 4 tens and 8 ones. You have 27 left.

 Mathematical Discussion Support

When generating ideas, ask students to explain or show what regrouping means. Ask them to identify the place values in the problem and explain what they will regroup to solve the problem and why. Encourage them to verbalize the value of each digit, such as 70 or 7 tens for the 7, and 40 or 4 tens for 4.

When Do You Multiply?

Lesson at a Glance

Prior Learning Needed

- Solve addition, subtraction, and multiplication word problems
- Understand mathematical symbols

Lesson Preparation

- Study Lesson Foundation
- Review Teaching Guide and Student Pages
- Prepare stapled packet of Student Pages 1–4 for each student
- Copy and cut in half Student Pages 5 and 6
- Post *Discussion Builders* poster

Mathematical goals

✳ Recognize story problem situations with repeated groups

✳ Relate multiplication situations to their number sentences

Mathematical language and reasoning goals

✳ Discuss reasons a number sentence is correct or incorrect for a situation

✳ Differentiate between needed and extra numbers in a story problem

LESSON ROADMAP			MATERIALS
CORE LESSON: DAY 1	GROUPING	TIME	○ *Discussion Builders* poster
Opener			○ Projector (optional)
Discussion Builders			○ Student Page 1
Purpose	👥	🕐	○ Student Page 2
Math Words			○ Teaching Guide
Starter Problem	👤	🕐	○ Clear bags, cups, and counters (suggested)
Discussion			
Student Thinking	👤 👥 👥	🕧	
Things to Remember Reflection	👥	🕜	
CORE LESSON: DAY 2			○ Clipboard Prompts, page 37
Review and Practice			○ Student Page 2 (completed day 1)
Review Day 1 Lesson	👥	🕐	○ Student Pages 3 and 4
Our Turn	👥 👥	🕜	○ Teaching Guide
My Turn	👤	🕜	○ Clear bags, cups, and counters (suggested)
MINI LESSONS: 2–3 DAYS LATER			○ Student Pages 5 and 6
Assess and Reinforce			○ Teaching Guide
Multiple Choice Mini Lesson	👤 👥 👥	🕧	○ Counters, place value materials (suggested)
Writing Task Mini Lesson	👤 👥	🕧	

Lesson Foundation

Starter Problem

Mike has 3 boxes. There are 5 cars and 2 marbles in each box. Which number sentence gives the total number of marbles? Write the total in the blank.

$3 + 2 =$ _____ $3 \times 2 =$ _____

$3 \times 5 =$ _____ $3 + 5 + 2 =$ _____

Student Thinking

Martin

I drew 3 boxes and put 2 marbles in each. That's 3 times 2 equals the total number of marbles. It's 6 marbles.

OK

Gina

There are 3 numbers to add. Total means how many in all. It's 3 plus 5 plus 2. That's 10 marbles.

Oops!

MATHEMATICAL INSIGHTS & TEACHING TIPS

Repeated Groups of the Same Number or Size

Martin was not distracted by extra numbers in the problem and correctly interpreted the important mathematical phrase "in each." He drew 3 simple boxes with 2 items in each to represent the marbles, and he related this situation to the number sentence 3 x 2. Students should also recognize that multiplication sentences could be written as repeated addition number sentences. So, 2 + 2 + 2 = ___ is also a correct number sentence for this problem, even though it is not given as one of the choices.

 Oops! Gina chose the addition number sentence, falsely assuming that the word "total," combined with three numbers in the problem, must indicate addition.

Repeated group problems use phrases such as "for every," "for each," or "per" to express a multiplication relationship. These problems involve a measured or counted quantity, such as "3 pounds each week."

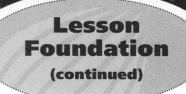

Lesson Foundation
(continued)

MATHEMATICAL INSIGHTS & TEACHING TIPS (CONTINUED)

 Set up experiences in which students learn to: (1) model multiplication problems, (2) say phrases such as 5 cups with 4 in each cup, and (3) write the number sentences, such as 5 x 4 = ___ and 4 + 4 + 4 + 4 + 4 = ___, to match the situation. Help them see that they can add, multiply, or skip count to find the total.

Comprehending Word Problems

In order to truly comprehend a word problem, it is necessary to recognize and understand the mathematical relationship involved. Gina, like many students, falsely assumed that when a word problem has three numbers, you will probably add to find the solution. It is true that you could add to solve this problem; however, it is not correct to add 3 + 5 + 2. Also, students who focus on key words may automatically associate the word "total" with addition and look for any number sentence that qualifies. A strategy based on key words becomes less and less reliable as students move into later grades, and it takes attention away from the meaning of the problem's situation.

 Encourage students to restate a word problem in their own words before they predict which operation they should use.

Matching Word Problems to Number Sentences

In this problem, students choose a number sentence to match a problem situation. It is also important for students to be able to reverse the activity. For example, give them a number sentence such as 3 x 2 = ___ and ask them to make up a story problem having "3 groups with 2 things in each." Such flexibility helps students read a situation into a number sentence and model both the situation and the number sentence.

 Give students problems of simple multiplication facts, such as 4 x 2. Ask them to orally make up a matching problem situation and to model it with materials, such as counters and cups.

MATHEMATICAL DISCUSSION SUPPORT

Ask students to explain why it is necessary in multiplication situations to give every box or group the same number of things. Help students develop flexibility using a variety of such mathematical phrases as "in each," "for every," "for each," and "per" while discussing repeated group multiplication situations. To help make the meaning clear, you may insert the word "one" in phrases such as "6 snacks for every 1 box."

Before discussing the numbers in the problem and how to solve it, encourage students to use reading comprehension strategies by visualizing the situation. Help students relate it to something they already know about. Encourage them to restate the problem in their own words, draw a representation for the problem, or use objects to act out the problem.

Core Lesson Day 1

Opener

Review *Discussion Builders*

Read the poster. **Suggest** a section to focus on today:
Presenting Our Ideas, Adding to Others' Ideas, or *Asking More Questions.*

Purpose

Distribute stapled packets of Student Pages 1–4. **Project** an image of page 1 (optional).

Call on a student to read the purpose.

Math Words

Point to and say the first math word. **Ask** students to repeat it aloud or silently.

Read the sentence containing the word.

Give an example using objects or drawings.

Repeat for the other math word.

Starter Problem

Read the Starter Problem. **Call on** a student to restate it in his/her own words.

 Please use what you already know to help you solve this problem on your own. This will prepare you to talk about the math and how to avoid pitfalls in our discussion later on.

I'll walk around and make notes about things we need to discuss. Look out for oops, or pitfalls! **WAIT**

Look at your work. It's easy to have an oops, or pitfall, in this type of problem. You might also have made a pitfall if your problem has a 5 in it.

Don't worry. Next we'll discuss how two imaginary students solved this problem. One has a pitfall! You may keep your solution private, but bring up your ideas in the discussion.

STUDENT PAGE 1

Purpose
To solve multiplication problems with the same number in each group

Math Words

group	A collection of things or people, like a team, is a group.
each	If there is money in each pocket, then that means every pocket has money in it.

Starter Problem

Mike has 3 boxes. There are 5 cars and 2 marbles in each box. Which number sentence gives the total number of marbles? Write the total in the blank.

$$3 + 2 = \underline{\hspace{1cm}} \qquad 3 \times 2 = \underline{\hspace{1cm}}$$

$$3 \times 5 = \underline{\hspace{1cm}} \qquad 3 + 5 + 2 = \underline{\hspace{1cm}}$$

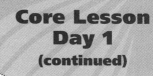

Discussion

Student Thinking

Martin

I drew 3 boxes and put 2 marbles in each. That's 3 times 2 equals the total number of marbles. It's 6 marbles.

 OK

Ask students to refer to page 2. **Read** the statement marked OK.

Explain that this statement is about the same problem students worked on earlier.

We can learn a lot about the math by studying what this student did.

Read each sentence silently and look at the drawing. Think about what they mean. **WAIT**

Now talk with a partner about what each sentence and each part of the drawing means.

Listen in, ask questions, and observe. **Note** potential contributions for the discussion.

Who can restate this problem in their own words? What do we want to find out?

Who can come up to explain why Martin drew 3 boxes and put 2 marbles in each box to solve this problem? Why didn't he draw the cars?

Talk to your neighbor about why Martin chose the number sentence 3 x 2 = ___. **WAIT**

In mathematics, 3 x 2 means 3 groups with 2 in each group. How does Martin's picture show 3 groups with 2 in each group? Why is it correct to use multiplication to write a number sentence to go with Martin's picture?

If the boxes didn't have the same number of marbles in each, could you still multiply?

Who can make up a word problem and drawing for 4 x 3 = ___?

Call on students to state things to remember about solving problems like this.

Start a Things to Remember list on the board.

MORE DAY 1

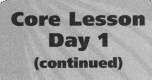

Discussion

Student Thinking, continued

 STUDENT PAGE 2

 There are 3 numbers to add. Total means how many in all. It's 3 plus 5 plus 2. That's 10 marbles.

Oops!

Gina

$3+5+2=10$

Read the statement marked Oops. **Remind** students that this is a common pitfall.

 Gina made a pitfall when she decided to add the three numbers in the problem. Talk with your neighbor about why this doesn't make sense. **WAIT**

Who would like to come up and explain why it doesn't make sense to use the number 5 in the number sentence?

Why is it correct to multiply 3 times 2 for this problem?

Write the following problem on the board. **Ask** students to talk with their neighbor about which number sentence can be used to solve each part of the problem. **Remind** them to look out for pitfalls. **Call on** students to explain.

James made 3 bouquets, each with 3 tulips, 2 roses, and 4 daisies.

How many flowers are in 1 bouquet? 3 + 3 + 2 + 4 = _____ or 3 + 2 + 4 = _____

How many roses are in all 3 bouquets? 3 + 2 = _____ or 3 x 2 = _____

Things to Remember

Call on students to **add** to the Things to Remember list on the board. **Read** the list.

Help students summarize and record two important Things to Remember.

> **Things to Remember List (sample)**
> 1. Restate the problem in your own words and draw a picture to help solve it.
> 2. For 5 x 3, you can say, "5 groups with 3 things in each group."

Reflection

Ask students to reflect on the discussion process using one of the sample prompts.

> **Reflection Prompts (sample)**
> - Name a *Discussion Builder* that we used today. How did it help the discussion?
> - What *Discussion Builder* could we use next time to make the discussion even better?
> - What did someone do or say today that helped you understand the math?

Review and Practice

Review

Ask students to review page 2 to jog their memory.

Read the statement marked OK. **Call on** a student to explain how the problem was solved.

Read the statement marked Oops. **Call on** a student to explain why it is incorrect or doesn't make sense.

Call on two or three students to read an item on their Things to Remember list.

Martin: I drew 3 boxes and put 2 marbles in each. That's 3 times 2 equals the total number of marbles. It's 6 marbles. **OK**

Gina: There are 3 numbers to add. Total means how many in all. It's 3 plus 5 plus 2. That's 10 marbles. **Oops!**

Our Turn

Ask students to refer to page 3.

Use the procedure below and the Clipboard Prompts to discuss students' solutions. **Discuss** the problems one at a time.

   Read the problem.

   Ask students to work with a neighbor to solve it.

   Discuss one or two students' solutions.

Answer Key
1. 3 x 5 = <u>15</u>
2. 2 + 3 + 5 = <u>10</u>
3. 4 x 3 = <u>12</u>

Our Turn

Draw a picture for each problem.
Circle and solve the correct number sentence.

1. Mr. Holden bought 3 boxes with 5 bags of chips and 1 prize in each. Which number sentence gives the total number of bags of chips?

   3 + 5 + 1 = _____   3 x 5 + 1 = _____

   3 x 5 = _____   3 x 1 = _____

2. Mrs. Fong has 2 bananas, 3 apples, and 5 oranges. She is making 2 bowls of fruit salad with the fruit. Which number sentence shows the number of pieces of fruit that Mrs. Fong has?

   2 + 2 + 3 + 5 = _____   5 x 2 = _____

   2 + 3 + 5 = _____   2 x 3 = _____

3. Alisha is making 4 sack lunches. She will put 2 sandwiches and 3 cookies in each bag. Which number sentence shows the number of cookies that Alisha needs?

   4 + 2 + 3 = _____   4 x 2 = _____

   4 x 2 x 3 = _____   4 x 3 = _____

My Turn

Ask students to solve the problems on page 4. **Remind** them to watch out for pitfalls!

After allowing time to work, **read** the answers. **Have** students mark and revise their papers using ink or crayon.

Answer Key
1. 3 x 2 = <u>6</u>
2. 8 + 4 + 6 = <u>18</u>
3. 4 x 2 = <u>8</u>

My Turn

Draw a picture for each problem.
Circle and solve the correct number sentence.

1. Mr. Velez brought 2 soft drinks and 3 health bars for each of his grandchildren on their camping trip. He has 3 grandchildren. Which number sentence gives the total number of soft drinks he brought?

   2 + 3 + 3 = _____   2 x 3 + 3 = _____

   3 x 2 = _____   3 x 3 = _____

2. Jenny has 8 tulips, 4 roses, and 6 snapdragons. She will put the flowers in 2 small baskets. Which number sentence shows the total number of flowers?

   8 + 4 + 6 = _____   8 x 4 x 6 = _____

   2 x 8 = _____   2 x 8 + 4 + 6 = _____

3. Kai has room for 2 file boxes, 3 magazine holders, and 2 CD boxes on each shelf. He has 4 shelves. Which number sentence shows the total number of CD boxes Kai will need?

   2 x 3 x 2 x 4 = _____   2 x 3 x 2 = _____

   4 + 2 = _____   4 x 2 = _____

Mini Lessons
(2–3 Days Later)

Assess and Reinforce

Multiple Choice Mini Lesson

Distribute Student Page 5.

Problem 1

Please read problem 1.

Talk with your neighbor about which choices don't make sense. [WAIT]

How could you show why 4 x 2 = _____ is the correct number sentence?

(i)▶ *Students may incorrectly choose the number sentence 4 + 2 + 1 = _____ because it uses all numbers given in the problem. Point out that problems sometimes contain extra numbers.*

Problem 2

Read the problem and find the correct choice. [WAIT]

Which response is correct? Explain why.

Why doesn't it make sense to choose the number sentence that shows 4 (teams) + 1 (captain) + 2 (soccer balls) + 3 (basketballs) = 10 (somethings)? Explain.

Writing Task Mini Lesson

Distribute Student Page 6.

Ask a student to read the task. **Call on** students to respond with their ideas.

Jot the ideas on the board.

Write an explanation together using their ideas. **Read** it aloud.

Ask students to write an explanation on their page.

Multiple Choice Mini Lesson
Fill in the circle next to the answer you choose.

1. Kim has 4 bottles. There are 2 cups of juice and 1 straw in each bottle. Which number sentence gives the total number of cups of juice?

   ○ 4 + 2 + 1 = _____   ○ 4 + 2 = _____   ● 4 x 2 = _____

2. There are 4 third grade teams. Every team has 1 captain, 2 soccer balls, and 3 basketballs. Which number sentence gives the number of balls for one team?

   ○ 4 + 1 + 2 + 3 = _____   ○ 4 x 2 = _____   ● 2 + 3 = _____

STUDENT PAGE 6

Writing Task Mini Lesson
Explain why the drawing below can be used to solve the problem.

Mrs. James got 6 markers and 4 pens for each of her 5 children. How many pens did she get?

Sample Explanation: The drawing shows 5 boxes, 1 box for each child. Each child should get 4 pens in the box. We don't need to draw the markers. The drawing shows 5 boxes with 4 pens for each child, or 5 x 4 = 20.

Mathematical Discussion Support

When generating ideas, ask students to restate the problem in their own words and identify what the problem is asking.

Invite students to explain what the boxes and lines represent in the problem.

Ask students to explain why they wouldn't use 6 in the drawing.

Making Sense and Multiplying

Lesson at a Glance

Prior Learning Needed

- Interpret single-digit multiplication word problems
- Use an algorithm to solve two-digit by one-digit multiplication problems

Lesson Preparation

- Study Lesson Foundation
- Review Teaching Guide and Student Pages
- Prepare stapled packet of Student Pages 1–4 for each student
- Copy and cut in half Student Pages 5 and 6
- Post *Discussion Builders* poster

Mathematical goals

✳ Find the product of a three-digit number and a one-digit number mentally

✳ Find the product of a three-digit number and a one-digit number using paper and pencil

Mathematical language and reasoning goals

✳ Use reasoning and drawings to make sense of multiplication problems

✳ Interpret word problems to distinguish addition and multiplication contexts

LESSON ROADMAP			MATERIALS
CORE LESSON: DAY 1	GROUPING	TIME	○ *Discussion Builders* poster
Opener			○ Projector (optional)
Discussion Builders			○ Student Page 1
Purpose	👥👥	🕐	○ Student Page 2
Math Words			○ Teaching Guide
Starter Problem	👤	🕐	○ Place value materials, scratch paper (suggested)
Discussion			
Student Thinking	👤 👥 👥👥	🕜	
Things to Remember	👥👥	🕐	
Reflection			
CORE LESSON: DAY 2			○ Clipboard Prompts, page 37
Review and Practice			○ Student Page 2 (completed day 1)
Review Day 1 Lesson	👥👥	🕐	○ Student Pages 3 and 4
Our Turn	👥👥 👥👥	🕜	○ Teaching Guide
My Turn	👤	🕜	○ Place value materials, scratch paper (suggested)
MINI LESSONS: 2–3 DAYS LATER			○ Student Pages 5 and 6
Assess and Reinforce			○ Teaching Guide
Multiple Choice Mini Lesson	👤 👥👥 👥👥	🕜	○ Place value materials, scratch paper (suggested)
Writing Task Mini Lesson	👤 👥👥	🕜	

Lesson Foundation

···**Starter Problem**····································

Solve.

The third grade class made 125 cupcakes for the school fair. Each cupcake had 3 candy kisses on top. How many candy kisses were needed all together? _____

Student Thinking

Joy

For 100 cupcakes you need 3 times 100 candies. For 25 cupcakes you need 3 times 25 candies. So 300 plus 75 is 375 candies. I can multiply 125 x 3 to check.

OK

100 cupcakes 25 cupcakes

$$\begin{array}{r} 125 \\ \times\ \ 3 \\ \hline 375 \end{array}$$

3 candies each is 300 candies

3 candies each is 75 candies

Tim

I needed to find how many candy kisses all together, so I added. It's 128 in all.

Oops!

$$\begin{array}{r} 125 \\ +\ \ 3 \\ \hline 128 \end{array}$$

MATHEMATICAL INSIGHTS & TEACHING TIPS

Multiplying Mentally Using the Distributive Property

Joy solved this problem intuitively by making sense of the problem context through her drawing. She recognized that problems involving equal-sized groups, such as putting 3 candy kisses on each cupcake, could be solved by multiplication. In other words, multiplication is an efficient way to add equal-sized groups. So, instead of adding 3 + 3 + 3 + 3 (125 times), you can multiply 3 x 125.

Oops! Tim focused on the words "all together" and mistakenly assumed that the problem could be solved using addition instead of multiplication.

Joy's method breaks the problem into parts so that it can easily be solved mentally. To find 3 times 125, she found 3 times 100, 3 times 25, and then added the products together (300 plus 75) to get 375. Another way to show what Joy did is: 3(100 + 25) = 300 + 75. This method uses the distributive property, which states that a(b + c) = ab + ac. She could also break 125 into 3 addends, using an extension of the distributive property, to get: 3(100 + 20 + 5) = 300 + 60 + 15. Either method results in the same answer, 375.

MATHEMATICAL INSIGHTS & TEACHING TIPS (CONTINUED)

Misleading Key Words in Word Problems

Instead of trying to understand what the problem meant, Tim noticed the key words "all together" and then looked for two numbers to add. To use addition to solve the problem, which is a correct method, Tim would have had to add 3 together 125 times, not add 3 and 125. Focusing on key words can undermine sense making and lead to incorrect solutions. Tim should have realized that his answer, 128 candy kisses, doesn't make sense because it allows for only a little more than one candy on each cupcake!

 Encourage students to draw a picture to illustrate the relationships in the word problem and then use their drawing to show how they know their solution makes sense.

Multiplication Algorithm

The distributive property is often used to facilitate mental computation, but it is also the foundation for the steps in the traditional multiplication algorithm. We first multiply the ones, then the tens, and then the hundreds, using place value to indicate the amounts that make up the final product. It is important for students to solve problems in more than one way and to show that the answer is the same regardless of the method used. Students who choose to use the algorithm should be able to explain why their answer makes sense using mental math strategies.

MATHEMATICAL DISCUSSION SUPPORT

The words "each" and "every" are often used interchangeably in mathematical word problems. For example, we may say that each student has 2 cookies or that every student has 3 cookies. One of the best ways to develop understanding of words such as these is to use them in a variety of contexts that are meaningful to students. Ask students to act out or illustrate the situation to reinforce the meaning.

 To help students understand the word "each," draw 10 cupcakes on the board. Ask students to draw 3 candy kisses on "each" cupcake. Verify that 30 candies are needed in order to have 3 candies on "each" of 10 cupcakes.

Core Lesson Day 1

Opener

Review *Discussion Builders*

Read the poster. **Suggest** a section to focus on today:
Presenting Our Ideas, Adding to Others' Ideas, or *Asking More Questions.*

Purpose

Distribute stapled packets of Student Pages 1–4. **Project** an image of page 1 (optional).

Call on a student to read the purpose.

Math Words

Point to and say the first math word. **Ask** students to repeat it aloud or silently.

Read the sentence containing the word.

Give an example using objects or drawings.

Repeat for the other math word.

Starter Problem

Read the Starter Problem. **Call on** a student to restate it in his/her own words.

 Please use what you already know to help you solve this problem on your own. This will prepare you to talk about the math and how to avoid pitfalls in our discussion later on.

I'll walk around and make notes about things we need to discuss. Look out for oops, or pitfalls! (WAIT)

Look at your work. It's easy to have an oops, or pitfall, in this type of problem. You might also have made a pitfall if your answer is less than 300.

Don't worry. Next we'll discuss how two imaginary students solved this problem. One has a pitfall! You may keep your solution private, but bring up your ideas in the discussion.

STUDENT PAGE 1

Purpose
To solve multiplication problems using mental math or paper and pencil

Math Words

multiplication	We can use multiplication to combine or add equal-sized groups.
times	We find 3 times 100 by multiplying, or we can add 100 plus 100 plus 100.

Starter Problem

Solve.

The third grade class made 125 cupcakes for the school fair. Each cupcake had 3 candy kisses on top. How many candy kisses were needed all together? _____

Discussion

Student Thinking

STUDENT PAGE 2

For 100 cupcakes you need 3 times 100 candies. For 25 cupcakes you need 3 times 25 candies. So 300 plus 75 is 375 candies. I can multiply 125 x 3 to check.

Joy

OK

Ask students to refer to page 2. **Read** the statement marked OK.

Explain that this statement is about the same problem students worked on earlier.

 We can learn a lot about the math by studying what this student did.

Read each sentence silently and look at the drawing. Think about what they mean. WAIT

Now talk with a partner about what each sentence and each part of the drawing means.

Listen in, ask questions, and observe. **Note** potential contributions for the discussion.

 Who can restate this problem in their own words? What is the problem asking?

Use Joy's drawing to explain how many candies are needed in order to put 1 candy kiss on each of 100 cupcakes. What if you put 2 candies on each of 100 cupcakes? What if you put 3 candies on each of 100 cupcakes? What does 3 times 100 mean?

Explain why 75 candy kisses were needed to put 3 candies on each of 25 cupcakes. Why did Joy say you need 3 times 25 candies for 25 cupcakes?

Talk to your neighbor about why 375 candies were needed in all. WAIT

Why are 375 candies needed in order to put 3 candies on each of 125 cupcakes? How did Joy break the problem into parts to find the answer mentally? How did she multiply 125 times 3 to check? Why can you multiply to find the answer?

Call on students to state things to remember about solving problems like this.

Start a Things to Remember list on the board.

MORE DAY 1

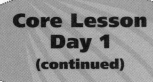

**Core Lesson
Day 1**
(continued)

Discussion

Student Thinking, continued

 I needed to find how many candy kisses all together, so I added. It's 128 in all.

Tim

$$\begin{array}{r} 125 \\ +3 \\ \hline 128 \end{array}$$

Oops!

Read the statement marked Oops. **Remind** students that this is a common pitfall.

 Tim made a pitfall by adding 125 + 3 instead of multiplying 3 x 125. Talk with your neighbor about why his answer doesn't make sense. **WAIT**

Is Tim's answer too high or too low? How do you know? Who would like to come up and explain why Tim should have multiplied instead of added?

Write the following problem on the board. **Ask** students to talk with their neighbor about whether to multiply or add to solve the problem. **Remind** them to look out for pitfalls. **Call on** students to explain.

June reads 35 pages each day. In 5 days, how many pages will she read in all?

Things to Remember

Call on students to **add** to the Things to Remember list on the board. **Read** the list.

Help students summarize and record two important Things to Remember.

> **Things to Remember List (sample)**
> 1. Restate the problem in your own words and draw a picture to help solve it.
> 2. Break the problem into easy steps to find the answer mentally.

Reflection

Ask students to reflect on the discussion process using one of the sample prompts.

> **Reflection Prompts (sample)**
> - Name a *Discussion Builder* that we used today. How did it help the discussion?
> - What *Discussion Builder* could we use next time to make the discussion even better?
> - What did someone do or say today that helped you understand the math?

Review and Practice

Review

Ask students to review page 2 to jog their memory.

Read the statement marked OK. **Call on** a student to explain how the problem was solved.

Read the statement marked Oops. **Call on** a student to explain why it is incorrect or doesn't make sense.

Call on two or three students to read an item on their Things to Remember list.

STUDENT PAGE 2

 Joy

For 100 cupcakes you need 3 times 100 candies. For 25 cupcakes you need 3 times 25 candies. So 300 plus 75 is 375 candies. I can multiply 125 x 3 to check.   **OK**

100 cupcakes   25 cupcakes

$\begin{array}{r} 125 \\ \times\ 3 \\ \hline 375 \end{array}$

3 candies each is 300 candies   3 candies each is 75 candies

 Tim

I needed to find how many candy kisses all together, so I added. It's 128 in all.   **Oops!**

$\begin{array}{r} 125 \\ +\ 3 \\ \hline 128 \end{array}$

Our Turn

Ask students to refer to page 3.

Use the procedure below and the Clipboard Prompts to discuss students' solutions. **Discuss** the problems one at a time.

>   **Read** the problem.
>
>   **Ask** students to work with a neighbor to solve it.
>
>   **Discuss** one or two students' solutions.

Answer Key		
	1.	128
	2.	325
	3.	744

STUDENT PAGE 3

Our Turn

Solve each problem using mental math or paper and pencil. It may help to make a drawing.

1. Amy made 32 birthday treat bags for her classmates. Each bag had 4 treats. How many treats did she need in all?

2. Eddie packs baskets with fruit to sell at the farmer's market. Each basket holds 7 plums or 5 peaches. How many peaches will he need to fill 65 baskets with peaches?

3. The outdoor theater has 124 rows; each row has 6 seats. How many seats does the theater have all together?

My Turn

Ask students to solve the problems on page 4. **Remind** them to watch out for pitfalls!

After allowing time to work, **read** the answers. **Have** students mark and revise their papers using ink or crayon.

Answer Key		
	1.	140
	2.	408
	3.	64

STUDENT PAGE 4

My Turn

Solve each problem using mental math or paper and pencil. It may help to make a drawing.

1. The pep band had 28 rows with 5 students in each row when it marched on the field. How many students were in the pep band?

2. The after-school clubs made 136 greeting cards for children in hospitals. Each card had 3 stickers. How many stickers were used on the cards all together?

3. Irma helped her neighbor plant flowers. They planted 16 tulips and 5 daffodils in each of 4 pots. How many tulips did they plant in all?

Mini Lessons
(2–3 Days Later)

Assess and Reinforce

Multiple Choice Mini Lesson

Distribute Student Page 5.

Problem 1

 Please read problem 1.

Talk with your neighbor about which choices don't make sense. **WAIT**

How could you show why 192 is the correct choice?

 Students may incorrectly choose 32 because they think "in all" means to add the two numbers. To combine equal groups, you can multiply the number of groups by the number in each group.

Problem 2

 Read the problem and find the correct choice. **WAIT**

Which response is correct? Explain why.

Why doesn't it make sense to choose 138 or 175? What pitfalls do we need to look out for so we don't choose these incorrect answers?

Writing Task Mini Lesson

Distribute Student Page 6.

Ask a student to read the task. **Call on** students to respond with their ideas.

Jot the ideas on the board.

Write an explanation together using their ideas. **Read** it aloud.

Ask students to write an explanation on their page.

Multiple Choice Mini Lesson

Fill in the circle next to the answer you choose.

1. The committee ordered 24 packages of hot dog buns for the picnic. Each package had 8 buns. How many buns did they order in all?

   ● 192   ○ 32   ○ 132

2. The school printed 135 programs for the outdoor fiesta. Each program had 3 pages. How many pages were printed all together?

   ○ 138   ● 405   ○ 175

Writing Task Mini Lesson

Explain how to use mental math to solve the problem below.

Each student got 6 free tickets for events at the school fair. If there are 62 students, how many tickets were given out?

Sample Explanation: If 60 students each got 6 free tickets, that's 6 times 60, or 360, tickets. It's the same as $60 + 60 + 60 + 60 + 60 + 60 = 360$. Then 2 more students would get 6 times 2, or 12, tickets. For 62 students, you add 360 and 12 to get 372 tickets.

Mathematical Discussion Support

Ask students to restate the problem in their own words and to draw a picture.

Students may suggest alternative ways to break the problem into parts, such as 6 times 50 and 6 times 12.

Encourage students to explain why both addition and multiplication can be used to solve the problem.

Student Pages

NAME:

Purpose

To name a number for a point on a number line

Math Words

number line	A number line shows numbers in order along a line.
point	A dot on a number line shows where the point for a number is.
unit	Each unit has a length of 1.

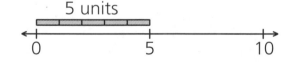

Starter Problem

Which point on the number line shows about 38?

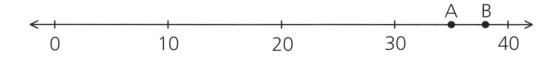

NAME:

Which point on the number line shows about 38?

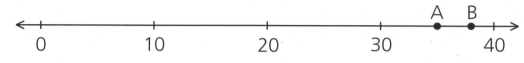

Student Thinking

Amir

Point A is about halfway between 30 and 40. So, that's not 38. It's point B because it's about 2 units before 40.

 OK

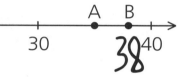

Kelly

It's point A because I marked the 8 units after 30.

 Oops!

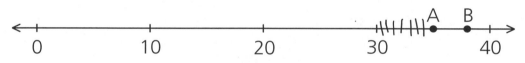

Things to Remember

* _____

_____

* _____

_____

 STOP

NAME:

Our Turn

Write the answer.

1. Which point on the number line shows about 27? _____

2. Which point on the number line shows about 44? _____

3. Which point on the number line shows about 18? _____

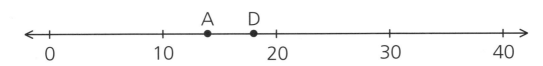

216   Math Pathways & Pitfalls® ✳ Unit 2 ✳ Lesson 1

NAME:

My Turn

Write the answer.

1. Which point on the number line shows about 15? _____

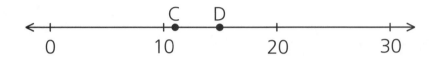

2. Which point on the number line shows about 22? _____

3. Which point on the number line shows about 36? _____

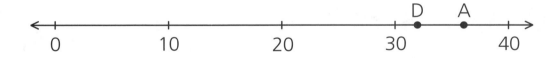

Math Pathways & Pitfalls® ✳ Unit 2 ✳ Lesson 1

NAME:

Multiple Choice Mini Lesson

Fill in the circle next to the answer you choose.

1. What number is a good estimate for point C?

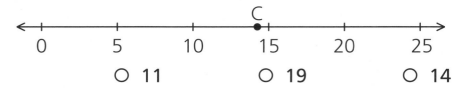

○ 11   ○ 19   ○ 14

2. What number is a good estimate for point X?

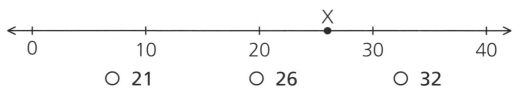

○ 21   ○ 26   ○ 32

NAME:

Multiple Choice Mini Lesson

Fill in the circle next to the answer you choose.

1. What number is a good estimate for point C?

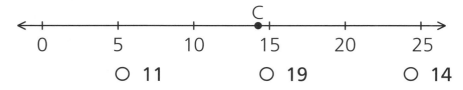

○ 11   ○ 19   ○ 14

2. What number is a good estimate for point X?

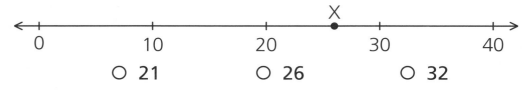

○ 21   ○ 26   ○ 32

218   Math Pathways & Pitfalls® ✳ Unit 2 ✳ Lesson 1

NAME:

Writing Task Mini Lesson

Explain how you know that a good estimate for point C is 25. You may draw a picture on the back to help explain.

....

....

....

....

Number Line Points

STUDENT PAGE 6

NAME:

Writing Task Mini Lesson

Explain how you know that a good estimate for point C is 25. You may draw a picture on the back to help explain.

....

....

....

....

NAME:

Purpose

To use estimation to mark a point for a number on a number line

Math Words

halfway between	15 is halfway between 10 and 20 on the number line.

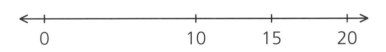

point	A dot on a number line shows where the point for a number is.

units	10 equal units fit between 0 and 10 on a number line.

Starter Problem

Draw a point to show about where 26 is on this number line.

NAME:

Draw a point to show about where 26 is on this number line.

Student Thinking

Amy

Halfway between 20 and 30 is 25. So, 26 is 1 more unit. I could check by drawing equal units.

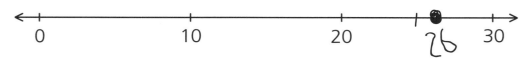

Michael

I need 6 marks after 20 to find the point for 26.

Things to Remember

✱ ....

....

✱ ....

....

NAME:

Our Turn

Draw a point to show about where the number is on each number line. Label the point.

1.   28

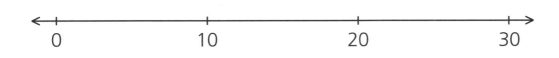

2.   14

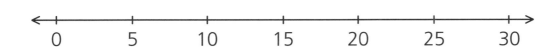

3.   37

NAME:

My Turn

Draw a point to show about where the number is on each number line. Label the point.

1.　23

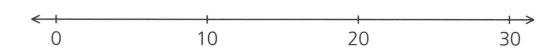

2.　19

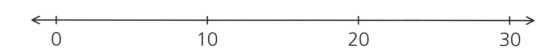

3.　45

NAME:

Multiple Choice Mini Lesson

Fill in the circle next to the answer you choose.

1. Which number line correctly shows the point for 14?

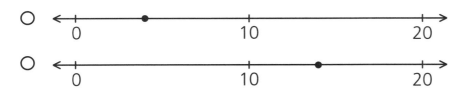

2. Which number line correctly shows the point for 27?

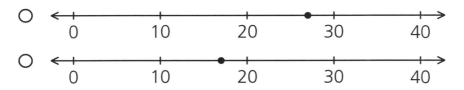

STUDENT PAGE 5 **Marking Points on a Number Line**

NAME:

Multiple Choice Mini Lesson

Fill in the circle next to the answer you choose.

1. Which number line correctly shows the point for 14?

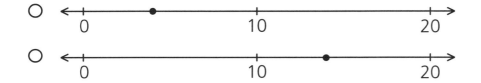

2. Which number line correctly shows the point for 27?

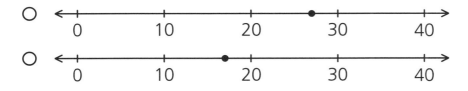

224   Math Pathways & Pitfalls® ✳ Unit 2 ✳ Lesson 2

NAME:

Writing Task Mini Lesson

Explain how you know where to mark and label the number 39 on this number line.

Marking Points on a Number Line

STUDENT PAGE 6

NAME:

Writing Task Mini Lesson

Explain how you know where to mark and label the number 39 on this number line.

NAME:

Purpose

To add a few more to a number

Math Words

add on   I can start with 28 shells and add on 2 more to make 30.

sum   When you add 8 and 5, you get 13 as the sum.

Starter Problem

Think about the meaning. Solve.

$$68 + 7 = \underline{\qquad}$$

NAME:

Starter Problem

Think about the meaning. Solve.

68 + 7 = _____

Student Thinking

Katie

I added 7 in my head using easy steps. 68 and 2 more made 70. Then 5 more made 75. I could add on paper too.

OK

68 + 7 = **75**

Sam

I just lined them up and added. It's 138.

Oops!

$$\begin{array}{r} 68 \\ +\ 7 \\ \hline 138 \end{array}$$

Things to Remember

✳ ....

....

✳ ....

....

Our Turn

Write the sum for each problem.

1.   45 + 8 = _____

2.   59 + 3 = _____

3.   4 + 60 = _____

NAME:

My Turn

Write the sum for each problem.

1.   48 + 6 = _____

2.   70 + 5 = _____

3.   8 + 39 = _____

NAME:

Multiple Choice Mini Lesson

Fill in the circle next to the answer you choose.

1. 63 + 8 = _____

    ○ 143   ○ 61   ○ 71

2. 59 + 6 = _____

    ○ 55   ○ 65   ○ 119

NAME:

Multiple Choice Mini Lesson

Fill in the circle next to the answer you choose.

1. 63 + 8 = _____

    ○ 143   ○ 61   ○ 71

2. 59 + 6 = _____

    ○ 55   ○ 65   ○ 119

NAME:

Writing Task Mini Lesson

Explain how to add 36 + 7 in easy steps. You may draw on this number line to help you explain.

Add a Few

STUDENT PAGE 6

NAME:

Writing Task Mini Lesson

Explain how to add 36 + 7 in easy steps. You may draw on this number line to help you explain.

NAME:

Purpose

To find the difference between two numbers

Math Words

difference between	Since I am 2 years older than my sister, the difference between our ages is 2 years.
find the difference	To find the difference between 5 and 3, find how much more 5 is than 3.

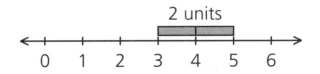

difference	The difference is the answer you get when you subtract.

Starter Problem

Adam has 11 toy trains. Marcos has 8 toy trains. What is the difference between the number of trains Adam has and the number of trains Marcos has? _____

NAME:

····Starter Problem····

Adam has 11 toy trains. Marcos has 8 toy trains. What is the difference between the number of trains Adam has and the number of trains Marcos has? _____

Student Thinking

Dan

To find the difference, I started with Marcos' trains and counted up 3 units between 8 and 11. It's easier to count up in easy steps than to take away in this problem. The difference is 3.

OK

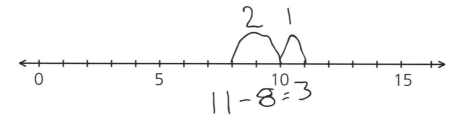

Olivia

I counted up from 8 to 11. There are 4 numbers: 8, 9, 10, 11. The difference is 4.

Oops!

8, 9, 10, 11   11 − 8 = 4

Things to Remember

* ··

* ··

NAME:

Our Turn

Find the difference. Use the number line to help you.

1. Eva's bean plant is 17 inches tall. Sophia's bean plant is 9 inches tall. Find the difference between the heights of Eva's and Sophia's plants. _____

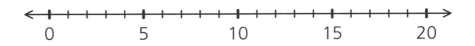

2. $\begin{array}{r} 21 \\ -\ 18 \\ \hline \end{array}$

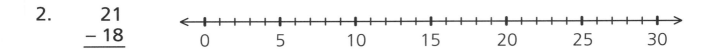

3. Find the difference between 20 and 5. _____

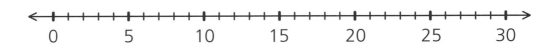

234   Math Pathways & Pitfalls® ✳ Unit 2 ✳ Lesson 4

My Turn

Find the difference. Use the number line to help you.

1. Avery is 13 years old. His little brother, Tom, is 9 years old.
    Find the difference in their ages. _____

2. $\begin{array}{r} 21 \\ -\ 17 \\ \hline \end{array}$

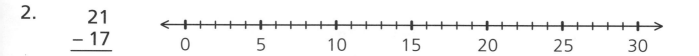

3. Find the difference between 25 and 19. _____

NAME:

Multiple Choice Mini Lesson

Fill in the circle next to the answer you choose.

1. Aida has 10 stuffed animals. Marta has 7 stuffed animals. Find the difference between the number of stuffed animals Aida has and the number of stuffed animals Marta has.

   ○ 17   ○ 7   ○ 3

2. Find the difference.

   $\begin{array}{r} 31 \\ -25 \\ \hline \end{array}$ ○ 6   ○ 4   ○ 14

STUDENT PAGE 5 **What's the Difference?**

NAME:

Multiple Choice Mini Lesson

Fill in the circle next to the answer you choose.

1. Aida has 10 stuffed animals. Marta has 7 stuffed animals. Find the difference between the number of stuffed animals Aida has and the number of stuffed animals Marta has.

   ○ 17   ○ 7   ○ 3

2. Find the difference.

   $\begin{array}{r} 31 \\ -25 \\ \hline \end{array}$ ○ 6   ○ 4   ○ 14

236   Math Pathways & Pitfalls® ✳ Unit 2 ✳ Lesson 4

NAME:

Writing Task Mini Lesson

Explain how to find the difference between 15 and 7. You may make a drawing to help you explain.

....

....

....

....

....

✂

What's the Difference? STUDENT PAGE 6

NAME:

Writing Task Mini Lesson

Explain how to find the difference between 15 and 7. You may make a drawing to help you explain.

....

....

....

....

NAME:

Purpose

To understand how to regroup when finding the sum of two numbers

Math Words

digit	There are ten digits: 0, 1, 2, 3, 4, 5, 6, 7, 8, and 9. The digits in 42 are 4 and 2.
regroup	I can regroup 14 ones into 1 ten and 4 ones, and 14 tens into 1 hundred and 4 tens.
place	The number 54 has 4 in the ones place and 5 in the tens place.

Starter Problem

Ellen has 36 seashells. Hillary has 28 seashells.

How many seashells do they have in all? _____

NAME:

····**Starter Problem**··········

Ellen has 36 seashells. Hillary has 28 seashells.
How many seashells do they have in all? _____

Student Thinking

Jerry

I added because I want to know how many shells in all.
I regrouped when I added 6 and 8. I got 64.

$$\begin{array}{r} \overset{1}{3}6 \\ +\ 28 \\ \hline 64 \end{array}$$

OK

Li Nan

I added. 6 and 8 is 14. 3 and 2 is 5. It's 514.

$$\begin{array}{r} 36 \\ +\ 28 \\ \hline 514 \end{array}$$

Oops!

Things to Remember

✷ ....

....

✷ ....

....

STOP

NAME:

Our Turn

Solve.

Is your answer reasonable? Circle Yes or No.

1.   64   Yes   No
     + 29

2.   87   Yes   No
     + 8

3.   55   Yes   No
     + 35

NAME:

My Turn

Solve.

Is your answer reasonable? Circle Yes or No.

1. $\begin{array}{r} 58 \\ + 13 \\ \hline \end{array}$ Yes   No

2. $\begin{array}{r} 34 \\ + 9 \\ \hline \end{array}$ Yes   No

3. $\begin{array}{r} 67 \\ + 41 \\ \hline \end{array}$ Yes   No

NAME:

Multiple Choice Mini Lesson

Fill in the circle next to the answer you choose.

1.   63
    + 29   ○ 812   ○ 82   ○ 92

2.   56
    + 8   ○ 64   ○ 54   ○ 514

STUDENT PAGE 5 **Don't Squeeze the Digits**

NAME:

Multiple Choice Mini Lesson

Fill in the circle next to the answer you choose.

1.   63
    + 29   ○ 812   ○ 82   ○ 92

2.   56
    + 8   ○ 64   ○ 54   ○ 514

242   Math Pathways & Pitfalls® ✳ Unit 2 ✳ Lesson 5

NAME:

Writing Task Mini Lesson

Explain how you know to regroup when you add 45 and 18.

....

....

....

....

....

....

Don't Squeeze the Digits

STUDENT PAGE 6

NAME:

Writing Task Mini Lesson

Explain how you know to regroup when you add 45 and 18.

....

....

....

....

....

....

NAME: _____

Purpose

To add on more tens or ones to a number

Math Words

place	In the number 257, 7 is in the ones place, 5 is in the tens place, and 2 is in the hundreds place.
ones	In the number 257, 7 means 7 ones.
tens	In the number 257, 5 means 5 tens.
hundreds	In the number 257, 2 means 2 hundreds.

Starter Problem

What number is 30 more than 328? _____

244   Math Pathways & Pitfalls® ✳ Unit 2 ✳ Lesson 6

NAME: _____

Starter Problem

What number is 30 more than 328? _____

Student Thinking

Carla

328 has 2 in the tens place. So 3 more tens is 358.

OK

Russ

30 more than 328 is 628. You just add.

$$\begin{array}{r} 328 \\ +30 \\ \hline 628 \end{array}$$

Oops!

Things to Remember

❋ ....

....

❋ ....

....

STOP

Our Turn

Write the answer.

1.   What number is 20 more than 571? _____

2.   What number is 3 more than 206? _____

3.   613 + 10 = _____

NAME:

My Turn

Write the answer.

1. What number is 40 more than 612? _____

2. What number is 4 more than 453? _____

3. 10 + 321 = _____

NAME:

Multiple Choice Mini Lesson

Fill in the circle next to the answer you choose.

1. What number is 20 more than 673? _____

     ○ 873   ○ 675   ○ 693

2. 40 + 432 = _____

     ○ 472   ○ 436   ○ 832

STUDENT PAGE 5 **Adding On More Tens or Ones**

NAME:

Multiple Choice Mini Lesson

Fill in the circle next to the answer you choose.

1. What number is 20 more than 673? _____

     ○ 873   ○ 675   ○ 693

2. 40 + 432 = _____

     ○ 472   ○ 436   ○ 832

248   Math Pathways & Pitfalls® ✳ Unit 2 ✳ Lesson 6

NAME:

Writing Task Mini Lesson

Explain how you know that 10 more than 368 is 378. You may draw a picture on the back to help you explain.

Adding On More Tens or Ones

STUDENT PAGE 6

NAME:

Writing Task Mini Lesson

Explain how you know that 10 more than 368 is 378. You may draw a picture on the back to help you explain.

NAME:

Purpose

To understand and solve addition equations that have missing numbers

Math Words

equation	An equation like 5 + 3 = 8 shows that 5 + 3 and 8 are equal amounts.
equals sign	An equals sign means "is the same amount as."
both sides	The amounts on both sides of the equals sign in this equation are equal to 4. 3 + 1 = 2 + 2

Starter Problem

Copy and complete this equation.
Think about the meaning.

$$5 + 2 = \underline{\hspace{2cm}} + 1$$

NAME:

Copy and complete this equation.
Think about the meaning.

$$5 + 2 = \underline{\hspace{2cm}} + 1$$

Student Thinking

James

I asked myself, "What number is missing so both sides have the same amount?" It's 6. Both sides equal 7. It checks.

OK

$$5 + 2 = \underline{6} + 1$$

Anna

It says to add, so 5 plus 2 is 7.

$$5 + 2 = \underline{7} + 1$$

Oops!

Things to Remember

✳ ....

....

✳ ....

....

NAME:

Our Turn

Complete each equation.

1. 3 + 7 = _____ + 6

2. 8 + _____ = 9 + 2

3. 4 + _____ = 15

NAME:

My Turn

Complete each equation.

1.   6 + 6 = _____ + 5

2.   _____ + 1 = 8 + 8

3.   9 + _____ = 15

NAME:

Multiple Choice Mini Lesson

Fill in the circle next to the answer you choose.

1. 10 = 9 + _____

    ○ 19   ○ 10   ○ 1

2. _____ + 11 = 5 + 8

    ○ 2   ○ 13   ○ 23

STUDENT PAGE 5 **What Goes in the Blank?**

NAME:

Multiple Choice Mini Lesson

Fill in the circle next to the answer you choose.

1. 10 = 9 + _____

    ○ 19   ○ 10   ○ 1

2. _____ + 11 = 5 + 8

    ○ 2   ○ 13   ○ 23

NAME:

Writing Task Mini Lesson

Explain how you know that 2 is the correct number to put in the blank. You may draw a picture on the back to help you explain.

$$9 + \underline{\hspace{2cm}} = 5 + 6$$

What Goes in the Blank?

STUDENT PAGE   6

NAME:

Writing Task Mini Lesson

Explain how you know that 2 is the correct number to put in the blank. You may draw a picture on the back to help you explain.

$$9 + \underline{\hspace{2cm}} = 5 + 6$$

Purpose

To understand place value and solve addition equations

Math Words

place	The number 645 has 6 in the hundreds place, 4 in the tens place, and 5 in the ones place.
hundreds, tens, and ones	6 hundreds, 4 tens, and 5 ones is the same as 600 + 40 + 5, or 645.

Starter Problem

Copy and complete this equation.
Think about the meaning.

$$400 + \underline{\hspace{2cm}} + 3 = 453$$

NAME:

Starter Problem

Copy and complete this equation.
Think about the meaning.

$$400 + \underline{\hspace{2cm}} + 3 = 453$$

Student Thinking

Daisy

"Four hundred **fifty** three." That's 4 hundreds, 5 tens, and 3 ones. So the 5 tens, or 50, is missing. I checked by adding another way.

$$400 + \underline{50} + 3 = 453$$

AJ

I saw a pattern. 453 is 400, then 5, then 3. The 5 is missing.

$$400 + \underline{5} + 3 = 453$$

Things to Remember

✳ ....

....

✳ ....

....

NAME:

Our Turn

Complete each equation.

1.   _____ + 40 + 5 = 645

2.   40 + 7 + _____ = 347

3.   207 = 7 + _____

NAME:

My Turn

Complete each equation.

1. _____ + 50 + 2 = 652

2. 30 + 1 + _____ = 931

3. 205 = 5 + _____

Math Pathways & Pitfalls® ✳ Unit 2 ✳ Lesson 8

NAME:

Multiple Choice Mini Lesson

Fill in the circle next to the answer you choose.

1.   724 = _____ + 20 + 700

         ○ 720　　　　○ 400　　　　○ 4

2.   724 = _____ hundreds + 2 tens + 4 ones

         ○ 700　　　　○ 72　　　　○ 7

STUDENT PAGE 5 **Place Value Hints**

NAME:

Multiple Choice Mini Lesson

Fill in the circle next to the answer you choose.

1.   724 = _____ + 20 + 700

         ○ 720　　　　○ 400　　　　○ 4

2.   724 = _____ hundreds + 2 tens + 4 ones

         ○ 700　　　　○ 72　　　　○ 7

NAME:

Writing Task Mini Lesson

Explain how you know that 2 is the correct number to put in the blank. Draw a picture on the back or use numbers to help show your ideas.

527 = _____ tens + 7 ones + 5 hundreds

Place Value Hints

STUDENT PAGE 6

NAME:

Writing Task Mini Lesson

Explain how you know that 2 is the correct number to put in the blank. Draw a picture on the back or use numbers to help show your ideas.

527 = _____ tens + 7 ones + 5 hundreds

NAME:

Purpose

To know when and how to regroup when subtracting

Math Words

ones	The 4 in the number 24 is in the ones place, so it means 4 ones.
tens	The 4 in 42 is in the tens place, so it means 4 tens, or 40, not 4.
regroup	One way to regroup 2 tens and 3 ones is into 1 ten and 13 ones. These amounts are equal.

Starter Problem

Think about the meaning.
Solve.

$$\begin{array}{r} 42 \\ -7 \\ \hline \end{array}$$

NAME:

···**Starter Problem**···

Think about the meaning.   42
Solve.   − 7

Student Thinking

Conner

I needed more ones. I got a ten to put with the 2 ones to make 12 ones. Then I subtracted 7. It's 35. It checks.

OK

$$\begin{array}{r} 3\;12 \\ 4\;2 \\ -\;\;\;7 \\ \hline 35 \end{array}$$

check

$$35 + 7 = 42$$

Zina

It's easier if I turn the ones upside down. 7 take away 2 is 5, and 4 take away 0 is 4. That's 45.

Oops!

$$\begin{array}{r} 42 \\ -\;7 \\ \hline 45 \end{array}$$

Things to Remember

✳ ....

....

✳ ....

....

Math Pathways & Pitfalls® ✳ Unit 2 ✳ Lesson 9

NAME:

Our Turn

Write the answer for each problem.

1.   23
     − 8
     ‾‾‾‾

2.   65 − 6 = _____

3.   20
     − 9
     ‾‾‾‾

NAME:

My Turn

Write the answer for each problem.

1.
$$\begin{array}{r} 42 \\ -\ 6 \\ \hline \end{array}$$

2.
$$\begin{array}{r} 30 \\ -\ 8 \\ \hline \end{array}$$

3.   37 − 5 = _____

NAME: _____

Multiple Choice Mini Lesson

Fill in the circle next to the answer you choose.

1. 34 − 7 = _____

     ○ 37   ○ 33   ○ 27

2.   56
    − 8
    _____
     ○ 48   ○ 52   ○ 42

STUDENT PAGE 5 **Minus a Few**

NAME: _____

Multiple Choice Mini Lesson

Fill in the circle next to the answer you choose.

1. 34 − 7 = _____

     ○ 37   ○ 33   ○ 27

2.   56
    − 8
    _____
     ○ 48   ○ 52   ○ 42

266   Math Pathways & Pitfalls® ✳ Unit 2 ✳ Lesson 9

NAME:

Writing Task Mini Lesson

Explain how you could regroup to solve this problem.

$$25 - 8 = \underline{\hspace{2cm}}$$

....

....

....

....

....

Minus a Few

STUDENT PAGE 6

NAME:

Writing Task Mini Lesson

Explain how you could regroup to solve this problem.

$$25 - 8 = \underline{\hspace{2cm}}$$

....

....

....

....

NAME:

Purpose

To practice regrouping when subtracting and to check by adding

Math Words

tens and ones	6 tens and 4 ones is the same amount as 60 + 4, or 64.
regroup	One way to regroup 6 tens and 4 ones is 5 tens and 14 ones. They are both equal to 64.

Starter Problem

Think about the meaning.
Find the difference.

$$\begin{array}{r} 64 \\ -\ 25 \\ \hline \end{array}$$

NAME:

Starter Problem

Think about the meaning.
Find the difference.

$$64 - 25$$

Student Thinking

Megan

5 is more than 4, so I needed more ones. I regrouped a ten and put it with the 4 to make 14. I got 39. It checks.

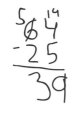

Luke

I borrowed 1 and put it with the 4. Then, I subtracted.

Things to Remember

✳ ....

....

✳ ....

....

Math Pathways & Pitfalls® ✳ Unit 2 ✳ Lesson 10

NAME:

Our Turn

Write the answer for each problem. Check your work.

1.   42   Check
     − 27
     ⎯⎯⎯

2.   60   Check
     − 42
     ⎯⎯⎯

3.   54 − 19 = ⎯⎯⎯⎯⎯   Check

NAME:

My Turn

Write the answer for each problem. Check your work.

1.   46
     − 27   Check

2.   90
     − 39   Check

3.   74 − 28 = _____   Check

    Math Pathways & Pitfalls® ✳ Unit 2 ✳ Lesson 10

NAME:

Multiple Choice Mini Lesson

Fill in the circle next to the answer you choose.

1. 53 − 27 = _____

    ○ 34   ○ 36   ○ 26

2. 83 − 6 = _____

    ○ 23   ○ 77   ○ 87

STUDENT PAGE 5 **Regroup and Subtract**

NAME:

Multiple Choice Mini Lesson

Fill in the circle next to the answer you choose.

1. 53 − 27 = _____

    ○ 34   ○ 36   ○ 26

2. 83 − 6 = _____

    ○ 23   ○ 77   ○ 87

272   Math Pathways & Pitfalls® ✳ Unit 2 ✳ Lesson 10

NAME:

Writing Task Mini Lesson

Explain how you know the answer to this subtraction problem is 14.

$$
\begin{array}{r}
32 \\
- 18 \\
\hline
\end{array}
$$

....

....

....

....

....

✂

NAME:

Writing Task Mini Lesson

Explain how you know the answer to this subtraction problem is 14.

$$
\begin{array}{r}
32 \\
- 18 \\
\hline
\end{array}
$$

....

....

....

....

....

Student Pages

NAME:

Purpose

To name a number for a point on a number line

Math Words

number line	A number line shows numbers in order along a line.
point	A dot on a number line shows where the point for a number is.
unit	A unit has a length of 1.

····Starter Problem····

Which point on the number line shows about 160?

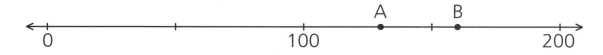

Math Pathways & Pitfalls® ✷ Unit 3 ✷ Lesson 1

NAME:

Which point on the number line shows about 160?

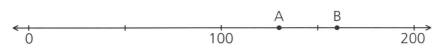

Student Thinking

Scott

Point A is less than 150. So it's not point A. It's point B because it's about 10 more than 150.

OK

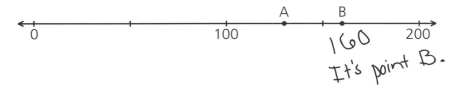

160
It's point B.

Stacy

I tried drawing 60 units after 100, but they were too little to count. I guessed point A.

Oops!

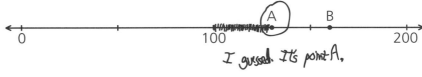

I guessed. It's point A.

Things to Remember

* ....

....

* ....

....

STOP

NAME:

Our Turn

Write the letter for the point that shows the number.

1.   Which point on the number line shows about 120? _____

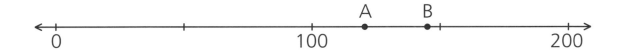

2.   Which point on the number line shows about 180? _____

3.   Which point on the number line shows about 90?   _____

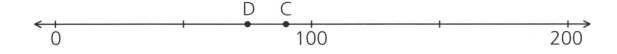

NAME:

My Turn

Write the letter for the point that shows the number.

1.   Which point on the number line shows about 80? _____

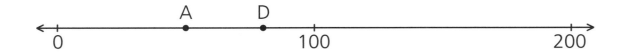

2.   Which point on the number line shows about 170? _____

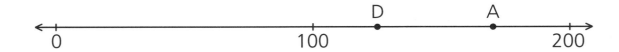

3.   Which point on the number line shows about 175? _____

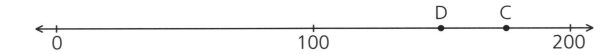

Math Pathways & Pitfalls® ✳ Unit 3 ✳ Lesson 1

NAME:

Multiple Choice Mini Lesson

Fill in the circle next to the answer you choose.

1.   What number is the best estimate for point X?

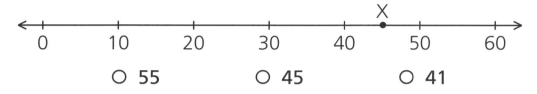

   ○ 55   ○ 45   ○ 41

2.   What number is the best estimate for point X?

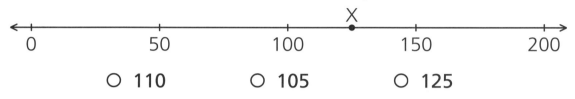

   ○ 110   ○ 105   ○ 125

STUDENT PAGE 5 **Number Line Sense**

NAME:

Multiple Choice Mini Lesson

Fill in the circle next to the answer you choose.

1.   What number is the best estimate for point X?

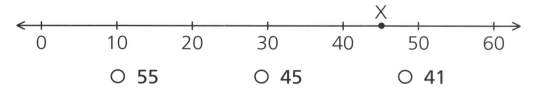

   ○ 55   ○ 45   ○ 41

2.   What number is the best estimate for point X?

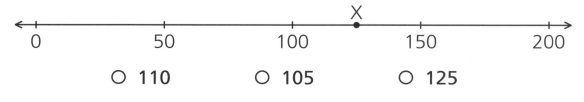

   ○ 110   ○ 105   ○ 125

NAME:

Writing Task Mini Lesson

Explain how you know that a good estimate for point X is 150. You may draw a picture on the back to help explain.

....

....

....

....

✂

Number Line Sense

STUDENT PAGE 6

NAME:

Writing Task Mini Lesson

Explain how you know that a good estimate for point X is 150. You may draw a picture on the back to help explain.

....

....

....

....

NAME:

Purpose

To use estimation to mark and label a point
on a number line

Math Words

units	The space between 0 and 10 on a number line is 10 units long.

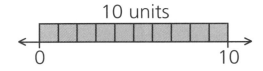

10 units

0   10

halfway between	25 is halfway between 0 and 50 on a number line.

benchmarks	Benchmark numbers, like 10, 50, and 100, help you estimate.

Starter Problem

Draw a point to show about where 128 is on
this number line. Label the point.

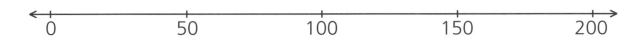

0   50   100   150   200

NAME:

Draw a point to show about where 128 is on this number line. Label the point.

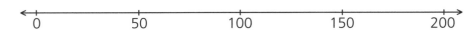

Student Thinking

Christy

I marked off the tens after 100. I put 128 just before 130. It checks because it's a little bit more than halfway between 100 and 150.

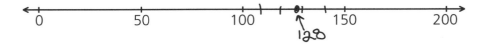

Tommy

It's 128, so I tried to put 28 marks after 100, but it's hard to fit them all in.

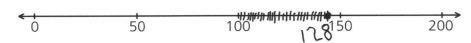

Things to Remember

✳ ....

....

✳ ....

....

Our Turn

Draw a point to show about where the number is on each number line. Label the point.

1.   131

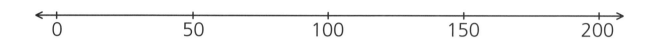

2.   162

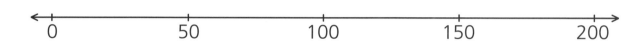

3.   180

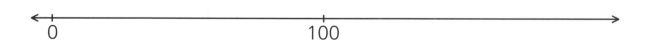

NAME:

My Turn

Draw a point to show about where the number is on each number line.
Label the point.

1. 92

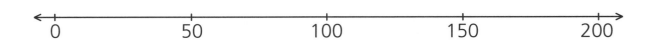

2. 92

3. 152

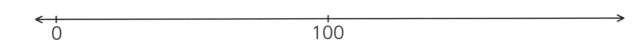

NAME:

Multiple Choice Mini Lesson

Fill in the circle next to the answer you choose.

1. Which number line correctly shows the number 137?

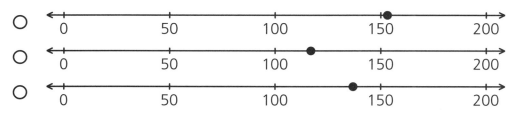

2. Which number line correctly shows the number 121?

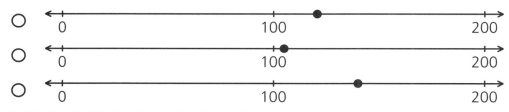

✂ -

STUDENT PAGE 5 **Marking Points for Numbers**

NAME:

Multiple Choice Mini Lesson

Fill in the circle next to the answer you choose.

1. Which number line correctly shows the number 137?

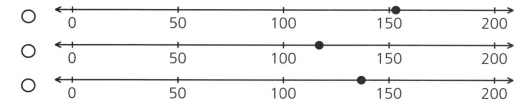

2. Which number line correctly shows the number 121?

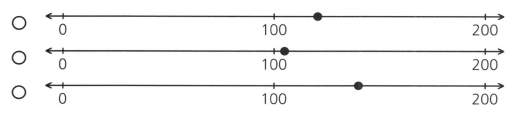

Math Pathways & Pitfalls® ✳ Unit 3 ✳ Lesson 2

NAME:

Writing Task Mini Lesson

Explain how you know about where to mark and label the number 70 on this number line.

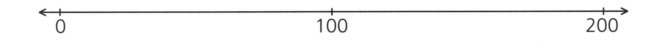

Marking Points for Numbers

STUDENT PAGE 6

NAME:

Writing Task Mini Lesson

Explain how you know about where to mark and label the number 70 on this number line.

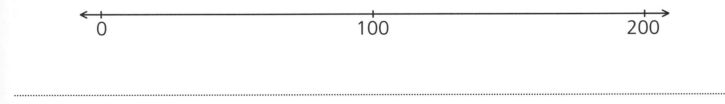

NAME:

Purpose

To add a few more to a large number

Math Words

sum	When I add 55 + 2, the sum is 57.
add on	I can start with 55 beads and add on 2 more to make 57 beads.

Starter Problem

Think about the meaning. Solve.

$$285 + 7 = \underline{\hspace{2cm}}$$

NAME:

> **Starter Problem**
>
> Think about the meaning. Solve.
>
> $$285 + 7 = \underline{\hspace{2cm}}$$

Student Thinking

Jackson

I added in my head with easy steps. First, I added on 5 to get to 290. Then, I needed to add on 2 more. It's 292. I could add using paper to check.

OK

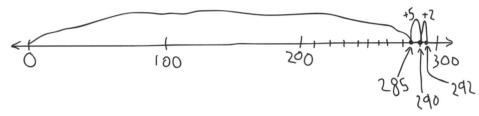

Alika

I rewrote the numbers up and down on paper. It's 985.

$$\begin{array}{r} 285 \\ +\ 7 \\ \hline 985 \end{array}$$

Oops!

Things to Remember

✳ ....

....

✳ ....

....

STOP

NAME:

Our Turn

Write the answer for each problem on the line.

1. $135 + 8 =$ _____

2. $427 + 5 =$ _____

3. $209 + 7 =$ _____

NAME:

My Turn

Write the answer for each problem on the line.

1.   239 + 4 = _____

2.   432 + 9 = _____

3.   152 + 8 = _____

NAME:

Multiple Choice Mini Lesson

Fill in the circle next to the answer you choose.

1.   7 + 226 = _____

       ○ 926   ○ 230   ○ 233

2.   8 + 254 = _____

       ○ 252   ○ 260   ○ 262

NAME:

Multiple Choice Mini Lesson

Fill in the circle next to the answer you choose.

1.   7 + 226 = _____

       ○ 926   ○ 230   ○ 233

2.   8 + 254 = _____

       ○ 252   ○ 260   ○ 262

NAME:

Writing Task Mini Lesson

Explain how you know how to add 7 + 156 in easy steps. You may draw
a picture on the back to help explain.

....

....

....

....

....

....

....

✂ -

Add On a Bit More   STUDENT PAGE 6

NAME:

Writing Task Mini Lesson

Explain how you know how to add 7 + 156 in easy steps. You may draw
a picture on the back to help explain.

....

....

....

....

....

Purpose

To find an amount less than a number

Math Words

less than	A penny is 4 cents less than a nickel.
count back	To count back from 100, you say "99, 98, 97, . . . "

Starter Problem

What is 5 less than 402?

NAME:

---Starter Problem---

What is 5 less than 402?

Student Thinking

Nan

I count back 2 and get to 400. Then I count back 3 more. It's 397. It's the same answer if I subtract.

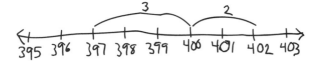

OK

Victor

Less than means subtract. The answer is 403.

$$\begin{array}{r} 402 \\ -5 \\ \hline 403 \end{array}$$

Oops!

Things to Remember

✳ ....

....

✳ ....

....

STOP

NAME:

Our Turn

Write the answer for each problem on the line.

1.   What is 3 less than 52? _____

2.   What is 7 less than 205? _____

3.   510 − 9 = _____

A Little Less

NAME:

My Turn

Write the answer for each problem on the line.

1.   What is 6 less than 205? _____

2.   What is 1 less than 400? _____

3.   302 – 8 = _____

NAME: _____

Multiple Choice Mini Lesson

Fill in the circle next to the answer you choose.

1. What is 8 less than 305? _____

   ○ 303   ○ 297   ○ 307   ○ 203

2. 208 – 9 = _____

   ○ 201   ○ 211   ○ 199   ○ 191

STUDENT PAGE 5 **A Little Less**

NAME: _____

Multiple Choice Mini Lesson

Fill in the circle next to the answer you choose.

1. What is 8 less than 305? _____

   ○ 303   ○ 297   ○ 307   ○ 203

2. 208 – 9 = _____

   ○ 201   ○ 211   ○ 199   ○ 191

NAME:

Writing Task Mini Lesson

Explain how you know that 7 less than 403 is 396. Draw a picture or a number line on the back to show how you know.

A Little Less

STUDENT PAGE 6

NAME:

Writing Task Mini Lesson

Explain how you know that 7 less than 403 is 396. Draw a picture or a number line on the back to show how you know.

NAME:

Purpose

To find a difference using counting strategies or subtraction

Math Words

difference | The difference between two numbers can be found by subtracting.

find the difference | To find the difference between 15 and 10, you can count the units from 10 up to 15 on the number line.

benchmark numbers | Numbers that are easy to use, like 10, 50, 100, and 200, are benchmark numbers.

Starter Problem

Alisha read to page 198 the first week. Then, she read to page 304 the second week. How many pages did she read the second week? _____

NAME:

Starter Problem

Alisha read to page 198 the first week. Then, she read to page 304 the second week. How many pages did she read the second week? _____

Student Thinking

Yolanda

To find the difference, I started at 198 and added on to make 304. It's 106 pages. I can subtract to check.

OK

Raymond

I subtracted to find the difference.

Oops!

Things to Remember

* ....

....

* ....

....

STOP

Our Turn

Solve each problem. Write the answer.

1. Kelly's team made 197 paper flowers in the morning and the rest in the afternoon. At the end of the day, they had 405 flowers. How many flowers did they make in the afternoon? _____

2. Sarah made a chain with 86 paper clips. Then, her friend put on more to make a chain with 212 paper clips. How many did the friend put on? _____

3. 302
   − 185
   ‾‾‾‾‾

NAME: _____

My Turn

Solve each problem. Write the answer.

1. J.R. had 280 pennies last year. Now, he has 402 pennies.
    How many pennies did he get this year? _____

2. John made a chain with 77 paper clips. Then, his friends
    put on more to make a chain with 315 paper clips. How many
    did the friends put on? _____

3.   502
      − 175
      _____

NAME:

Multiple Choice Mini Lesson

Fill in the circle next to the answer you choose.

1. Alice baked 36 cookies. She needs 100 for the bake sale. How many cookies does she still need to bake?

   ○ 136   ○ 64   ○ 74

2. Allen had 280 trading cards last year. Now he has 410. How many more trading cards did he get this year?

   ○ 410   ○ 130   ○ 270

STUDENT PAGE 5 **Finding the Difference**

NAME:

Multiple Choice Mini Lesson

Fill in the circle next to the answer you choose.

1. Alice baked 36 cookies. She needs 100 for the bake sale. How many cookies does she still need to bake?

   ○ 136   ○ 64   ○ 74

2. Allen had 280 trading cards last year. Now he has 410. How many more trading cards did he get this year?

   ○ 410   ○ 130   ○ 270

NAME:

Writing Task Mini Lesson

Explain how you know that the difference between 405 and 296 is 109.
Draw a picture on the back to show how you know.

....

....

....

....

....

....

✂

Finding the Difference

STUDENT PAGE 6

NAME:

Writing Task Mini Lesson

Explain how you know that the difference between 405 and 296 is 109.
Draw a picture on the back to show how you know.

....

....

....

....

....

NAME:

Purpose

To use place value to understand how to add on to a number

Math Words

thousands	The 5 in the number 5,382 has a value of 5 thousands, or 5,000.
hundreds	The 3 in the number 5,382 has a value of 3 hundreds, or 300.
tens	The 8 in the number 5,382 has a value of 8 tens, or 80.
ones	The 2 in the number 5,382 has a value of 2 ones, or 2.

Starter Problem

What number is 100 more than 1,357? _____

NAME:

Starter Problem

What number is 100 more than 1,357? _____

Student Thinking

Ernesto

1,357 has 3 in the hundreds place. So, 1 more hundred is 1,457. It's the short way to write 1,000 + 400 + 50 + 7.

 OK

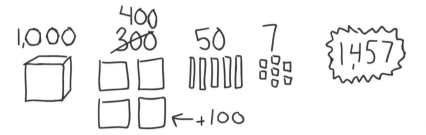

Kendra

100 more than 1,357 is 2,357. I added.

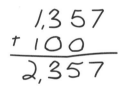

 Oops!

Things to Remember

✳ ....

....

✳ ....

....

 STOP

Math Pathways & Pitfalls™ ✳ Unit 3 ✳ Lesson 6

NAME:

Our Turn

Solve each problem. Write the answer on the line.

1. What number is 20 more than 8,742? _____

2. What number is 900 more than 3,051? _____

3. 300 + 4,670 = _____

NAME:

My Turn

Solve each problem. Write the answer on the line.

1.   What number is 400 more than 7,568? _____

2.   What number is 50 more than 204? _____

3.   10 + 5,640 = _____

NAME:

Multiple Choice Mini Lesson

Fill in the circle next to the answer you choose.

1. What number is 100 more than 5,238?

   ○ 6,238   ○ 52,138   ○ 5,338

2. $8,092 + 600 =$ _____

   ○ 80,692   ○ 8,692   ○ 1,492

STUDENT PAGE 5 **Add On Using Place Value**

NAME:

Multiple Choice Mini Lesson

Fill in the circle next to the answer you choose.

1. What number is 100 more than 5,238?

   ○ 6,238   ○ 52,138   ○ 5,338

2. $8,092 + 600 =$ _____

   ○ 80,692   ○ 8,692   ○ 1,492

NAME:

Writing Task Mini Lesson

Explain how you know that 300 more than 4,205 is 4,505. Draw a picture on the back to show how you know.

....

....

....

....

....

....

✂

NAME:

Writing Task Mini Lesson

Explain how you know that 300 more than 4,205 is 4,505. Draw a picture on the back to show how you know.

....

....

....

....

NAME:

Purpose

To understand and solve addition equations
with missing numbers

Math Words

equation   An equation like 5 + 30 = 35 shows
that 5 + 30 and 35 are equal.

equals sign   An equals sign means "is the same
amount as."

both sides   The amounts on both sides of the equals
sign in this equation are equal to 20.

10 + 10 = 19 + 1

Starter Problem

Copy and complete this equation.
Think about the meaning.

20 + _____ = 54

NAME:

Starter Problem

Copy and complete this equation.
Think about the meaning.

$$20 + \underline{\hspace{2cm}} = 54$$

Student Thinking

Anita

I read it to myself: "20 plus a missing number is equal to 54." Both sides of the equals sign need to be the same amount. The left side needs 34 more. It checks.

$$20 + \underline{34} = 54$$

Joel

It says to add, so 20 plus 54 is 74.

$$20 + \underline{74} = 54$$

Things to Remember

✱ ....

....

✱ ....

....

NAME:

Our Turn

Write a number on the line to complete each equation.
You may use drawings to help you.

1.   30 + _____ = 50

2.   68 = 62 + _____

3.   4 + _____ = 75

NAME:

My Turn

Write a number on the line to complete each equation.
You may use drawings to help you.

1.   15 + _____ = 25

2.   20 + _____ = 85

3.   53 = 49 + _____

NAME:

Multiple Choice Mini Lesson

Fill in the circle next to the answer you choose.

1. 4 + _____ = 30

    ○ 34   ○ 26   ○ 24   ○ 30

2. 40 + 10 + _____ = 60

    ○ 110   ○ 50   ○ 10   ○ 0

STUDENT PAGE 5 **What Number Is Missing?**

NAME:

Multiple Choice Mini Lesson

Fill in the circle next to the answer you choose.

1. 4 + _____ = 30

    ○ 34   ○ 26   ○ 24   ○ 30

2. 40 + 10 + _____ = 60

    ○ 110   ○ 50   ○ 10   ○ 0

316   Math Pathways & Pitfalls® ✳ Unit 3 ✳ Lesson 7

NAME:

Writing Task Mini Lesson

Explain how you know that 32 is the correct number to write in the blank to complete the equation.

$$8 + \rule{2cm}{0.4pt} = 40$$

What Number Is Missing?

STUDENT PAGE 6

NAME:

Writing Task Mini Lesson

Explain how you know that 32 is the correct number to write in the blank to complete the equation.

$$8 + \rule{2cm}{0.4pt} = 40$$

NAME:

Purpose

To understand the value of each digit in a number

Math Words

place	The number 3,204 has a 3 in the thousands place, a 2 in the hundreds place, a 0 in the tens place, and a 4 in the ones place.
thousands, hundreds, tens, and ones	3 thousands, 7 hundreds, 4 tens, and 5 ones is the same amount as 3,000 + 700 + 40 + 5.
digits	The number 3,204 has 4 digits: 3, 2, 0, and 4.

Starter Problem

Copy and complete this equation.
Think about the meaning.

$$2{,}409 = 2{,}000 + \underline{\hspace{2cm}} + 9$$

NAME:

Copy and complete this equation.
Think about the meaning.

$$2{,}409 = 2{,}000 + \underline{\hspace{2cm}} + 9$$

Student Thinking

John

I read 2,409 out loud: "Two thousand, **four hundred** nine." The 4 means 4 hundreds. I checked by adding another way.

OK

$$2{,}409 = 2{,}000 + \underline{400} + 9$$

$$
\begin{array}{r}
2{,}000 \\
400 \\
+\quad 9 \\
\hline
2{,}409
\end{array}
$$

Trina

I added the numbers and got 2,009. Then I wrote the answer in the blank.

Oops!

$$2{,}409 = 2{,}000 + \underline{2{,}009} + 9$$

Things to Remember

✳ ....

....

✳ ....

....

STOP

NAME:

Our Turn

Write the answer for each problem on the line.

1. $1,345 = 300 + 5 + 1,000 +$ _____

2. $5,027 = 5,000 +$ _____ $+ 7$

3. $200 + 5,000 + 6 =$ _____

NAME:

My Turn

Write the answer for each problem on the line.

1.   60 + 4 + _____ + 1,000 = 1,264

2.   5,803 = 3 + _____ + 5,000

3.   8,041 = 8,000 + _____ + 1

NAME:

Multiple Choice Mini Lesson

Fill in the circle next to the answer you choose.

1.   3,654 = _____ + 50 + 600 + 3,000

     ○ 3000   ○ 3,654   ○ 54   ○ 4

2.   3,654 = _____ hundreds + 5 tens + 3 thousands + 4 ones

     ○ 600   ○ 654   ○ 6   ○ 3

STUDENT PAGE 5   **Values of Digits**

NAME:

Multiple Choice Mini Lesson

Fill in the circle next to the answer you choose.

1.   3,654 = _____ + 50 + 600 + 3,000

     ○ 3000   ○ 3,654   ○ 54   ○ 4

2.   3,654 = _____ hundreds + 5 tens + 3 thousands + 4 ones

     ○ 600   ○ 654   ○ 6   ○ 3

322   Math Pathways & Pitfalls® ✳ Unit 3 ✳ Lesson 8

NAME:

Writing Task Mini Lesson

Explain how you know that 400 is the correct number to put in the blank. Use a picture or numbers on the back to show your ideas.

$$6,405 = 6,000 + \underline{\hspace{2cm}} + 5$$

--------------------------------✂

Values of Digits

STUDENT PAGE 6

NAME:

Writing Task Mini Lesson

Explain how you know that 400 is the correct number to put in the blank. Use a picture or numbers on the back to show your ideas.

$$6,405 = 6,000 + \underline{\hspace{2cm}} + 5$$

Math Pathways & Pitfalls® ✳ Unit 3 ✳ Lesson 8

NAME:

Purpose

To know when and how to regroup when subtracting

Math Words

hundreds, tens, and ones	235 is the same amount as 2 hundreds, 3 tens, and 5 ones, or 200 + 30 + 5.
regroup	You can regroup 2 hundreds, 3 tens, and 5 ones into 2 hundreds, 2 tens, and 15 ones. Both amounts are equal.

Starter Problem

Think about the meaning.
Solve.

$$\begin{array}{r} 262 \\ -38 \\ \hline \end{array}$$

NAME:

Starter Problem

Think about the meaning.
Solve.

262
− 38

Student Thinking

Patty

I needed more ones. I regrouped a ten and put it with the 2 to make 12 ones. Then I subtracted and got 224. It checks.

OK

$$\begin{array}{r} 2\overset{5}{\cancel{6}}\overset{12}{\cancel{2}} \\ -\ 38 \\ \hline 224 \end{array} \qquad \begin{array}{r} \overset{1}{2}24 \\ +\ 38 \\ \hline 262 \end{array}$$

Ray

First, I just subtracted the ones: 8 minus 2 is 6. Then I subtracted the tens: 6 minus 3 is 3. Then I wrote down the 2 from the hundreds. It's 236.

Oops!

$$\begin{array}{r} 262 \\ -38 \\ \hline 236 \end{array}$$

Things to Remember

✳ ....

....

✳ ....

....

Our Turn

Write the answer for each problem. Check your work by adding.

1.   357   Check
   – 49

2.   165   Check
   – 36

3.   50   Check
   – 27

NAME:

My Turn

Write the answer for each problem. Check your work by adding.

1.   542
   − 26
   _____

Check

2.   70
   − 48
   _____

Check

3.   346
   − 39
   _____

Check

NAME:

Multiple Choice Mini Lesson

Fill in the circle next to the answer you choose.

1. 64 – 27 = _____

    ○ 33   ○ 37   ○ 43   ○ 47

2. 50 – 38 = _____

    ○ 12   ○ 18   ○ 22   ○ 28

NAME:

Multiple Choice Mini Lesson

Fill in the circle next to the answer you choose.

1. 64 – 27 = _____

    ○ 33   ○ 37   ○ 43   ○ 47

2. 50 – 38 = _____

    ○ 12   ○ 18   ○ 22   ○ 28

Math Pathways & Pitfalls® ✳ Unit 3 ✳ Lesson 9

NAME:

Writing Task Mini Lesson

Explain how regrouping could be used to solve this problem.

$$75 - 48 = \underline{\hspace{2cm}}$$

....

....

....

....

....

✂

Regroup a Ten

STUDENT PAGE 6

NAME:

Writing Task Mini Lesson

Explain how regrouping could be used to solve this problem.

$$75 - 48 = \underline{\hspace{2cm}}$$

....

....

....

....

....

NAME:

Purpose

To solve multiplication problems with the same number in each group

Math Words

group A collection of things or people, like a team, is a group.

each If there is money in each pocket, then that means every pocket has money in it.

Starter Problem

Mike has 3 boxes. There are 5 cars and 2 marbles in each box. Which number sentence gives the total number of marbles? Write the total in the blank.

$3 + 2 = $ _____ $3 \times 2 = $ _____

$3 \times 5 = $ _____ $3 + 5 + 2 = $ _____

NAME:

Starter Problem

Mike has 3 boxes. There are 5 cars and 2 marbles in each box.
Which number sentence gives the total number of marbles?
Write the total in the blank.

$3 + 2 =$ _____ $3 \times 2 =$ _____

$3 \times 5 =$ _____ $3 + 5 + 2 =$ _____

Student Thinking

Martin

I drew 3 boxes and put 2 marbles in each. That's 3 times 2 equals the total number of marbles. It's 6 marbles.

OK

Gina

There are 3 numbers to add. Total means how many in all. It's 3 plus 5 plus 2. That's 10 marbles.

  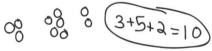

Oops!

Things to Remember

✳ ....

....

✳ ....

....

STOP

NAME:

Our Turn

Draw a picture for each problem.
Circle and solve the correct number sentence.

1. Mr. Holden bought 3 boxes with 5 bags of chips and 1 prize in each.
   Which number sentence gives the total number of bags of chips?

   $3 + 5 + 1 =$ _____ $3 \times 5 + 1 =$ _____

   $3 \times 5 =$ _____ $3 \times 1 =$ _____

2. Mrs. Fong has 2 bananas, 3 apples, and 5 oranges. She is making
   2 bowls of fruit salad with the fruit. Which number sentence shows
   the number of pieces of fruit that Mrs. Fong has?

   $2 + 2 + 3 + 5 =$ _____ $5 \times 2 =$ _____

   $2 + 3 + 5 =$ _____ $2 \times 3 =$ _____

3. Alisha is making 4 sack lunches. She will put 2 sandwiches and
   3 cookies in each bag. Which number sentence shows the
   number of cookies that Alisha needs?

   $4 + 2 + 3 =$ _____ $4 \times 2 =$ _____

   $4 \times 2 \times 3 =$ _____ $4 \times 3 =$ _____

NAME:

My Turn

Draw a picture for each problem.
Circle and solve the correct number sentence.

1. Mr. Velez brought 2 soft drinks and 3 health bars for each of his grandchildren on their camping trip. He has 3 grandchildren. Which number sentence gives the total number of soft drinks he brought?

   2 + 3 + 3 = _____   2 x 3 + 3 = _____

   3 x 2 = _____   3 x 3 = _____

2. Jenny has 8 tulips, 4 roses, and 6 snapdragons. She will put the flowers in 2 small baskets. Which number sentence shows the total number of flowers?

   8 + 4 + 6 = _____   8 x 4 x 6 = _____

   2 x 8 = _____   2 x 8 + 4 + 6 = _____

3. Kai has room for 2 file boxes, 3 magazine holders, and 2 CD boxes on each shelf. He has 4 shelves. Which number sentence shows the total number of CD boxes Kai will need?

   2 x 3 x 2 x 4 = _____   2 x 3 x 2 = _____

   4 + 2 = _____   4 x 2 = _____

NAME:

Multiple Choice Mini Lesson

Fill in the circle next to the answer you choose.

1. Kim has 4 bottles. There are 2 cups of juice and 1 straw in each bottle. Which number sentence gives the total number of cups of juice?

   ○ 4 + 2 + 1 = _____   ○ 4 + 2 = _____   ○ 4 x 2 = _____

2. There are 4 third grade teams. Every team has 1 captain, 2 soccer balls, and 3 basketballs. Which number sentence gives the number of balls for one team?

   ○ 4 + 1 + 2 + 3 = _____   ○ 4 x 2 = _____   ○ 2 + 3 = _____

STUDENT PAGE 5 **When Do You Multiply?**

NAME:

Multiple Choice Mini Lesson

Fill in the circle next to the answer you choose.

1. Kim has 4 bottles. There are 2 cups of juice and 1 straw in each bottle. Which number sentence gives the total number of cups of juice?

   ○ 4 + 2 + 1 = _____   ○ 4 + 2 = _____   ○ 4 x 2 = _____

2. There are 4 third grade teams. Every team has 1 captain, 2 soccer balls, and 3 basketballs. Which number sentence gives the number of balls for one team?

   ○ 4 + 1 + 2 + 3 = _____   ○ 4 x 2 = _____   ○ 2 + 3 = _____

NAME:

Writing Task Mini Lesson

Explain why the drawing below can be used to solve the problem.

Mrs. James got 6 markers and 4 pens for each of her 5 children. How many pens did she get?

....

....

....

....

✂

When Do You Multiply?

STUDENT PAGE   6

NAME:

Writing Task Mini Lesson

Explain why the drawing below can be used to solve the problem.

Mrs. James got 6 markers and 4 pens for each of her 5 children. How many pens did she get?

....

....

....

....

NAME:

Purpose

To solve multiplication problems using mental math or paper and pencil

Math Words

multiplication   We can use multiplication to combine or add equal-sized groups.

times   We find 3 times 100 by multiplying, or we can add 100 plus 100 plus 100.

Starter Problem

Solve.

The third grade class made 125 cupcakes for the school fair. Each cupcake had 3 candy kisses on top. How many candy kisses were needed all together? _____

NAME:

Starter Problem

Solve.

The third grade class made 125 cupcakes for the school fair. Each cupcake had 3 candy kisses on top. How many candy kisses were needed all together? _____

Student Thinking

For 100 cupcakes you need 3 times 100 candies. For 25 cupcakes you need 3 times 25 candies. So 300 plus 75 is 375 candies. I can multiply 125 x 3 to check.

Joy

OK

100 cupcakes

3 candies each is 300 candies

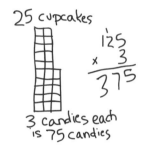

25 cupcakes

3 candies each is 75 candies

$$\begin{array}{r} 1\overset{1}{2}5 \\ \times\ \ 3 \\ \hline 375 \end{array}$$

I needed to find how many candy kisses all together, so I added. It's 128 in all.

Tim

Oops!

$$\begin{array}{r} 125 \\ +\ \ \ 3 \\ \hline 128 \end{array}$$

Things to Remember

* ....

....

* ....

....

NAME:

Our Turn

Solve each problem using mental math or paper and pencil.
It may help to make a drawing.

1. Amy made 32 birthday treat bags for her classmates.
   Each bag had 4 treats. How many treats did she need in all?

2. Eddie packs baskets with fruit to sell at the farmer's market.
   Each basket holds 7 plums or 5 peaches. How many peaches
   will he need to fill 65 baskets with peaches?

3. The outdoor theater has 124 rows; each row has 6 seats.
   How many seats does the theater have all together?

NAME:

My Turn

Solve each problem using mental math or paper and pencil.
It may help to make a drawing.

1. The pep band had 28 rows with 5 students in each row when it marched on the field. How many students were in the pep band?

2. The after-school clubs made 136 greeting cards for children in hospitals. Each card had 3 stickers. How many stickers were used on the cards all together?

3. Irma helped her neighbor plant flowers. They planted 16 tulips and 5 daffodils in each of 4 pots. How many tulips did they plant in all?

NAME:

Multiple Choice Mini Lesson

Fill in the circle next to the answer you choose.

1. The committee ordered 24 packages of hot dog buns for the picnic. Each package had 8 buns. How many buns did they order in all?

   ○ 192   ○ 32   ○ 132

2. The school printed 135 programs for the outdoor fiesta. Each program had 3 pages. How many pages were printed all together?

   ○ 138   ○ 405   ○ 175

STUDENT PAGE 5 **Making Sense and Multiplying**

NAME:

Multiple Choice Mini Lesson

Fill in the circle next to the answer you choose.

1. The committee ordered 24 packages of hot dog buns for the picnic. Each package had 8 buns. How many buns did they order in all?

   ○ 192   ○ 32   ○ 132

2. The school printed 135 programs for the outdoor fiesta. Each program had 3 pages. How many pages were printed all together?

   ○ 138   ○ 405   ○ 175

NAME:

Writing Task Mini Lesson

Explain how to use mental math to solve the problem below.

Each student got 6 free tickets for events at the school fair. If there are 62 students, how many tickets were given out?

....

....

....

....

✂

Making Sense and Multiplying

STUDENT PAGE 6

NAME:

Writing Task Mini Lesson

Explain how to use mental math to solve the problem below.

Each student got 6 free tickets for events at the school fair. If there are 62 students, how many tickets were given out?

....

....

....

....

About the Authors

Carne Barnett-Clarke, Senior Research Associate at WestEd and Codirector of *Math Pathways & Pitfalls,* investigates and develops effective, engaging, and pragmatic instructional materials for teachers and students. She is principal investigator of research projects funded by the National Science Foundation and the U.S. Department of Education that seek to understand how these materials contribute to equitable mathematics learning. Her current work draws on her prior experience as a teacher in ethnically and linguistically diverse communities and as a teacher educator at the University of California, Berkeley. Barnett-Clarke is lead author on a National Council of Teachers of Mathematics (NCTM) publication (in press) focusing on the essential understandings of rational numbers needed by teachers. Earlier, her groundbreaking work using case methods for professional development resulted in two casebooks, *Mathematics Teaching Cases: Fractions, Decimals, Ratios, and Percents* and *Number Sense and Operations in the Primary Grades.* She is also the author of K–8 mathematics supplementary materials and textbooks and has published in the *Journal of Teacher Education, Teaching and Teacher Education,* the *National Council of Teachers of Mathematics Sixty-sixth Yearbook, Mathematics Teachers in Transition,* and the *Journal of Mathematics for Teacher Education.*

Alma B. Ramírez began her career as a bilingual elementary and middle school teacher of English learners in urban settings. Currently, as Senior Research Associate at WestEd and Codirector of *Math Pathways & Pitfalls,* her work focuses on increasing equity in mathematics education for students and developing the capacity of diverse teachers to become leaders in mathematics education. Ramírez has served as a consultant and teacher for a variety of mathematics projects, including EQUALS, Family Math, and the Head Start Math Readiness Project. She has expertise in mathematics teaching and learning, second language acquisition, and teacher professional development. She coedited a book for teachers entitled *Mathematics Teaching Cases: Number Sense and Operations in the Primary Grades* (Heinemann, 2003), coauthored a chapter entitled "Language Pitfalls and Pathways to Mathematics" for the 2004 NCTM Yearbook *Perspectives on the Teaching of Mathematics,* and coauthored an advocacy publication for middle school parents and children, *The Journey Through Middle School Mathematics* (EQUALS, Lawrence Hall of Science, 2005). She has also served as a pre-K–8 mathematics author for well-known textbook publishers.

Debra Coggins is a mathematics education consultant with experience coaching teachers, writing materials for teachers, developing and scoring state assessments, and developing and delivering professional development. She has 18 years of experience teaching in elementary and middle schools, experience as a coach in several districts, and recently served as a mathematics coach for the Bay Area Coalition for Equitable Schools. She holds a bachelor's degree from the University of California, Berkeley, and a master's degree with a focus on serving organizations as a mathematics specialist. Coggins is the lead author of *English Language Learners in the Mathematics Classroom* and *A Mathematics Source Book for Elementary and Middle School Teachers.* She also is a contributor to *Mathematics Teaching Cases: Fractions, Decimals, Ratios, and Percents* and to *Number Sense and Operations in the Primary Grades.*

Also Available from WestEd

More *Math Pathways & Pitfalls®* Publications

Carne Barnett-Clarke and Alma B. Ramírez with Debra Coggins

This K–8 intervention curriculum helps students tackle stubborn pitfalls head-on and transform them into pathways for learning key topics. Each grade-span volume includes 20 or more complete lessons, a teaching manual, DVD with classroom footage, CD-ROM with black line masters of handouts, quizzes, and resources, *Discussion Builders* classroom poster, and teacher professional development tasks, activities, and video footage. Download sample lessons and research results at WestEd.org/mpp.

Grades K–2 ≫ Early and Whole Number Concepts with Algebra Readiness
$165.00 • 320 pages • Trade Paper with DVD, CD-ROM, & Poster
8.5 x 11 • 2010 • WestEd
978-0-914409-58-8 • MPP-09-01

Grades 4–6 ≫ Fractions and Decimals with Algebra Readiness
$165.00 • 368 pages • Trade paper with DVD, CD-ROM, & Poster
8.5 x 11 • 2010 • WestEd
978-0-914409-60-1 • MPP-09-03

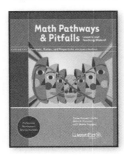

Grades 6–8 ≫ Percents, Ratios, and Proportions with Algebra Readiness
$165.00 • 368 pages • Trade Paper with DVD, CD-ROM, & Poster
8.5 x 11 • 2010 • WestEd
978-0-914409-61-8 • MPP-09-04

For more information ≫ WestEd.org/mpp

Also Available from WestEd

Math Pathways & Pitfalls® Institutes

Probably the best training I have ever participated in. The content is excellent and life changing. The concept of PITFALLS is huge. — First grade teacher

What Are *Math Pathways & Pitfalls* Institutes?

Math Pathways & Pitfalls institutes help K–8 teachers solidify key concepts and tackle persistent pitfalls using research-based strategies with *Math Pathways & Pitfalls* lessons and their district-adopted curriculum. The institutes enhance implementation of *Math Pathways & Pitfalls* lessons and support the development of effective and equitable teaching habits, even in non-*Math Pathways & Pitfalls* lessons. Participants learn:

* Instructional approaches for turning pitfalls into pathways for learning.

* Effective strategies for developing students' mathematical language.

* Practical tools for developing a community of learners in which students learn how to participate in the discourse practices of mathematics.

* How to address multiple modalities in their lessons.

Who Should Participate?

* K–8 teachers

* Mathematics coaches and instructional leaders

* Staff developers

What Is the Format?

We offer *Math Pathways & Pitfalls* institutes in different formats to accommodate your scheduling and professional development needs.

Format One: Implementation Institute Hosted by WestEd. This three-day institute provides everything needed to successfully use *Math Pathways & Pitfalls* lessons, including *Math Pathways & Pitfalls* strategies and *Discussion Builders*. Participants also learn ways to apply these strategies in their adopted curriculum. K–8 institute participants receive a complete set of *Math Pathways & Pitfalls* materials, including a *Math Pathways & Pitfalls* book with intervention lessons and teaching guides, a DVD that has video for students and teachers, a CD with black line masters, and a *Discussion Builders* poster and guide. Visit WestEd.org/mpp for upcoming dates and costs.

Format Two: Implementation Institute Hosted by Your Organization. Host this three-day institute at your organization to provide staff everything needed to successfully use *Math Pathways & Pitfalls* strategies and lessons. Contact us for costs and scheduling.

Format Three: Customized Institute Hosted by Your Organization. Professional development institutes are available with flexible dates and can be tailored for your district and state needs. Costs for customized institutes are calculated per day for school or district teams in increments of 24 participants. Other institute formats and follow-up professional development can be provided on request. Contact us to inquire about costs and customization options.

Contact Information >> Alma B. Ramírez >> 510.302.4249 >> aramire@WestEd.org

Also Available from WestEd

Discussion Builders™ Workshop

When one of my 5th grade students was at the board showing they really didn't have a solid understanding, another would say, "I'm confused about what you put up there. Can you prove your thinking?" Then as a class they would work through those mistakes until they had a solid understanding. — Teacher

Who Should Attend?

K–8 classroom teachers who want practical, evidence-based teaching strategies that foster oral and written academic language development. Excellent for teachers with English learners in their classroom.

What Are *Discussion Builders*?

Originally created for teaching math, *Discussion Builders* are at the core of a suite of classroom posters, teaching guides, and classroom strategies, developed and field-tested with funding from the National Science Foundation. *Discussion Builders* promote academic language use and help students build their communications skills. Sentence stems on the posters provide students with a scaffold for voicing their ideas and questions and valuing others' contributions. The three levels of posters and teaching guides support progressively more sophisticated language and reasoning across the grades. The teaching guide includes tasks and a black line master for introducing and sustaining the use of *Discussion Builders* in any subject area.

What Do Teachers Get Out of the Workshop?

* Powerful, easy-to-implement strategies using *Discussion Builders* classroom posters and teaching guide

* Proven techniques for building students' communication and reasoning skills

* Practical ways to help all students overcome academic, linguistic, and social barriers in classroom discussions

* Overview of current research on the role of academic language development in academic success

* Practice facilitating productive discussions

* High comfort level in leading effective discussions that boost collaborative and respectful critical thinking among students

What Is the Format?

One-day workshop. Participants receive a poster and teaching guide. Visit WestEd.org/mpp for upcoming dates and costs.

End-user License Agreement

WestEd grants the purchaser of this *Math Pathways & Pitfalls*® book a nonexclusive license to use the printable material on the accompanying CD for individual classroom implementation only. The CD may not be duplicated, nor may any files or content from the CD be electronically shared or transferred, or stored in a database or retrieval system, without permission from WestEd. Furthermore, the CD may not be treated as a "master" copy for duplicating print materials for multiple users.

A single user may reproduce printable materials from this CD, including classroom sets of the Lesson Masters, Pitfalls Quiz files, and *Discussion Builders*™ teaching guide. The Pitfalls Quiz files on this CD may be modified to create customized quizzes. Reproduction of the Professional Development Handout for members of a group implementing *Math Pathways & Pitfalls* is also permissible. No other copies of these files or their contents may be made without explicit written permission from the publisher.